MW01601799

# EVERY DAY
## WITH
# Jesus

# EVERY DAY
## WITH

*Jesus*

LIFE-CHANGING INSPIRATIONAL DEVOTIONALS

# BRADLEY BOOTH

 **Remnant**
Publications

Coldwater, Michigan 49036
www.remnantpublications.com

Published by
Remnant Publications
649 East Chicago Road
Coldwater MI 49036
517-279-1304
www.remnantpublications.com

Cover by David Berthiaume
Edited by Verlyne Starr
Text Design by Greg Solie • AltamontGraphics.com

ISBN 978-1-933291-71-0

# DEDICATION

This book is dedicated to Ellen White who was chosen by God as a messenger for these end times in which we find ourselves so precariously living. May her message of Jesus and His righteousness shine from these pages until we meet our Savior face to face!

—— ☙ ——

# PREFACE

*E*very Day with Jesus has been prayerfully written using inspirational vignettes to partner with Ellen White's *Steps to Christ*.[1] Her inspired themes of righteousness by faith in Jesus laid the foundation for the work presented here. Daily readings are adapted from the 13 chapters of *Steps to Christ*. Each selection or "Reading" is usually four to six paragraphs and is followed by an illustrative sketch that includes commentary from one or more of the following sources: nature, the Bible, an anecdotal story, a poem, or a hymn.

One of the goals for this book is to use *Steps to Christ* by Ellen G. White in its entirety without paraphrasing or substitutions of any kind by the author. One simple modification has been made, however. In the readings taken from *Steps to Christ*, the New King James Version of the Bible is substituted for the traditional King James Version, to provide for easier reading. Throughout the rest of the book the New King James Version of the Bible is used, unless otherwise specified.

---

1   Ellen G. White, *Steps to Christ* (Hagerstown, MD: Review and Herald Publishing Association, 1997).

# CONTENTS

# CHAPTER 1

# God's Love for Man

**God's Second Book—Reading #1**

"Nature and revelation alike testify of God's love. Our Father in heaven is the source of life, of wisdom, and of joy. Look at the wonderful and beautiful things of nature. Think of their marvelous adaptation to the needs and happiness, not only of man, but of all living creatures. The sunshine and the rain, that gladden and refresh the earth, the hills and seas and plains, all speak to us of the Creator's love. It is God who supplies the daily needs of all His creatures. In the beautiful words of the psalmist: "*The eyes of all look expectantly to You, and You give them their food in due season. You open Your hand and satisfy the desire of every living thing.*" *Psalm 145:15, 16.*

"God made man perfectly holy and happy; and the fair earth, as it came from the Creator's hand, bore no blight of decay or shadow of the curse. It is transgression of God's law—the law of love—that has brought woe and death. Yet even amid the suffering that results from sin, God's love is revealed. It is written that God cursed the ground for man's sake. Genesis 3:17. The thorn and the thistle—the difficulties and trials that make his life one of toil and care—were appointed for his good as a part of the training needful in God's plan for his uplifting from the ruin and degradation that sin has wrought. The world, though fallen, is not all sorrow and misery. In nature itself are messages of hope and comfort. There are flowers upon the thistles, and the thorns are covered with roses.

"'God is love' is written upon every opening bud, upon every spire of springing grass. The lovely birds making the air vocal with their happy songs, the delicately tinted flowers in their perfection perfuming the air, the lofty trees of the forest with their rich foliage of living green—all testify to the tender, fatherly care of our God and to His desire to make His children happy."[2]

**Illustrative Sketch:**

God has given us the wonderful world in which we live, and although sin has blighted its grandeur, creation still holds breathtaking examples of His masterful design. Consider the birds of the air. They are among the most colorful and exquisite of God's creatures, portraying His handiwork in design and function.

Peacocks sport showy fantails of blues, greens, and eye-like patterns that baffle even the staunchest of evolutionists. Other birds like the Arctic ptarmigans have the ability to camouflage themselves, changing with the colors of the seasons. Quail learn to remain motionless in order to blend in, but can suddenly take flight in a burst of feathers to startle predators and give themselves a better chance to escape.

Birds cheer us with beautiful melodies that can stir the soul. Garden birds such as orioles, robins, and cardinals have distinctive calls, and canaries are favorite household pets because of their cheerful sonnets. Parrots and mina birds have the ability to imitate many kinds of sounds, and mockingbirds can mimic the songs of 40 different birds. Some birds enjoy singing so much they never seem to stop. The red-eyed vireo probably holds the record at 22,197 songs in just a 10-hour period.[3]

Most birds fly, giving them advantages for adaptation in an ever-changing world. Their hollow bones make them lightweight and flexible for flight. Feathers give their wings lift on the morning breeze. They also help birds shed water and insulate their bodies in cold weather.

Humming birds beat their wings in a figure-eight pattern at over 4200 beats per minute, allowing them to fly forward, backward, from side to side, and even to hover. The Arctic tern flies fantastic distances

---

2    White, 9.

3    Lawrence, L. de K., "Nesting Life and Behavior of the Red-Eyed Vireo," *Canadian Field Naturalist,* 67 (1953), 47-77.

from the North Pole to the South Pole, and the Sooty Tern can fly three to four years, non-stop, never landing anywhere to rest.[4]

Some birds live in the clouds, like condors and eagles, hardly moving their wings, riding on updrafts of warm air. The peregrine falcon can fall from the sky, diving at speeds as high as 180 miles per hour. Penguins have been known to dive in water at depths of 872 feet and stay there for as long as 18 minutes. Oil birds are extremely versatile. They live deep in caves, have dolphin-like sonar, navigate like a bat, have eyes like a deep-sea fish, and can hover like a kingfisher.

And one of the most amazing stories of them all is the life cycle of a type of gull that nests on remote islands in the Pacific. The bird raises its young long enough to fatten them on fish, and then seemingly abandons them to fend for themselves. But God has instilled within the baby birds a driving instinct to adjust and survive. The young are too fat to fly, but after a few months when they are mature enough to travel and the fat reserves have worn off, they teach themselves to fly and take flight. And then, with only an inner gyroscope and no mentor to guide them, they migrate as one giant flock to join their parents thousands of miles away in a place they've never been. Now that's phenomenal!

And so we see God's love and care for His creatures in nature. If He watches over the lowly birds of His incredibly diverse creation, will He not most certainly care for you and me? You don't need to worry about what He can or cannot do for you. His words of assurance continue to inspire us today. *"'Therefore I tell you, do not worry about your life, what you will eat; or about your body, what you will wear. Life is more than food, and the body more than clothes. Consider the ravens: They do not sow or reap, they have no storeroom or barn; yet God feeds them. And how much more valuable you are than birds! Who of you by worrying can add a single hour to his life? Since you cannot do this very little thing, why do you worry about the rest?'" Luke 12:22-26 NIV.*

*"'Do not fear ... you are of more value than many sparrows.'" Luke 12:7. "Humble yourselves, therefore, under God's mighty hand, that he may lift you up in due time. Cast all your anxiety on him because he cares for you." 1 Peter 5:6, 7 NIV.*

---

4    Flying is almost effortless for these birds, and they are known to sleep only seconds at a time while in the air.

This is my Father's world,
    and to my listening ear
All nature sings, and round me rings
    the music of the spheres.
This is my Father's world:
    I rest me in the thought
Of rocks and trees, of skies and seas;
    His hand the wonders wrought.

This is my Father's world,
    the birds their carols raise,
The morning light, the lily white,
    declare their maker's praise.
This is my Father's world:
    He shines in all that's fair;
In the rustling grass I hear him pass;
    He speaks to me everywhere.

This is my Father's world.
    O let me ne'er forget
That though the wrong seems oft so strong,
    God is the ruler yet.
This is my Father's world:
    why should my heart be sad
The Lord is King; let the heavens ring!
    God reigns; let the earth be glad!

—Maltbie D. Babcock, "This Is My Father's World"

**You Have Done It Unto Me—Reading #2**

"The word of God reveals His character. He Himself has declared His infinite love and pity. When Moses prayed, "*Show me Your glory,*" the Lord answered, "*I will make all My goodness pass before you.*" *Exodus 33:18, 19.* This is His glory. The Lord passed before Moses, and proclaimed, "'*The Lord, The Lord God, merciful and gracious, long-suffering, and abounding in goodness and truth, keeping mercy for thousands, forgiving iniquity and transgression and sin.*'" *Exodus 34:6, 7.* He is "*slow to anger, and abundant in loving kindness,*" "*because He delights in mercy.*" *Jonah 4:2; Micah 7:18.*

"God has bound our hearts to Him by unnumbered tokens in heaven and in earth. Through the things of nature, and the deepest and tenderest earthly ties that human hearts can know, He has sought to reveal Himself to us. Yet these but imperfectly represent His love. Though all these evidences have been given, the enemy of good blinded the minds of men, so that they looked upon God with fear; they thought of Him as severe and unforgiving. Satan led men to conceive of God as a being whose chief attribute is stern justice,—one who is a severe judge, a harsh, exacting creditor. He pictured the Creator as a being who is watching with jealous eye to discern the errors and mistakes of men, that He may visit judgments upon them. It was to remove this dark shadow, by revealing to the world the infinite love of God, that Jesus came to live among men.

"The Son of God came from heaven to make manifest the Father. "'*No man has seen God at any time; the only begotten Son, who is in the bosom of the Father, He has declared Him.*'" *John 1:18.* "'*Nor does anyone know the Father, except the Son, and he to whom the Son wills to reveal Him.*'" *Matthew 11:27.* When one of the disciples made the request, "'*Show us the Father,*'" Jesus answered, "'*Have I been with you so long, and yet you have not known Me, Philip? He who has seen Me has seen the Father; so how can you say, ""Show us the Father?""*'" *John 14:8, 9.*

"In describing His earthly mission, Jesus said, The Lord "*has anointed Me to preach the gospel to the poor; He has sent Me to heal the brokenhearted, to preach deliverance to the captives, and recovery of sight to the blind, to set at liberty those who are oppressed.*'" *Luke 4:18.* This was His work. He went about doing good and healing all that were oppressed by Satan. There were whole villages where there was not a moan of sickness in any house, for He had passed through them and healed all their sick. His work gave evidence of His divine anointing. Love, mercy, and compassion were revealed in every act of His life; His heart went out in tender sympathy to the children of men. He took man's nature, that He might reach man's wants. The poorest and humblest were not afraid to approach Him. Even little children were attracted to Him. They loved to climb upon His knees and gaze into the pensive face, benignant with love."[5]

**Illustrative Sketch:**

Gideon Randle sat on the hard train seat, staring out the window, a worried expression on his careworn face. At 70 years-of-age traveling was not his favorite pastime, though this journey was only a hundred miles to Harrowtown. It was a warm sunny day in November, but that didn't make the journey any less tiring for the feeble old man. Several times already he had startled himself from slumber when the conductor called out the name of some upcoming train station. "How long before we reach Harrowtown?" he finally asked the busy conductor.

"At half past eight this evening."

Assured that all would be well, Gideon once again settled himself in his seat for a short nap. Darkness came as the train roared on mile after mile. Behind him sat Albert, a tall boy, also a passenger on the train. A bright handsome lad, but he had a nasty streak in him that could make him mean and even cruel at times. "I'm going to have some fun," he bragged to his seatmate as they watched the old man nod off. "Watch what I do."

Presently the train pulled to a stop again at a local station, and Albert jumped from his seat to shake Mr. Randle violently. "Get up!" he said roughly. "This is Harrowtown! You've got to get off here!"

The old man stood to his feet quickly, dazed and confused by the change of daylight to darkness. He grabbed his traveling bag and limped off the train to the station platform. Unfortunately, in all the commotion and squealing of train brakes none of the other passengers realized what had happened before the train pulled out of the station leaving Gideon behind.

Albert and his seatmate laughed hysterically. "What fun!" they snickered.

Meanwhile Gideon Randle was asking the ticket agent at the train station if he knew where Luke Conway lived.

"There's no one living here by that name," he replied.

---

5    White, 10.

"Isn't this Harrowtown?" asked Mr. Randle, looking very much confused.

"I'm afraid not. It's Whipple Village."

Mr. Randle was distraught. "Then I got off at the wrong station!" His face grew troubled, and he sighed heavily. "That boy on the train tricked me." Gideon spent the night in a hotel room that he couldn't afford, on a bed that was far from comfortable. By dawn he was more weary and careworn than ever.

When he got to the station, there were many people rushing about on the station platform. The old man appeared overwhelmed and a little confused. Among those passengers waiting to board the train was an honest-looking boy, accompanied by his mother who was there to see him off. "Lyman, that's a sad looking old man," she said to her son. "He looks distressed. When you board the train, see what you can do for him, will you?"

Lyman stepped beside the elderly man and offered his arm for support. "Thank you, son," Gideon smiled weakly at the strong looking lad beside him. "I'm not what I used to be. You're a real gentleman," he said as they boarded the train. "Where are you going, and what's your name?"

"To Harrowtown, sir. I'm applying for a job in a store, and I hope to get the position. My name is Lyman Dean."

"I'm sure you'll do fine, Lyman. You're a good boy," he smiled at Lyman. "I'm hoping my journey will turn out as well. I've had a bit of misfortune come my way now that I'm too old to run the farm. I've got a few debts, and I must find a man named Luke Conway to see if he can advise me."

"Luke Conway?" Lyman said with interest. "That's exactly who I'm going to see. I'll take you there!" he added cheerfully.

Half an hour later they stopped in Harrowtown and were soon at Luke Conway's business establishment. Gideon didn't recognize Albert, the rude boy from the train, who was also there applying for the job in Luke Conway's store.

Presently Mr. Conway came out of his office. He greeted the two applicants for the job, and then noticed Gideon standing there, crumpled hat in hand. "Mr. Randle!" he grasped the old man's hand. "What a surprise to see you here!"

In Mr. Conway's office, Gideon related the tale of his misfortune as best he could, but Mr. Conway finally stopped him. "Don't worry yourself, Gideon. Your troubles are over. You helped me along when I was a young man just getting started in life, and I'm forever grateful. I shall clear your debt, and you can come to live with me here in Harrowtown, if you wish."

Mr. Conway returned to the boys sitting in his waiting room. "And now boys, I suppose you'd like to know about the job."

"What is your name?" he turned to Albert, a frown creasing his forehead.

"Albert Gregory, and I think I'm the man for the job," the arrogant boy said quickly. I have testimonials here for you, letters of recommendation from Esquire Jenks, Reverend Joseph Lee, and Dr. Henshaw." He held out the envelopes to Mr. Conway, but the businessman ignored them.

"I don't care to see them," he said almost crossly. "I've seen you before, and I know your character well enough."

"And how about you, lad?" he looked intently at Lyman.

"Well, all I can say is, I will work hard for you. My family is poor, but my mother taught me to do an honest day's work. Unfortunately, I have no testimonials to recommend me, sir."

"Oh, yes, you have," Gideon spoke up as he stepped toward Lyman, and then he told Mr. Conway how polite Lyman had been to him that morning.

"That's good enough in my estimation," Mr. Conway said briskly. "With a recommendation like that, I'll give you the job, son." Lyman's mouth dropped open in surprise.

"But," Albert demanded impatiently, "I'm the one with all the credentials!"

"You?" Mr. Conway stared at Albert coldly. "I saw you in action on the train last evening. I was sitting behind you taking a nap like Gideon. By the time I realized what was happening, it was too late to help him. It was a nasty trick you played on him." He turned to Gideon, "Is this the boy who treated you so rudely at Whipple Village?"

"Why, yes, I believe it is." Gideon squinted at Albert. "Yes, that's the boy," and he pointed a finger at Albert. "You should be ashamed of yourself, young man! If you were more like Lyman, here, maybe you could get a good job, too."

Albert squirmed uneasily, stood, and made a quick exit.

"You are a boy after God's own heart," Mr. Conway said proudly as he laid a hand on Lyman's shoulder, "and my dear friend Mr. Randle here can testify to that. Kindness goes a long way toward qualifying us for blessings in this life, and in the life to come."[6]

*"Then the King will say to those on His right hand, 'Come, you blessed of My Father, inherit the kingdom prepared for you from the foundation of the world.' ... 'Inasmuch as you did it to one of the least of these My brethren, you did it to Me.'" Matthew 25:34, 40.*

We may not always realize that everything we do
    Affects not only our lives but touches others too.
A single happy smile can always brighten up the day
    For anyone who happens to be passing by your way.

And a little bit of thoughtfulness that shows someone you care
    Creates a ray of sunshine for both of you to share.
Yes, every time you offer someone a helping hand,
    Every time you show a friend you understand.

Every time you have a kind and gentle word to give,
    You help someone to find beauty in this precious life we live.
For happiness brings happiness and loving ways bring love,
    And giving is the treasure that contentment is made of.

—Author Unknown, "Everything We Do"

**Lamb of God—Reading #3**

"Jesus did not suppress one word of truth, but He uttered it always in love. He exercised the greatest tact and thoughtful, kind attention in His intercourse with the people. He was never rude, never needlessly spoke a severe word, never gave needless pain to a sensitive soul. He

---

6    M. A. Vroman, "Lyman Dean's Testimonials," in *Sabbath Readings for the Home Circle* (South Lancaster, MA: South Lancaster Printing Co., 1905), 251.

did not censure human weakness. He spoke the truth, but always in love. He denounced hypocrisy, unbelief, and iniquity; but tears were in His voice as He uttered His scathing rebukes. He wept over Jerusalem, the city He loved, which refused to receive Him, the way, the truth, and the life. They had rejected Him, the Savior, but He regarded them with pitying tenderness. His life was one of self-denial and thoughtful care for others. Every soul was precious in His eyes. While He ever bore Himself with divine dignity, He bowed with the tenderest regard to every member of the family of God. In all men He saw fallen souls whom it was His mission to save.

"Such is the character of Christ as revealed in His life. This is the character of God. It is from the Father's heart that the streams of divine compassion, manifest in Christ, flow out to the children of men. Jesus, the tender, pitying Savior, was God *"manifest in the flesh."* *1 Timothy 3:16.*

"It was to redeem us that Jesus lived and suffered and died. He became "a Man of Sorrows," that we might be made partakers of everlasting joy. God permitted His beloved Son, full of grace and truth, to come from a world of indescribable glory, to a world marred and blighted with sin, darkened with the shadow of death and the curse. He permitted Him to leave the bosom of His love, the adoration of the angels, to suffer shame, insult, humiliation, hatred, and death. *"The chastisement of our peace was upon Him; and with His stripes we are healed."* *Isaiah 53:5.* Behold Him in the wilderness, in Gethsemane, upon the cross! The spotless Son of God took upon Himself the burden of sin. He who had been one with God, felt in His soul the awful separation that sin makes between God and man. This wrung from His lips the anguished cry, *"'My God, My God, why have You forsaken Me?'"* *Matthew 27:46.* It was the burden of sin, the sense of its terrible enormity, of its separation of the soul from God—it was this that broke the heart of the Son of God.

"But this great sacrifice was not made in order to create in the Father's heart a love for man, not to make Him willing to save. No, no! *"God so loved the world that He gave His only-begotten Son."* *John 3:16.* The Father loves us, not because of the great propitiation, but He provided the propitiation because He loves us. Christ was the medium through which He could pour out His infinite love upon a fallen world. *"God was in Christ, reconciling the world to Himself."* *2 Corinthians 5:19.* God suffered with His Son. In the agony of Gethsemane, the death of Calvary, the heart of Infinite Love paid the price of our redemption.

"Jesus said, *"'Therefore My Father loves Me, because I lay down My life, that I may take it again.'"* *John 10:17.* That is, 'My Father has so loved you that He even loves Me more for giving My life to redeem you. In becoming your Substitute and Surety, by surrendering My life, by taking your liabilities, your transgressions, I am endeared to My Father; for by My sacrifice, God can be just, and yet the Justifier of him who believes in Jesus.'"[7]

**Illustrative Sketch:**

Hundreds of prophecies in the Bible point to the coming of Jesus as the Savior of the world. Standing above them all is one poignant passage: the saga of Abraham's offering of Isaac on Mount Moriah. I believe the event was watched breathlessly by the inhabitants of un-fallen worlds because it pre-figured dramatically the coming sacrifice of Jesus.

Can you imagine them? Abraham and Isaac walking that stren-uous three-day journey as they make the dreaded pilgrimage? A wealthy sheik and his prince-like son travel by foot from Beersheba to Salem in the hill country of Canaan. The day is hot with no breeze to stir the waves of shimmering heat rising from the dusty, rock-strewn pathway. Pesky biting flies buzz everywhere landing first on Abraham's neck, and then on Isaac's arms and legs. The two of them swat at the flies impatiently, but the insects keep coming back for more.

For Abraham the annoyance of this inconvenience is eclipsed by his knowledge that he must soon give up his son, must sacrifice Isaac on a lonely hill called Moriah. In this shocking story, father and son become two of the most important figures of Old Testament lore. Abraham, directed by God to sacrifice his son, was willing to go through the heart-wrenching, mind-bending ordeal.

Perhaps greatest of all, and just as inspiring, is the fact that Isaac himself was willing to surrender himself in this test of faith. Why?

7    White, 12.

Because God asked it of him. The event was a mutual, collaborate effort by Abraham and Isaac to fulfill the will of the Lord and obey His explicit command: *"'Take now your son, your only son Isaac, ... and offer him there as a burn offering on one of the mountains of which I shall tell you.'" Genesis 22:2.*

This event portrays the coming of the world's Redeemer. This sacred hill, Mt. Moriah, is where God comes near to mankind. King David purchased it as a place to pitch the legendary tabernacle from Israel's wilderness wanderings. Then Solomon erected his world-famous temple atop Moriah, constructing the Most Holy Place on the spot traditionally believed to be the location of Abraham's and Isaac's altar. It was here that the Ark of the Covenant rested for over 600 years before Judah was finally taken captive by the Babylonians.

But the crowning honor of all for Mount Moriah was when Jesus, God's Son, came to live among men. He walked on the holy hill in the sacred halls of the temple and blessed the nation of Israel with His presence. Then just a few hundred yards north of this sacred spot, on a sister hill called Calvary, God gave up His only Son to die as the Sacrificial Lamb for the human race. He perished so that you and I might live, thereby establishing us once and for all as His children, heirs to the kingdom of God. We can ask no greater display of God's love, no more impressive gift than Jesus. *"Behold! The Lamb of God who takes away the sin of the world.'" John 1:29.*

The lyrics from a well-known gospel song express this sentiment, inviting us to be led by Jesus, the Lamb of God, to serve Him all of our days.

> Your only Son no sin to hide,
>     but You have sent Him from Your side
> To walk upon this guilty sod
>     and to become the Lamb of God.
> Oh, Lamb of God, sweet Lamb of God,
>     I love the holy Lamb of God.
> Oh wash me in His precious blood,
>     My Jesus Christ the Lamb of God.

Your gift of love they crucified,
    they laughed and scorned Him as He died,
The humble King they named a fraud
    and sacrificed the Lamb of God.
Oh, Lamb of God, sweet Lamb of God,
    I love the holy Lamb of God.
Oh wash me in His precious blood,
    My Jesus Christ the Lamb of God.

I was so lost, I should have died,
    but You have brought me to Your side
To be led by Your staff and rod,
    and to be called the Lamb of God
Oh, Lamb of God, sweet Lamb of God,
    I love the holy Lamb of God.
Oh wash me in His precious blood,
    My Jesus Christ the Lamb of God.

—Twila Paris, "Lamb of God"

## What More Could He Do?—Reading #4

"None but the Son of God could accomplish our redemption; for only He who was in the bosom of the Father could declare Him. Only He who knew the height and depth of the love of God could make it manifest. Nothing less than the infinite sacrifice made by Christ in behalf of fallen man could express the Father's love to lost humanity.

"'*God so loved the world, that He gave His only-begotten Son.' John 3:16.* He gave Him not only to live among men, to bear their sins, and die their sacrifice. He gave Him to the fallen race. Christ was to identify Himself with the interests and needs of humanity. He who was one with God has linked Himself with the children of men by ties that are never to be broken. Jesus is *"not ashamed to call them brethren"* *Hebrews 2:11*; He is our Sacrifice, our Advocate, our Brother, bearing our human form before the Father's throne, and through eternal ages one with the race He has redeemed—the Son of man. And all this that man might be uplifted from the ruin and degradation of sin that he might reflect the love of God and share the joy of holiness.

"The price paid for our redemption, the infinite sacrifice of our heavenly Father in giving His Son to die for us, should give us exalted conceptions of what we may become through Christ. As the inspired apostle John beheld the height, the depth, the breadth of the Father's love toward the perishing race, he was filled with adoration and reverence; and, failing to find suitable language in which to express the greatness and tenderness of this love, he called upon the world to behold it. *"Behold, what manner of love the Father has bestowed upon us, that we should be called the sons of God." 1 John 3:1.*

"What a value this places upon man! Through transgression the sons of man become subjects of Satan. Through faith in the atoning sacrifice of Christ the sons of Adam may become the sons of God. By assuming human nature, Christ elevates humanity. Fallen men are placed where, through connection with Christ, they may indeed become worthy of the name "sons of God."

"Such love is without a parallel. Children of the heavenly King! Precious promise! Theme for the most profound meditation! The matchless love of God for a world that did not love Him! The thought has a subduing power upon the soul and brings the mind into captivity to the will of God. The more we study the divine character in the light of the cross, the more we see mercy, tenderness, and forgiveness blended with equity and justice, and the more clearly we discern innumerable evidences of a love that is infinite and a tender pity surpassing a mother's yearning sympathy for her wayward child."[8]

**Illustrative Sketch:**

Volney Beckner was an Irish lad, the son of a poor fisherman. His father had always intended the boy should sail the seven seas, and took great pains to teach him such things as are useful for a sailor to know. He tried to make him brave and hardy, teaching him to swim when he was little more than a baby. As he grew, the father reminded Volney that strength of character is the most awesome of virtues, and no sacrifice should be considered too great in the line of duty.

---

8    White, 14.

Volney was just nine when he first went to sea with his father as a cabin boy on a merchant ship. Life was hard for the boy as he scrubbed decks and mended sails and peeled potatoes. Some days his fingers bled from all the work. Some nights he could hardly sleep lying in his hammock in the oppressive heat below deck.

But he was a Beckner, and his father had taught him to be proud of it. He worked hard and soon grew calluses where there had been blisters. His body grew tough; he never got sick, and he feared nothing.

During violent storms when the rain was coming down in sheets and the winds howled like demons, the Irish boy climbed the stays and sail yards without a word of complaint. He would mount the topmast, hanging on for dear life as he tied down the sails. No job was beyond his strength. No job was too hard or too simple. His father was proud of the boy, but as a sailor he never showed it.

When Volney turned twelve the captain promoted him as the most clever and trustworthy of lads, and doubled his pay. His mates on board the ship thought him a most generous chap and knew he deserved the awards, but Volney was uneasy at being praised for things he considered his duty. Not surprisingly, the crew loved him all the more for it. Young though he was, they felt he was the heart and soul of the sailing ship. Many a time Volney had shown himself ready and able to brave the dangers at sea, and to risk his own life if necessary for the good of the crew.

Finally, there came a day when he was faced with the most awesome of challenges, a truly heroic deed that defied logic. The vessel in which Volney and his father sailed was headed to Port au Prince, in Santo Domingo. On board a little girl, the daughter of one of the passengers, slipped away from her nanny and ran up to the deck to see the sights. Unfortunately, the heaving swell of the ocean tide made her dizzy, and she suddenly fell overboard.

Volney's father was the first to see the accident and sprang to action. Diving over the side of the ship, he swam to the little girl and caught her by the dress. With one hand he swam to reach the small row boat that the crew was lowering to him, and with the other he held tight to the child. Suddenly, to his horror he caught sight of a shark swimming at top speed toward them.

The sailor was a strong swimmer, but he hadn't a moment to spare, and the race was on. He shouted frantically for help, but there was little anyone could do for him or the little girl until they should reach the boat. No one dared to jump to their rescue for it would mean certain death.

None, except one. Urged on by a boy's love for his father, Volney did something grown men dared not attempt. Without hesitation he grabbed a sharp saber and leaped into the sea. Diving under the fast approaching shark, he drove the weapon up to its hilt into the shark's body.

The shark was stunned momentarily, but then suddenly turned on the boy. Again and again the boy attacked with the saber, and it seemed he would make short work of the shark. The shark began to list to one side, and ropes were thrown to rescue the father and his son. They both grasped the lines, and a shout of joy was raised, "They are saved!"

But it was not to be so. The shark, cheated of his prey, revived now and in one last desperate attempt lunged at the courageous, noble-hearted boy. The struggle was a horrible mismatch, and within seconds the battle was over. Volney's father and the young girl were saved, but the life of the lad was snuffed out, sacrificed for the good of those he had dared to save.[9] "Greater *love has no one than this, than to lay down his life for his friends.*" *John 15:13.*

> Through the eyes of faith I picture
>   God's Son stepping down,
> Humbly taking off His robes
>   And laying down His crown.
>
> He left Heaven's home
>   To help a world that was enslaved,
> Led by love He came to seek and save.
>   Though some people walked away,

---

9    Marmaduke Park, "Volney Beckner," in *Thrilling Stories of the Ocean* (1852), Archive Children's Library, Project Gutenberg, http://www.archive.org/details/thrillingstories13604gut (accessed 5 Dec. 2010), Released 6 Oct. 2004.

He loved them just the same.
    And though He gave them all He could,
They still despised His name.
    From Bethlehem to Calvary

He healed the wounds of man.
    On the cross His death fulfilled the plan.
What more could He do?
    I ask you, what more could He do?

To show His matchless love for man
    Was always just and true?
What more could He do?
    What more could He do?
He gave His life for you,
    What more could He do?

—Pete McCloud, "What More Could He Do?"

---⟨✦⟩---

# CHAPTER 2

# The Sinner's Need of Christ

**Breathe on Me Breath of God—Reading #1**

"Man was originally endowed with noble powers and a well-balanced mind. He was perfect in his being, and in harmony with God. His thoughts were pure, his aims holy. But through disobedience, his powers were perverted, and selfishness took the place of love. His nature became so weakened through transgression that it was impossible for him, in his own strength, to resist the power of evil. He was made captive by Satan, and would have remained so forever had not God specially interposed. It was the tempter's purpose to thwart the divine plan in man's creation, and fill the earth with woe and desolation. And he would point to all this evil as the result of God's work in creating man.

"In his sinless state, man held joyful communion with Him *"in whom are hidden all the treasures of wisdom and knowledge."* *Colossians 2:3.* But after his sin, he could no longer find joy in holiness, and he sought to hide from the presence of God.

"Such is still the condition of the unrenewed heart. It is not in harmony with God, and finds no joy in communion with Him. The sinner could not be happy in God's presence; he would shrink from the companionship of holy beings. Could he be permitted to enter heaven, it would have no joy for him. The spirit of unselfish love that reigns there—every heart responding to the heart of Infinite Love—would touch no answering chord in his soul. His thoughts, his interests, his motives, would be alien to those that actuate the sinless dwellers there. He would be a discordant note in the melody of heaven. Heaven would be to him a place of torture; he would long to be hidden from Him who is its light, and the center of its joy. It is no arbitrary decree on the part of God that excludes the wicked from heaven; they are shut out by their own unfitness for its companionship. The glory of God would be to them a consuming fire. They would welcome destruction, that they might be hidden from the face of Him who died to redeem them.

"It is impossible for us, of ourselves, to escape from the pit of sin in which we are sunken. Our hearts are evil, and we cannot change them. *"Who can bring a clean thing out of an unclean? no one." "The carnal mind is enmity against God: for it is not subject to the law of God, nor indeed can be." Job 14:4; Romans 8:7.* Education, culture, the exercise of the will, human effort, all have their proper sphere, but here they are powerless. They may produce an outward correctness of behavior, but they cannot change the heart; they cannot purify the springs of life. There must be a power working from within, a new life from above, before men can be changed from sin to holiness. That power is Christ. His grace alone can quicken the lifeless faculties of the soul, and attract it to God, to holiness."[10]

**Illustrative Sketch:**

Charles William Post was one of the success stories of the 19th Century, but you wouldn't have known it by his first attempts in business. He quit college at age 15, borrowed $500, and started a general store in Kansas. The store failed, so he tried his hand at designing farm implements, but that venture failed too. A few years later he bought 200,000 acres in Texas to build a utopian city called Post City, but that was a bust. He even tinkered with science to "dynamite" rain out of the Texas sky, but again he was unsuccessful.

Eventually he had a nervous breakdown and ended up in John Harvey Kellogg's world-famous sanitarium in Battle Creek, Michigan. It was here that Mr. Post learned to love the vegetarian diet promoted by Dr. Kellogg, and shortly thereafter he built his own health food factory in Battle Creek near the famous Kellogg's Cereal Company. One of his products—Grape Nuts cereal—is still on the market today.

Mr. Post's instincts for business came from his father's, but his wit for advertising inherited from his mother eventually made him one of

---

10   White, 17.

the most successful industrialists in the country. Not surprisingly, he became extremely wealthy from his various enterprises.

But although money could buy success, it couldn't buy his happiness. He was never very spiritual and as he grew older, he became more and more bitter towards God. Before his death by suicide in 1914, Post left unusual instructions in his will that when he was buried, they should pour a massive slab of concrete over his grave. The reason? If there was going to be a final resurrection, he didn't want God disturbing him.[11]

Those who have never learned to surrender themselves to God are the most unhappy in life. The Apostle Paul offers us this truth. "If you confess with your mouth the Lord Jesus and believe in your heart that God has raised Him from the dead, you will be saved. For with the heart one believes unto righteousness, and with the mouth confession is made unto salvation." Romans 10:9, 10.

Those who learn to partner with God, on the other hand, are content and make a real impact in the lives of others. Dorcas (her story is told in Acts 9) was just such a person, and the New Testament Church in Joppa came to love her for her "good works and charitable deeds" among them. Acts 9:36.

One day she got sick and died. At the funeral all the widows stood around weeping, showing Peter the garments Dorcas had made for them. Her reputation as expressed by the affection of her sisters and brothers in the local Church is enviable.

But that funeral wasn't the end of the story. When Peter miraculously raised Dorcas to life, it was a glorious day. Through the power of God, she was restored to them to continue her good works among the people of Joppa.

The resurrection of Dorcas is an example of what it will be like someday for those who are raised to eternal life when Jesus comes again. In that glorious morning Jesus will tell all those who have labored in service for Him, "'You did well. You are a good and loyal servant. Because you were loyal with small things, I will let you care for much greater things. Come and share my joy with me.'" Matthew 25:21 NCV.

---

11   Battle Creek Historical Tours, HistoricTour Battle Creek and Marshall, www.battlecreekvisitors.org.

Breathe on me, Breath of God,
　　Fill me with life anew,
That I may love what Thou dost love,
　　And do what Thou wouldst do.

Breathe on me, Breath of God,
　　Until my heart is pure,
Until with Thee I will one will—
　　To do and to endure.

Breathe on me, Breath of God,
　　Till I am wholly Thine,
Till all this earthly part of me
　　Glows with Thy fire divine.

Breathe on me, Breath of God,
　　So shall I never die,
But live with Thee the perfect life
　　Of Thine eternity.

　　　—Edwin Hatch, "Breathe on Me, Breath of God"

## Change of Heart—Reading #2

"The Savior said, "*Except a man be born from above,*'" unless he shall receive a new heart, new desires, purposes, and motives, leading to a new life, "*he cannot see the kingdom of God.*'" *John 3:3.* The idea that it is necessary only to develop the good that exists in man by nature, is a fatal deception. *"But the natural man does not receive the things of the Spirit of God, for they are foolishness to him; nor can he know them, because they are spiritually discerned." "'Do not marvel that I said to you, "You must be born again."'" 1 Corinthians 2:14; John 3:7.* Of Christ it is written, *"In Him was life; and the life was the light of men"*—the only *"name under heaven given among men, by which we must be saved." John 1:4; Acts 4:12.*

"It is not enough to perceive the loving-kindness of God, to see the benevolence, the fatherly tenderness, of His character. It is not enough to discern the wisdom and justice of His law, to see that it is founded upon the eternal principle of love. Paul the apostle saw all this when he exclaimed, *"I agree with the law that it is good." "The law is holy, and the commandment holy, and just, and good." Romans 7:16, 12.*

"But he added, in the bitterness of his soul-anguish and despair, *"I am carnal, sold under sin." Romans 7:14.* He longed for the purity, the righteousness, to which in himself he was powerless to attain, and cried out, *"O wretched man that I am! who will deliver me from this body of death?" Romans 7:24.* Such is the cry that has gone up from burdened hearts in all lands and in all ages. To all, there is but one answer, *"'Behold the Lamb of God, who takes away the sin of the world.'" John 1:29."* [12]

**Illustrative Sketch:**

Jesus came to seek and to save that which was lost, but He is a God of free will. He will not force Himself on anyone. As with the first couple in paradise, choice has always been an option. History is full of men and women who sold themselves to the world for what it could give them. Kings and queens, presidents, army generals, church leaders, unscrupulous businessmen, and a host of ordinary people illustrate the point well.

John D. Rockefeller is said to be one of the most famous men of our modern era, and one of the most brilliant businessmen of all time. As an entrepreneur, industrialist, and philanthropist, he changed the face of American business.

As a devout Baptist he believed in total abstinence from alcohol and tobacco. Although he was a tithe payer to his church and gave his money to charities freely, it is said he cared little for the people to which he gave.

His biographer Ron Chernow[13] says that while Rockefeller's good side was good, his bad side was bad. Not surprisingly, Rockefeller's dark side made it a habit to swindle others in business whenever he could,

---

12  White, 18.

13  Ron Chernow, *Titan: The Life of John D. Rockefeller, Sr.* ( New York: Random House, 1998).

leveraging millions from under his competitors. By 1880, according to his critics, Rockefeller's oil company became a large, cruel, and grasping monopoly. He never lost a chance to turn a dollar, and used unscrupulous methods to get it, caring nothing it seemed for anyone but himself.

John D. Rockefeller made his first million as one of the founders of Standard Oil during the late 1800s. As kerosene and gasoline grew in importance, his wealth soared, and he became the first American worth more than a billion dollars. In today's money that would have been worth about $300 billion. At the height of his glory, his vast American industrial empire included over 20,000 oil wells, 4,000 miles of pipeline, 5,000 tank cars, over 100,000 employees, and 90% of the world's oil refineries.

In his 50s, Rockefeller's health became so broken that his doctors were greatly concerned for his well-being. He had lost most of his hair, and was reduced to eating little more than crackers and milk. His habits of business and disregard for the welfare of others had driven him to become a selfish, grasping, evil man by anyone's standards. He was now a broken and discouraged man, and began to question his reasons for living. Then one cold, rainy night he was compelled to help someone in need, and he discovered how good it felt to be kind.

It was the beginning of a new life for Rockefeller, and the dawning of a new-birth experience as the Holy Spirit began to change him. He began giving money to those in need and often gave to complete strangers just to see the look of wonder on their faces. At retirement, he devoted himself to fulltime philanthropic giving to charities and other worthy causes. Over the course of time he became one of the greatest benefactors to public and private institutions in the history of the United States. His foundations gave to medical research and helped eradicate hookworm and yellow fever. He is also the founder of the University of Chicago and Rockefeller University.

John D. Rockefeller was a contradictory figure who sold himself to the love of money, but regained his soul through compassion for others. Jesus said that we cannot serve two masters. It's either God or money. Not both. They are mutually exclusive, as John D. Rockefeller found out. *"For what is a man profited if he gains the whole world, and loses his own soul? Or what will a man give in exchange for his soul?"* *Matthew 16:26.* Fortunately, Rockefeller came out the winner on several counts. His end was better than his beginning because he chose to ally himself with the One who holds the keys to life and death.

> He called me first in the early morn,
>     As I stood by the smiling sea,
> But I heeded not, for the day that was born,
>     Was a day that was all to me.
>
> So I builded my castles, and dreamed my dreams,
>     And wondered why she should fall,
> 'Til the night drew near, and the sunset gleams
>     Brought back the thought of His call.
>
> He called again one busy noon,
>     But my plans loomed large that day
> So I set full sail and forgot so soon
>     That the Master had come my way.
>
> But the winds were fierce that day, ah me!
>     And I struggled alone through the storm,
> Through the shadows, returning, off there in the quay
>     Me thought 'twas the Master's dorm.
>
> And as I entered the harbor at last,
>     I saw Him quietly stand,
> And though I needed Him not in the past,
>     He gently helped me to land.
>
> And So He called me again that day,
>     As we stood by the raging sea,
> Now He holds my hand and I walk His way,
>     As He comes through the storm with me.[14]

---

14  Nell Ruth Roffe, "Call of the Master," in *God's Minutes,* ed. C. L. Paddock (Nashville: Southern Publishing Association, 1963).

---

Jesus calls us to walk with Him. He knows the way ahead because He's already been through the rugged trails of life. Sometimes our stubborn streaks get in the way, and He understands that, but we must never let our pride keep us from doing the right thing. Surrendering to His will is our only hope for salvation and happiness—complete and unreserved surrender.

**Angels Watching Over Me—Reading #3**

"Many are the figures by which the Spirit of God has sought to illustrate truth, and make it plain to souls that long to be freed from the burden of guilt. When, after his sin in deceiving Esau, Jacob fled from his father's home, he was weighed down with a sense of guilt. Lonely and outcast as he was, separated from all that had made life dear, the one thought that above all others pressed upon his soul, was the fear that his sin had cut him off from God, that he was forsaken of Heaven. In sadness he lay down to rest on the bare earth, around him only the lonely hills, and above, the heavens bright with stars.

"As he slept, a strange light broke upon his vision; and lo, from the plain on which he lay, vast shadowy stairs seemed to lead upward to the very gates of heaven, and upon them angels of God were passing up and down; while from the glory above, the divine voice was heard in a message of comfort and hope. Thus was made known to Jacob that which met the need and longing of his soul—a Savior. With joy and gratitude he saw revealed a way by which he, a sinner, could be restored to communion with God. The mystic ladder of his dream represented Jesus, the only medium of communication between God and man.

"This is the same figure to which Christ referred in His conversation with Nathanael, when He said, *'You shall see heaven open, and the angels of God ascending and descending upon the Son of man.'* *John 1:51.* In the apostasy, man alienated himself from God; earth was cut off from heaven. Across the gulf that lay between, there could be no communion. But through Christ, earth is again linked with heaven. With His own merits, Christ has bridged the gulf which sin had made, so that the ministering angels can hold communion with man. Christ connects fallen man in his weakness and helplessness with the Source of infinite power."[15]

**Illustrative Sketch:**

Many are the stories to be told of heavenly angels come to comfort and protect God's people. Pressed in on every side by the forces of evil, they have been rescued from danger and even death by holy warriors sent from the throne of God.

Years ago when the modern missionary movement was getting started, John Paton and his wife went as pioneer missionaries to the New Hebrides Islands in the Western Pacific. It was culture shock at its worst. Times were hard, and the couple had to brave the elements to provide for their needs. No help was offered John by the locals as he struggled to build a crude home for himself and his wife. There were no stores or markets where they could buy food. No communication with the outside world. And the natives of the island to which they had come were anything but friendly. In fact they were cannibals. They were intrigued by the white folks who had come to live among them, but John was sure that if given the chance, they would not hesitate to kill and eat the missionaries for one of their local feasts.

But John and his wife stayed. Here among these primitive tribes of people were countless souls who had never heard the name of Jesus. They needed the hope the message of salvation could bring them. For John no sacrifice was too great if he could bring them the light of the gospel. No hardship too difficult to bear.

When sickness came to the village in the form of a deadly measles epidemic, scores began to die. John and his wife took food, water, and medicines to the sickest of the villagers, but most did not take the medicine as directed. Some jumped into the sea instead, to cool their fevered bodies and died shortly thereafter. Others dug holes for themselves in the cool earth, and were soon buried in the graves which they had dug. Panic set in among the villagers. The natives began to reason among themselves that the missionaries were to blame for the tragedies that had come upon them. In their superstitious minds they could not see the good these missionaries had come to do for them.

---

15  White, 20.

One night John, his wife, and another young missionary helper knelt in their home as usual, consecrating themselves to God in a season of prayer. They knew now that it was a matter of time before the tensions would break loose, but they prayed that God might spare them to continue spreading the gospel to the cannibal islanders.

As they prayed, the chief and his fierce savages surrounded the missionaries' humble cottage of thatch and oaken wattles. Urged on by superstitious fears, and the influence of alcohol and demons, the evil men emerged from the jungle to attack. Armed with clubs, killing stones, and muskets, they had come to kill and eat these foreigners whose God, they were sure had brought all their troubles upon them.

When the missionaries had finished their prayers and worship, the young missionary helper left John's house to go back to his own sleeping quarters. He was viciously attacked and injured, but John was able to rescue him and bring him back into the house. The savages fled, but John could hear them returning later.

John and his wife prayed all night, knowing that unless God intervened they would not survive the next wave of attacks. But the attack never came. When dawn broke over the eastern horizon, the village cannibals were nowhere in sight, and the missionaries never had trouble from them again. John was perplexed at the sudden change toward the missionaries by the cannibals, and a year later when relations with the cannibals had improved, he had a chance to ask the chief about that late night raid.

"Why did you not attack us the second time?" he asked the chief. "You could have easily overpowered us."

"Oh, no!" the chief quickly said, his eyes wide with wonder and excitement. "We could not. When we came back, your house was surrounded by armed guards!"

"We had no one standing guard over us," replied John in surprise. "My wife and the young missionary were the only ones at the house with me."

"Well, we saw them!" the chief insisted. "They were there, and we knew we were no match for so many!"

Surely angels from heaven were there that night to protect the missionaries! God's arm is never short to come to the aid of those who serve him in all humbleness and call upon Him for help in time of need.

John Paton remained many years in the Islands of the Hebrides and helped bring many, many souls to the Kingdom of God. His work and testimony among the cannibals is reflected in the inspirational words he later wrote: "Life in such circumstances led me to cling very near to the Lord Jesus. With my trembling hand clasped in the hand once nailed on Calvary, and now swaying the scepter of the universe, calmness and peace abode in my soul."[16]

And so it has always been for God's people. He has had His Divine security forces in every age to protect his children who are the heirs of salvation. Hebrews 1:14. In their times of need Daniel and Peter and Paul all had heavenly bodyguards dispatched to deliver them from evil. Today Satan and his allies would harm God's people too, if they could, but it is a great source of comfort to know that our God is all-powerful. He is able to guard his children to the uttermost, keeping watch over them by day, and during the vigils of the night. Hebrews 7:25.

*"I sought the Lord, and he heard me; And delivered me from all my fears. They looked to Him and were radiant, and their faces were not ashamed....The angel of the Lord encamps all around those who fear Him, and delivers them... The eyes of the Lord are on the righteous and His ears are open to their cry...Many are the afflictions of the righteous, but the Lord delivers him out of them all." Psalm 34:4, 5, 7, 15, 19.*

Sleep, my child, and peace attend thee
　　All through the night
Guardian angels God will send thee
　　All through the night
Soft the drowsy hours are creeping
　　Hill and dale in slumber sleeping
I my loving vigil keeping
　　All through the night

---

16　Billy Graham, "Angels Protect and Deliver Us," in *Angels: God's Secret Agents* (Dallas: Word Publishing, 1975).

While the moon her watch is keeping
　　All through the night
While the weary world is sleeping
　　All through the night
O'er thy spirit gently stealing
　　Visions of delight revealing
Breathes a pure and holy feeling
　　All through the night

Though I roam a minstrel lonely
　　All through the night
My true harp shall praise sing only
　　All through the night
Love's young dream, alas, is over
　　Yet my strains of love shall hover
Near the presence of my lover
　　All through the night

Hark, a solemn bell is ringing
　　Clear through the night
Thou, my love, art heavenward winging
　　Home through the night
Earthly dust from off thee shaken
　　Soul immortal shalt thou awaken
With thy last dim journey taken
　　Home through the night

—Jane Siberry, "All Through the Night"

## The Friend of the King—Reading #4

"But in vain are men's dreams of progress, in vain all efforts for the uplifting of humanity, if they neglect the one Source of hope and help for the fallen race. *"Every good gift and every perfect gift"* is from God. *James 1:17.* There is no true excellence of character apart from Him.

And the only way to God is Christ. He says, *"'I am the way, the truth, and the life: No one comes to the Father except through Me.'"* *John 14:6.*

"The heart of God yearns over His earthly children with a love stronger than death. In giving up His Son, He has poured out to us all heaven in one gift. The Savior's life and death and intercession, the ministry of angels, the pleading of the Spirit, the Father working above and through all, the unceasing interest of heavenly beings,—all are enlisted in behalf of man's redemption.

"Oh, let us contemplate the amazing sacrifice that has been made for us! Let us try to appreciate the labor and energy that Heaven is expending to reclaim the lost, and bring them back to the Father's house. Motives stronger, and agencies more powerful, could never be brought into operation; the exceeding rewards for right-doing, the enjoyment of heaven, the society of the angels, the communion and love of God and His Son, the elevation and extension of all our powers throughout eternal ages—are these not mighty incentives and encouragements to urge us to give the heart's loving service to our Creator and Redeemer?

"And, on the other hand, the judgments of God pronounced against sin, the inevitable retribution, the degradation of our character, and the final destruction, are presented in God's word to warn us against the service of Satan.

"Shall we not regard the mercy of God? What more could He do? Let us place ourselves in right relation to Him who has loved us with amazing love. Let us avail ourselves of the means provided for us that we may be transformed into His likeness, and be restored to fellowship with the ministering angels, to harmony and communion with the Father and the Son."[17]

## Illustrative Sketch:

A long time ago in a country far away there once lived a good king who ruled his people with justice and mercy. The king was a benevolent sovereign, fair and just in every way, and the citizens of that blessed country loved him without reservation. Under his rule the nation prospered, and because of God's blessing, they were always at peace with their neighbors.

---

17  White, 21.

On top of a grand and majestic mountain overlooking the fertile valley lived a poor old hermit. The old hermit was a lazy man. He never washed his clothes, he never swept his house, and he never weeded his garden. In fact, it seemed he absolutely despised anything that had to do with work.

Now it just so happened that one day the king left the valley and rode his royal steed up to the top of that mountain. The king stood by the old hermit's house overlooking the entire kingdom, and the panoramic view was incredible. Every corner of the vast region was visible and it seemed to glow in brilliant detail. The king was delighted with his discovery and asked the hermit if he might sit a while on a stool to soak it all in.

The old man was honored, of course, and went inside his house to find a stool to offer the king. But to his dismay he discovered he had no stool worthy of the king. In fact, the only one he had was in terrible disrepair. It was incomprehensible that he should offer such a seat to the mighty monarch. Frantically he searched his house for a better seat, and while he was looking, the king went away.

"But he will come again!" the hermit said to himself. "I know he will. He was so inspired by the extraordinary view of his valley, and I must have a place for him to sit when he comes." And so the old hermit cut some wood and carefully fashioned a beautiful stool, and waited for the king to come again.

And, one day a few weeks later he heard a horse coming up the hill, and behold, it was the king. The hermit ran to get the stool he'd made, and the king sat on the stool and took in the fantastic view of the valley. "Thank you so much, Mr. Hermit, for the wonderful seat to sit on while I enjoy the beautiful view of our valley. You have been so kind. Might you have a cool drink of water for me? The ride up the mountain was steep, and I am so very thirsty!"

The old hermit was embarrassed and turned away red-faced. How could he have failed to extend the most common of such courtesies by not offering the king a refreshing drink? He ran into his house to prepare the drink, but his worst fears were soon realized. He had no clean cup to give to the king. Only a few dirty pieces of chipped pottery lay around, and while he stood in his dirty kitchen trying to figure out what to do, the king went away. "He'll come again,

I know he will," the old man said to himself once more, "and I must be prepared!"

The hermit went to his potter's wheel and fashioned a new cup of clay, one that he was proud of and could offer the king. Then he cleaned out the spring and drew fresh water and waited for the king to come again.

And one day he heard a horse coming up the hill again, and the old hermit saw it was the king. And he ran to get the stool for the king to sit in the shade, and brought him a drink of cool, clear water. "Thank you so much, Mr. Hermit. You are kind to let me come see this beautiful valley, and you have refreshed me with your cool, fresh water. I was wondering? Would you have a little something for me to eat? The day has been long and I am quite hungry."

Something to eat! The old hermit was nearly beside himself with anguish that he should have missed so great an opportunity to provide for his king! How could he have been so stupid? Again he rushed into his house, but the truth of the matter was already obvious! He had nothing to offer the king. Only a dry crust or two of bread, and a few half-rotten grapes occupied his cupboard. He hung his head in despair, and while he was there the king went away.

"The king will come again!" the hermit reassured himself for the third time. "He loves the view and he can't stay away for long! I must get ready for him!" So the old hermit cut some wood, loaded it up on a cart, and took it down the mountain into the valley. He sold the wood at the market, bought some corn meal, and took it home to makes some corn cakes. Then he noticed how cluttered his garden was, so he weeded his sweet potatoes. And every day now he cleared out the spring, drew fresh water, baked corn cakes and sweet potatoes, and waited for the king to come again.

And sure enough, one day he heard a horse coming up the hill again. And the old hermit looked and it was the king. And the hermit ran to get the stool for the king to sit in the shade, and brought him sparkling, clear water from the spring, and served him up some corn cakes and baked sweet potatoes. As the king basked in the glorious view enjoying the meal, he said, "Mr. Hermit, thank you so much for your hospitality! This cool water is so refreshing, and the food is delicious! Would you mind if I spent the night here with you on this grand mountain so that I could see the sun rise over my kingdom?"

Mr. Hermit couldn't believe his ears! Sleep here! He had no proper bed for a king! All he had in the house were a few old sacks that he slept on in the corner. In shame the hermit ran into the house wondering what he should do. And while he was there, the king went away.

"But he'll come again, I know he will," the hermit said to himself, "and I must be prepared!" Forgetting that he didn't like to work, he cut down some trees, and with skilled craftsmanship he made a beautiful new bed for the king. Then he cut some more wood and hauled it to the city to trade for a nice mattress and a warm blanket. Then he noticed how dirty his clothes were, so he sold some more wood and bought himself some nice new clothes. Then he noticed how dirty his house was, and how fly-specked his windows were. So he brought a bucket of water from the spring and scrubbed his house and windows from top to bottom. And every day now he drew fresh water, weeded his garden, baked corn cakes, and dressed in his nice new clothes while he waited for the king to come again.

And one day he heard a horse coming up the hill, and the old hermit saw it was the king, and he ran to meet him. And the king came to sit on the stool, and drank the refreshing water, and ate hot corncakes and sweet potatoes. Then he stayed that night, and slept in the new bed, and rose early in the morning to watch the gorgeous sunrise over the beautiful valley.

The hermit and the king became such good friends that the king finally asked the old man to come and live with him in his royal palace. The hermit accepted the king's offer, and they both lived to a ripe old age. From time to time, however, they would ride their horses together up the long winding trail to the mountain top, and there they would enjoy the view together. What a change had come over the old hermit! He wasn't lazy anymore, and he didn't want to be by himself all the time any more. And people didn't call him a dirty old hermit anymore. They called him the friend of the king.[18]

---

18   Eric B. Hare, *Classic Eric B. Hare Stories, Vol. 2* (Nampa, ID: Chapel Record Recordings).

*"And we, who with unveiled faces all reflect the Lord's glory, are being transformed into his likeness with ever-increasing glory, which comes from the Lord, who is the Spirit."* *(2 Corinthians 3:18, NIV, 1984.)*

---◎---

# CHAPTER 3

# Repentance

**A New Heart—Reading #1**

"How shall a man be just with God? How shall the sinner be made righteous? It is only through Christ that we can be brought into harmony with God, with holiness; but how are we to come to Christ? Many are asking the same question as did the multitude on the Day of Pentecost, when, convicted of sin, they cried out, "*What shall we do?*" The first word of Peter's answer was, "*Repent.*" Acts 2:37, 38. At another time, shortly after, he said, "*Repent, … and be converted, that your sins may be blotted out.*" Acts 3:19.

"Repentance includes sorrow for sin and a turning away from it. We shall not renounce sin unless we see its sinfulness; until we turn away from it in heart, there will be no real change in the life.

"There are many who fail to understand the true nature of repentance. Multitudes sorrow that they have sinned and even make an outward reformation because they fear that their wrongdoing will bring suffering upon themselves. But this is not repentance in the Bible sense. They lament the suffering rather than the sin. Such was the grief of Esau when he saw that the birthright was lost to him forever. Balaam, terrified by the angel standing in his pathway with drawn sword, acknowledged his guilt lest he should lose his life; but there was no genuine repentance for sin, no conversion of purpose, no abhorrence of evil. Judas Iscariot, after betraying his Lord, exclaimed, "*I have sinned by betraying the innocent blood.*" Matthew 27:4.

"The confession was forced from his guilty soul by an awful sense of condemnation and a fearful looking for of judgment. The consequences that were to result to him filled him with terror, but there was no deep, heartbreaking grief in his soul, that he had betrayed the spotless Son of God and denied the Holy One of Israel. Pharaoh, when suffering under the judgments of God, acknowledged his sin in order to escape further punishment, but returned to his defiance of Heaven as soon as the plagues were stayed. These all lamented the results of sin, but did not sorrow for the sin itself.

"But when the heart yields to the influence of the Spirit of God, the conscience will be quickened, and the sinner will discern something of the depth and sacredness of God's holy law, the foundation of His government in heaven and on earth. The *"... Light, which gives light to every man coming into the world"* illumines the secret chambers of the soul, and the hidden things of darkness are made manifest. *John 1:9.* Conviction takes hold upon the mind and heart. The sinner has a sense of the righteousness of Jehovah and feels the terror of appearing, in his own guilt and uncleanness, before the Searcher of hearts. He sees the love of God, the beauty of holiness, the joy of purity; he longs to be cleansed and to be restored to communion with Heaven."[19]

**Illustrative Sketch:**

The events surrounding the crucifixion of Jesus make for some of the most profound stories in the entire Bible, and the characters in them are unforgettable. The thief on the cross who accepted Jesus as his Savior hung at the crossroads of time with Jesus, who bore the penalty for sin. Like Jesus he was taken to Golgotha on Friday morning to be crucified on a cruel cross. Like Jesus he was stripped bare, shamed, and taunted mercilessly by the religious rabble. Like Jesus the thief suffered incredibly from the pain of cruel nails in his hands and feet, the elements of sun and wind on his parched skin, the flies and scavenging birds that landed on him to pick at his defenseless body.

But that is where the similarities end. Jesus was dying for the sins of the world. The thief was not. The thief agonized through the hours of that endless Friday to pay for his own sin. He suffered the excruciating reality of jagged nails tearing at his flesh because he committed crimes in a Roman regime. He endured the embarrassment of nakedness and public humility that executions of this sort brought to the guilty.

---

19   White, 23.

He was helpless on a hill called Calvary beside the Savior of the world, and though this was not where he would have chosen to come, it was where God brought him to save him. Nailed as a thief on a beam of hewn lumber, he was hanging in the shadow of the One who could save him from the wages of sin and eternal death. In the presence of the Son of God the thief did the wisest thing any man on death row could do—he surrendered himself to Jesus. Incensed by the taunts of the other thief hanging opposite him, and urged on by the calling of the Holy Spirit, this thief strung up between earth and heaven, threw himself on the mercies of God's only Son. In that moment he understood why Jesus was being lifted upon a cross. "'And I, if I be lifted up from the earth, will draw all men unto me.'" John 12:32, KJV

But to the thief Jesus was more than just the Redeemer of the world. He was a coming King, and it inspired him to make one final request. "'Remember me when You come into Your kingdom,'" he pleaded, and never were words more welcome to Jesus than this heart cry from a man whose earthly time had run out. Luke 23:42.

Although the thief's last day of life had come, he understood a far more serious issue for him was at hand. He understood that he was unprepared to stand before a Holy God in the judgment. But in Jesus he saw his Savior, the One who could take away the guilty stains of his life's record, and it was this that gave him hope beyond the grave.

On the cross that day the beauty of Jesus' Divinity flashed forth, and the thief recognized it for what it was. Unable to kneel at the feet of Jesus, nailed as he was to the cross, he bowed his head in submission to the One who could bring him peace and courage in the face of death. And because of the thief's humble surrender, Jesus promised him eternal life and a home in paradise. At that moment the dying criminal's record was cleared, and he was immediately restored to the image of God in which he was created. "Having been justified by His grace we … become heirs according to the hope of eternal life." Titus 3:7.

The cross of Jesus' day was a cruel instrument of torture, one of the worst ever invented for purposes of execution. And yet, we cannot deny that for the dying thief who gave his life to Jesus that day, it was exactly where he needed to be.

Jesus invites us all to take up our crosses and follow Him. If we are not willing to do this, we can have no part in Him. And so like the thief, the cross is the very best place we can be, humbly surrendering our lives and our hearts to our Savior daily. Only then can we find rest for our souls.

> Jesus, keep me near the cross,
>     There a precious fountain
> Free to all, a healing stream
>     Flows from Calvary's mountain.
>
> In the cross, in the cross,
>     Be my glory ever;
> Till my ransomed soul shall find
>     Rest beyond the river.
>
> Near the cross, a trembling soul,
>     Love and mercy found me;
> There the bright and morning star
>     Sheds its beams around me.
>
> Near the cross! O Lamb of God,
>     Bring its scenes before me;
> Help me walk from day to day,
>     With its shadows o'er me.
>
> Near the cross I'll watch and wait
>     Hoping, trusting ever,
> Till I reach the golden strand,
>     Just beyond the river.
>
> In the cross, in the cross,
>     Be my glory ever;
> Till my ransomed soul shall find
>     Rest beyond the river.
>
> —Frances J. Crosby, "Near the Cross"

## Thou Art the Man—Reading #2

"The prayer of David after his fall, illustrates the nature of true sorrow for sin. His repentance was sincere and deep. There was no effort to palliate his guilt; no desire to escape the judgment threatened, inspired his prayer. David saw the enormity of his transgression; he saw the defilement of his soul; he loathed his sin. It was not for pardon only that he prayed, but for purity of heart. He longed for the joy of holiness—to be restored to harmony and communion with God. This was the language of his soul:

*"Blessed is he whose transgression is forgiven, whose sin is covered. Blessed is the man to whom the LORD does not impute iniquity, and in whose spirit there is no deceit." Psalm 32:1, 2.*

*"Have mercy upon me, O God, according to Your loving-kindness; According unto the multitude of Your tender mercies blot out my transgressions. ... For I acknowledge my transgressions: and my sin is ever before me. ... Purge me with hyssop, and I shall be clean: wash me, and I shall be whiter than snow. ... Create in me a clean heart, O God; And renew a steadfast spirit within me. Do not cast me away from Your presence; And do not take Your Holy Spirit from me. Restore to me the joy of Your salvation; And uphold me with Your generous spirit. ... Deliver me from blood guiltiness, O God, the God of my salvation: And my tongue shall sing aloud of Your righteousness." Psalm 51:1-14.*

"A repentance such as this, is beyond the reach of our own power to accomplish; it is obtained only from Christ, who ascended up on high and has given gifts unto men. Just here is a point on which many may err, and hence they fail of receiving the help that Christ desires to give them. They think that they cannot come to Christ unless they first repent, and that repentance prepares for the forgiveness of their sins. It is true that repentance does precede the forgiveness of sins; for it is only the broken and contrite heart that will feel the need of a Savior. But must the sinner wait till he has repented before he can come to Jesus? Is repentance to be made an obstacle between the sinner and the Savior?

"The Bible does not teach that the sinner must repent before he can heed the invitation of Christ, *"Come to Me, all you who labor and are heavy laden, and I will give you rest."* *Matthew 11:28*. It is the virtue that goes forth from Christ, that leads to genuine repentance. Peter made the matter clear in his statement to the Israelites when he said, *"Him God has exalted to His right hand to be Prince and Savior, to give repentance to Israel and forgiveness of sins."* *Acts 5:31*. We can no more repent without the Spirit of Christ to awaken the conscience than we can be pardoned without Christ.

"Christ is the source of every right impulse. He is the only one that can implant in the heart enmity against sin. Every desire for truth and purity, every conviction of our own sinfulness, is an evidence that His Spirit is moving upon our hearts." [20]

**Illustrative Sketch:**

Then the Lord sent Nathan to David. And when the prophet had come into the royal palace, he stood before the king and said, "There were two men in a certain town, one rich and the other poor. The rich man owned several large tracts of land, which he farmed in wheat and barley mostly, although he did have several orchards of olives and sycamore fruit. He also had a large herd of cattle and over five hundred sheep, each one of them making him infinitely wealthy in the eyes of the villagers. But he was also one of the meanest men around, and a bully by nature. Although an Israelite by birth, he was not devout, and he had no heart for sympathy. He obviously cared more for himself that anyone else, least of all the men who worked for him.

Now, the poor man worked for the wealthy landowner as a day laborer, but he had nothing of this world's goods, save one little ewe lamb which he had raised from birth. It grew up with his children, shared his food and drink, and even slept in his arms at night. Not surprisingly the little lamb was like a daughter to him.

Now a distinguished traveler came to see the rich man one day. The rich man invited him to stay the night, and straightway began making extravagant preparations to see that his visitor should feel most

20   White, 24.

welcome. A banquet was to be prepared in honor of the celebrated guest, but the rich man refused to take from his own flocks and herds for such a feast. Instead, he sent one of his servants down to the poor man's house in broad daylight to take by force the little lamb the family held so dear. The servant made no apologies, and left the poor man with his family heartbroken over the loss of the little creature.

When Nathan finished his story, King David was very angry, and his heart burned within him toward the man of wealth. And the king said to Nathan, "As surely as the Lord lives, the man who did this deserves to die! Besides that, the Law of Moses says he must pay for that lamb four times over because he did such a thing and had no pity."[21]

Then the prophet looked steadfastly upon the king with righteous indignation. In scathing tones he fearlessly announced, "You are the man!"[22]

Immediately David's heart was stricken with remorse for his own sin of passion and treachery now public knowledge. Tragically he had dishonored an innocent woman, and one of his most trusted army officers was now slain on the battlefield. Although David was now ready to repent with bitter tears, he could not escape the noose he had put around his own neck. For the rest of his life he would experience the consequences of his infidelity and betrayal. Never again would his subjects see him as their ultimate leader. Never again would they respect and admire him as they once had, and his indiscretions now emboldened many to live their lives with a sense of spiritual recklessness.

But the price in his family for this sin was more tangible. The son conceived in sin with his adulteress died at birth, thus beginning the fulfillment of the prophecy David pronounced on his own head.

His other sons all fought among themselves with hatred and jealousy in competition for positions of power. Ammon committed a crime in defiling his sister Tamar, and in the absence of justice for this transgression, his brother Absalom retaliated and murdered him. Absalom fled the country but a few years later staged a coup against his father, King David, and then died violently in battle. And then finally, Adonijah the firstborn attempted to take his father's throne by force,

---

21  2 Samuel 12:5-6

22  2 Samuel 12:7

proclaiming himself to be king in place of the crown prince Solomon. After David's death, Adonijah paid with his life for his rebellion.[23]

Those whom God has greatly blessed should not forget that God alone can protect them from temptation by His power through faith. They must listen to His voice as He calls them to repentance with His cords of love. *"'I have loved you with an everlasting love; Therefore with loving kindness I have drawn you.'" Jeremiah 31:3.*

> Jesus is tenderly calling me home
> > Calling today, calling today
> Why from the sunshine of love will thou roam
> > Farther and farther away?
>
> Jesus is calling the weary to rest
> > Calling today, calling today
> Bring Him thy burden and thou shalt be blessed
> > He will not turn thee away.
>
> Jesus is pleading, O list to His voice
> > Hear Him today, hear Him today
> They who believe on His Name shall rejoice
> > Quickly arise and away.
>
> Calling today, calling today
> > Jesus is calling, He is tenderly calling today.
>
> —Fanny J. Crosby, "Jesus is Calling"

**No Leftovers for Jesus—Reading #3**

"Jesus has said, *"'And I, if I am lifted up from the earth, will draw all peoples to Myself.'" John 12:32.* Christ must be revealed to the sinner as the Savior dying for the sins of the world; and as we behold the Lamb of God upon the cross of Calvary, the mystery of redemption begins to unfold to our minds and the goodness of God leads us to repentance. In dying for sinners, Christ manifested a love that is incomprehensible;

---

23  1 Kings 1

and as the sinner beholds this love, it softens the heart, impresses the mind, and inspires contrition in the soul.

"It is true that men sometimes become ashamed of their sinful ways, and give up some of their evil habits, before they are conscious that they are being drawn to Christ. But whenever they make an effort to reform, from a sincere desire to do right, it is the power of Christ that is drawing them. An influence of which they are unconscious works upon the soul, and the conscience is quickened, and the outward life is amended. And as Christ draws them to look upon His cross, to behold Him whom their sins have pierced, the commandment comes home to the conscience. The wickedness of their life, the deep-seated sin of the soul, is revealed to them. They begin to comprehend something of the righteousness of Christ, and exclaim, "What is sin, that it should require such a sacrifice for the redemption of its victim? Was all this love, all this suffering, all this humiliation, demanded, that we might not perish, but have everlasting life?"

"The sinner may resist this love, may refuse to be drawn to Christ; but if he does not resist he will be drawn to Jesus; a knowledge of the plan of salvation will lead him to the foot of the cross in repentance for his sins, which have caused the sufferings of God's dear Son.

"The same divine mind that is working upon the things of nature is speaking to the hearts of men and creating an inexpressible craving for something they have not. The things of the world cannot satisfy their longing. The Spirit of God is pleading with them to seek for those things that alone can give peace and rest—the grace of Christ, the joy of holiness. Through influences seen and unseen, our Savior is constantly at work to attract the minds of men from the unsatisfying pleasures of sin to the infinite blessings that may be theirs in Him. To all these souls, who are vainly seeking to drink from the broken cisterns of this world, the divine message is addressed, "'*And let him who thirsts come. Whoever desires, let him take the water of life freely.*'" *Revelation 22:17.*"[24]

**Illustrative Sketch:**

The night was a cold one, but Tom didn't care. From where he sat on the floor in the corner of the tavern, he could hear the clink of beer

---

24  White, 26.

glasses and the buzz of conversation. All that seemed important right now was the warm feeling he had in the pit of his stomach from the umpteenth glass of alcohol he had drunk that night. Why he stayed he didn't know. At home his wife waited, not so patiently anymore. She had given up on him by now, he was sure, and gone to bed weary of his broken promises that he would be a decent husband. Once he had been a religious man, attending church services weekly with his wife and children. When the drinking began, those days ended.

His two children were his pride and joy, but they were growing up without a father, at least one they would be proud of. Alex was ten now, and baseball with his father wouldn't interest him much longer. Soon he would close his heart to the man his father had become. Little Edith was only seven, and she idolized her father though he was a hopeless drunk, out of control in his life, and now a poor man as well.

Tom had no job, had been in and out of work countless times. He had been an engineer down at the power plant, but they had let him go because of absenteeism. The foreman said he just had to have someone more reliable. Tom had liked his job well enough, but he guessed he had liked the liquor better.

The sting of icy temperatures hit him in the face every time the door to the tavern opened. "Do you want me to help you home?" his best friend asked him, and he struggled to grasp what Pete was asking.

"Leave him alone," the bartender laughed. "Let me sell him just one more drink. He's my best customer, spending his paycheck every week here as soon as it's cashed."

"He doesn't even have a job anymore!" Pete said.

"Yeah?"

"That's right, your liquor trade has cost him more than money! It's cost him his job!"

"He's still got money, doesn't he?"

"Maybe, but he's got a wife and kids!" Pete protested, anger rising in his voice.

"Aaah! She can have the leftovers," the bartender laughed again.

Tom stirred where he sat on the floor, drowsy from one too many drinks. What was that the bartender had said? His wife could have the leftovers? A fine husband he was, taking everything for himself, or worse, giving it to the bartender. For months now his dear wife had been managing the family food budget on scraps. He had known it, but had been selfishly living in a state of crippling denial.

In that brief moment something happened to Tom that he couldn't explain. The fog of alcohol lifted from his mind momentarily so that he saw things clearly. The words of the bartender hit the mark and made the impact on him that all the nights of his drinking had failed to do. God was calling to him in the darkness of his deepest night, and he knew he must respond now or all would be lost. There was no other decision to make.

He pulled himself to his feet and stumbled out the door. "Just one more drink!" the bartender called after him, but Tom ignored the invitation and somehow made it home.

He slept on the couch that night to avoid disturbing his wife, and before the dawn creased the eastern sky, he was up again. Grabbing himself some cold potatoes and a drink of something hot, he scooted out the kitchen door before his wife could notice. When she awoke, she found a ten dollar bill in a cup at the kitchen table, and her heart skipped a beat. Had Tom been home? Was he back to his usual self? She didn't want to get her hopes up, but where had he gone at this early hour? Surely not for another drink!

And indeed, Tom seemed to be his old self, or at least a semblance of it. As he stood under the vaulted ceiling at the power plant a few minutes later looking at the huge generator on its blocks, a familiar voice greeted him. "Is that you, Tom?" the foreman asked excitedly. "It's so good to see you back!"

Tom ran his hands over the generator's broad side and half smiled to himself.

"There's no one like you, Tom! You were always the best!" the foreman pointed to the huge generator, now silent and still. "Do you think you can get it running again, Tom? It broke down last week, and we haven't been able to do much with it?"

It had been a long time since Tom had worked. Too long. He always thought he was the master of the booze he drank, but when he recognized that he was a slave, God reached inside this shell of a man and gently placed him on the road to recovery. The Holy Spirit was working on his heart, and angels of God were doing battle with the tempter to keep Tom from being dragged into destruction.

When the town whistle blew at six that night and Tom did not return home, his wife's heart sank. She had been right not to trust him, she reasoned. He had failed her too many times to make a new start now. At half past six she heard footsteps on the back porch, and then to her joy, her man walked through that kitchen door again, sober and clear-eyed. Joyfully she threw her arms around his neck and cried tears of happiness as she heard him say, "I will never again leave you with the leftovers."[25]

*"Taste and see that the Lord is good; blessed is the man who trusts in him." Psalm 34:8.*

O soul, are you weary and troubled?
    No light in the darkness you see?
There's light for a look at the Savior,
    And life more abundant and free!

Turn your eyes upon Jesus,
    Look full in His wonderful face,
And the things of earth will grow strangely dim,
    In the light of His glory and grace.

—Helen H. Lemmel, "Turn Your Eyes Upon Jesus"

## A Friend Indeed—Reading #4

"You who in heart long for something better than this world can give, recognize this longing as the voice of God to your soul. Ask Him to give you repentance, to reveal Christ to you in His infinite love, in His perfect purity. In the Savior's life the principles of God's law—love to God and man—were perfectly exemplified. Benevolence, unselfish love, was the life of His soul. It is as we behold Him, as the light from our Savior falls upon us, that we see the sinfulness of our own hearts.

---

25    M. A. Vroman, "Only a Husk," in *Sabbath Readings for the Home Circle.* (South Lancaster, MA: South Lancaster Printing Co., 1905), 151.

"We may have flattered ourselves, as did Nicodemus, that our life has been upright, that our moral character is correct, and think that we need not humble the heart before God, like the common sinner: but when the light from Christ shines into our souls, we shall see how impure we are; we shall discern the selfishness of motive, the enmity against God, that has defiled every act of life. Then we shall know that our own righteousness is indeed as filthy rags, and that the blood of Christ alone can cleanse us from the defilement of sin, and renew our hearts in His own likeness.

"One ray of the glory of God, one gleam of the purity of Christ, penetrating the soul, makes every spot of defilement painfully distinct, and lays bare the deformity and defects of the human character. It makes apparent the unhallowed desires, the infidelity of the heart, the impurity of the lips. The sinner's acts of disloyalty in making void the law of God, are exposed to his sight, and his spirit is stricken and afflicted under the searching influence of the Spirit of God. He loathes himself as he views the pure, spotless character of Christ.

"When the prophet Daniel beheld the glory surrounding the heavenly messenger that was sent unto him, he was overwhelmed with a sense of his own weakness and imperfection. Describing the effect of the wonderful scene, he says, "... 'No strength remained in me; for my vigor was turned to frailty in me, and I retained no strength.'" Daniel 10:8. The soul thus touched will hate its selfishness, abhor its self-love, and will seek, through Christ's righteousness, for the purity of heart that is in harmony with the law of God and the character of Christ."[26]

**Illustrative Sketch:**

We may not likely desire this purity of heart that God wishes to see in us. Our lives of material secularism sometimes prevent it, but God knows our heart and He knows our need. If we let Him, He will reach down into the cherished place we hide and take us to Himself, rescuing us from certain disaster. Only He can save us.

Phil was a troubled child. He had no friends, was a drifter on the fringes of the school crowd, and spent his days in the streets of small-town Mississippi. He was an annoyance to his teachers, a bully to the

26  White, 28.

kids at school, and a punching bag for his often-drunk father. To most folks Phil was a thorn in the flesh and a nuisance, period. He trusted no one, and Aaron, it seemed, was the closest thing he had to a pal. Not that Aaron would know it, the way Phil treated him.

"Come on, let's go hang out at Cokey's Corner!" he swaggered in his rumpled leather jacket one day after school. "We can check out the girls and get a bite to eat."

"I can't," Aaron said bluntly, not wanting to offer a further explanation of what his parents would say if they knew he was hanging out with someone like Phil.

"Oh, your parents don't approve of me!" Phil grilled Aaron. "Not good enough for 'em, am I?"

"It's not that," Aaron lied. "It's just that I've got chores to do at home."

"Yeah, right!!" Phil eyed Aaron cynically. "Your problem is that your parents never let you have any fun! Take me now! I get to do what I want, when I want! No one tells me what to do! I'm my own man!" He said the words proudly, as if he were already actually a man.

"My parents are good to me," Aaron thought.

"Got a buck?" Phil asked, and Aaron was glad he had changed the subject. But he was also angry that Phil could make fun of him, and then ask for money. Why should he give Phil money knowing he would probably just use the money to buy cigarettes? How he got them was anybody's guess. He was street-hardened to be sure, but he certainly didn't look 18. Thirteen was more like it, to any store clerk's eye.

"Why don't you leave me alone!" Aaron finally snapped. "You don't need me! All you want is your stupid old cigarettes!"

"Aw, give a guy a break, Aaron! Honest! I just want to buy a hamburger. I ain't had a decent meal in two days." It was strange to hear Phil talk like that. For once he actually looked hurt.

Aaron pushed his bike to the hamburger stand and gave Phil the twenty-five cents. When he saw how Phil gobbled up the hamburger, he bought him two more.

"Thanks, you're a real friend," Phil grinned as they walked the street to Aaron's house. "Want to try something fun?" he asked as they put Aaron's bike away in the woodshed. Phil pulled out a pack of cigarettes and offered the small box to Aaron. "Try one," he said in a suave manner that awed Aaron and made him sick at the same time.

He felt strange being so close to the contraband, and he surprised himself when he didn't immediately refuse. Of course, he wouldn't smoke. His parents had raised him to be smarter than that. Cigarette smoking was a dirty habit. It wrecked your health and was a terrible waste of money. But he took the pack of cigarettes and held it in his hands. It didn't feel evil, and for a moment he imagined what it would be like to hold one of the cigarettes between his fingers. Not to smoke, of course. Just to look street smart like Phil. It shocked him to think he was tempted to be like Phil.

"Keep 'em," Phil offered, pushing the pack away as Aaron tried to give it back. "You don't have to smoke 'em now."

Phil left, and Aaron just stood there in the woodshed looking at the cigarettes. What was he doing? What would his parents say if they knew? Before he could feel any worse he found a safe place to hide the pack of cigarettes behind a shingle up under the eaves. Aaron felt bad when he went to the house for supper, knowing he was hiding such a thing from his parents. But he felt worse for Phil as he ate the warm soup his mother had prepared. Thoughts of Phil and the hungry, forlorn face kept coming back to Aaron, and it troubled him that Phil should have to live hand-to-mouth like he did. Aaron's parents could tell something was troubling him, and when they questioned him, the whole story tumbled out—Phil and his suave leather jacket, the hamburgers, the hidden cigarettes.

"I guess I'm sometimes tempted to forget just how good I have it here with you guys." Aaron bowed his head gratefully to God for such parents, and they listened wisely.

"Where does he live?" Aaron's father asked.

"Down near the railroad tracks in an old shack of a house. I've never seen his dad there, and the place looks like it would be ideal for rats."

"Let's go have a look," Aaron's father offered. "Maybe there's something we can do."

They got to Phil's place sometime after dark, and when they knocked on the door, Phil opened it a crack. "What do you want?" he asked, and by the dim light of the 40 watt bulb burning in the kitchen, Aaron thought he saw tears in the boy's eyes. The place was deplorable!

The windows were fly-specked, the dishes in the sink looked as if they hadn't been washed in weeks, and the little tumbled down shack smelled damp and moldy.

"Where's your dad?" Aaron's father asked, and Phil just hung his head and mumbled something about not seeing the man for over a week now.

Aaron felt bad for Phil, and he wondered what his father would do next, but he shouldn't have been surprised. "Why don't you come home with us tonight, Phil?" he heard his father say. "Aaron's got an extra bed in his room, and you could do with a good, home-cooked meal."

Phil didn't say anything at first, but then he finally stammered a "thanks," and they were on their way. It was the turning point in Phil's life. Unbeknownst to Phil, his father had deserted him, and was never seen again. Aaron's mother and father went through all the legal channels to adopt Phil as their own son. He and Aaron became like brothers, attended a boarding school together, and then went on to college where they studied to serve God.

Phil's life changed. Not just because someone was a friend and extended a compassionate helping hand in time of need—but because he saw the love of Jesus in the lives of his servants, just everyday people doing the work of the Master.[27]

*"'I say to you, inasmuch as you did it to one of the least of these My brethren, you did it to me.'" Matthew 25:40.*

**I Surrender All—Reading #5**

"Paul says that as "concerning the righteousness which is in the law"—as far as outward acts were concerned—he was *"blameless" Philippians 3:6*; but when the spiritual character of the law was discerned, he saw himself a sinner. Judged by the letter of the law as men apply it to the outward life, he had abstained from sin; but when he looked into the depths of its holy precepts, and saw himself as God saw

27 Josephine Cunnington Edwards, "Someone Who Cares" in *Secrets in the Hayloft, and Other Stories* (Nashville: Southern Publishing Association, 1969).

him, he bowed in humiliation and confessed his guilt. He says, *"I was alive once without the law: but when the commandment came, sin revived, and I died." Romans 7:9.* When he saw the spiritual nature of the law, sin appeared in its true hideousness, and his self-esteem was gone.

"God does not regard all sins as of equal magnitude; there are degrees of guilt in His estimation, as well as in that of man; but however trifling this or that wrong act may seem in the eyes of men, no sin is small in the sight of God. Man's judgment is partial, imperfect; but God estimates all things as they really are. The drunkard is despised and is told that his sin will exclude him from heaven; while pride, selfishness, and covetousness too often go unrebuked.

"But these are sins that are especially offensive to God; for they are contrary to the benevolence of His character, to that unselfish love which is the very atmosphere of the uncalled universe. He who falls into some of the grosser sins may feel a sense of his shame and poverty and his need of the grace of Christ; but pride feels no need, and so it closes the heart against Christ and the infinite blessings He came to give.

"The poor publican who prayed, *"God be merciful to me a sinner"" Luke 18:13*, regarded himself as a very wicked man, and others looked upon him in the same light; but he felt his need, and with his burden of guilt and shame he came before God, asking for His mercy. His heart was open for the Spirit of God to do its gracious work and set him free from the power of sin. The Pharisee's boastful, self-righteous prayer showed that his heart was closed against the influence of the Holy Spirit. Because of his distance from God, he had no sense of his own defilement, in contrast with the perfection of the divine holiness. He felt no need, and he received nothing.

"If you see your sinfulness, do not wait to make yourself better. How many there are who think they are not good enough to come to Christ. Do you expect to become better through your own efforts? *"Can the Ethiopian change his skin or the leopard its spots? Then may you also do good who are accustomed to do evil." Jeremiah 13:23.* There is help for us only in God. We must not wait for stronger persuasions, for better opportunities, or for holier tempers. We can do nothing of ourselves. We must come to Christ just as we are."[28]

---

28 White, 29.

**Illustrative Sketch:**

Tiger and Tom were the best of friends as only a dog and boy can be. That's the way the town's folk always saw them, together walking the streets of the little village where they lived, the boy whistling and the dog with his tail held high. Or, they might be seen sitting by the local fish pond together on a lazy spring day waiting for a fish to bite the hook.

They were inseparable. Tiger had been a gift for Tom's birthday, a great mass of shaggy fur with big affectionate eyes. Tom was handsome and likeable, and one of the most generous lads in town. There wasn't anything he wouldn't do for someone, if he thought they were in need. He might have been seen as a boy most envied for his gifts and talents, except for one major flaw in his personality. He had a violent temper.

The trait was a startling one. With red face he could quickly become the most irritable boy around. Within seconds he could slam a door impatiently, or speak unkindly to his mother, or even slap his little sister. It was a flaw that was most unappealing, and to his mother's troubled mind, posed a real threat to Tom's future success and happiness.

Tom knew it, too. It wasn't that he prided himself in these tantrums. He did not, and many a time he had apologized to those whom he had wronged, but his mother had warned him that this was not enough. He must learn to control the feelings that were beginning to control him as he grew older. She warned that some horrible disaster was sure to take him by surprise. He might become a wicked man of crime, or even commit murder.

One fateful day her prophecy came true. It was the beginning of summer, and school had let out for what seemed to Tiger and Tom an eternity of fun and frolic. Tom invited Matt Casey, one of his classmates from school, to play in the haymow with them at Tom's father's grain store.

"Let's do it!" Matt said excitedly. "I've already done all my chores at home for the day." The two boys and the dog had the most fun playing. But as often happens, the boys got into an argument and rolled over and over in the hay as they fought. Tom was on top when they stopped.

"There, now!" Tom shouted, "who's right? You or me?"

"I am," Matt insisted, getting to his feet, with hay in his hair and one eye blackened. "You're lying, and you know it!"

That was the straw that tipped the scales. Tom's face grew angry as he flew into one of his uncontrollable rages! In an instant he attacked Matt giving him a violent push, sending him falling backward out the haymow door to the hard sidewalk below.

An icy chill swept over Tom as he suddenly realized what he had done, and he hardly dared look for fear of what he might see. He stood frozen not knowing what to do at first, but then finally rushed down below. Some men were already lifting the unconscious Matt carefully from the sidewalk.

Tom's face was white as a sheet as he followed the men into the store, and the whole thing felt like a bad dream. What would happen now? Would Matt die? Would they charge Tom with attempted murder?

Tom could take it no more and ran out the door, followed by Tiger, his only true friend now, it seemed. He wandered out into the woods, and fell to the ground, tears of remorse stinging his eyes. At last it had come! The day his mother had warned him about should he fail to control his temper. He had almost become a murderer, and nothing but God's goodness had guided Matt's hands to the rope that broke his fall and saved him from a dreadful end.

Matt could yet die. Tom fell to his knees there in the forest and begged God to spare Matt's life. From that day forward he pledged that he would work to practice kindness and patience and work to control that temper.

But he knew that would not be enough. Matt's hands were badly torn from grabbing the rope in the haymow as he fell, so he would not be able to work and help his widow mother as he had before. And so all that summer vacation Tom came to Matt's house to help in whatever ways he could. He did the farm chores and cared for the few livestock they owned. He weeded the garden and picked the cabbages, potatoes, and beans, and sold them at the daily market. And always Tiger was there to help.

But still it was not enough. When the bandages were removed from Matt's hands, it was discovered that they had been unskillfully treated and were scarred and distorted in odd shapes. Without surgery by one of the city doctors they would never be normal again.

Tom went to the woods and talked it over with Tiger. He wanted to help raise the money for the trip to the city and the doctor's fees, but what could he do? And then he thought of Tiger. The dog was a valuable sheep dog, a border collie with some pedigree. He could sell Tiger, but the thought of such a thing was almost unthinkable. And then Tom thought of Matt's hands, and that he might never use them again properly, and he knew what he must do.

So he traipsed through the woods to Major White's house and sadly told him his plan. "If you would buy Tiger from me, I think the money I get might help Matt. With what I've already earned this summer, I've been told we can get Matt to a city doctor," Tom said bravely. The deal was made and Tom took the money and ran, afraid he might cry if he stayed longer. He didn't even take time to say goodbye to Tiger properly.

Tom's gift was accepted. A friend took little Matt to the city free of charge and Matt's poor, crooked fingers were soon almost as good as new. The whole town now loved Tom for his sacrifice and persistent deeds of kindness. There wasn't a finer lad anywhere, they said. His gentle ways and loving spirit were contagious and people even found themselves wanting to be more like Tom.

At the close of our story all ended well for Tom. On his birthday Tiger showed up with a letter in his mouth from Major White. "Tiger is homesick and pines for your friendship daily," the letter read, "and I feel compelled to return him to you. It is the least I can do for a boy that has learned to become his own master."[29]

Paul's words put such a transformation aptly. *"I have been crucified with Christ; it is no longer I who live, but Christ lives in me; and the life which I now live in the flesh I live by faith in the Son of God, who loved me and gave Himself for me." Galatians 2:20.*

**Don't Procrastinate—Reading #6**

"But let none deceive themselves with the thought that God, in His great love and mercy, will yet save even the rejecters of His grace. The exceeding sinfulness of sin can be estimated only in the light of the cross. When men urge that God is too good to cast off the sinner, let

---

29   M. A. Vroman, "Tom's Trial," in Sabbath Readings for the Home Circle. (South Lancaster, MA: South Lancaster Printing Co., 1905), 50.

them look to Calvary. It was because there was no other way in which man could be saved, because without this sacrifice it was impossible for the human race to escape from the defiling power of sin, and be restored to communion with holy beings—impossible for them again to become partakers of spiritual life—it was because of this that Christ took upon Himself the guilt of the disobedient and suffered in the sinner's stead. The love and suffering and death of the Son of God all testify to the terrible enormity of sin and declare that there is no escape from its power, no hope of the higher life, but through the submission of the soul to Christ.

"The impenitent sometimes excuse themselves by saying of professed Christians, "I am as good as they are. They are no more self-denying, sober, or circumspect in their conduct than I am. They love pleasure and self-indulgence as well as I do." Thus they make the faults of others an excuse for their own neglect of duty. But the sins and defects of others do not excuse anyone, for the Lord has not given us an erring human pattern. The spotless Son of God has been given as our example, and those who complain of the wrong course of professed Christians are the ones who should show better lives and nobler examples. If they have so high a conception of what a Christian should be, is not their own sin so much the greater? They know what is right, and yet refuse to do it.

"Beware of procrastination. Do not put off the work of forsaking your sins and seeking purity of heart through Jesus. Here is where thousands upon thousands have erred to their eternal loss. I will not here dwell upon the shortness and uncertainty of life; but there is a terrible danger—a danger not sufficiently understood—in delaying to yield to the pleading voice of God's Holy Spirit, in choosing to live in sin; for such this delay really is. Sin, however small it may be esteemed, can be indulged in only at the peril of infinite loss. What we do not overcome, will overcome us and work out our destruction." [30]

**Illustrative Sketch:**

*"Don't put off 'til tomorrow what you can do today."* That line penned by the famous Benjamin Franklin is sage advice for anyone who is a procrastinator, and a phrase Paul could certainly have used

---

30  White, 31.

---

when talking to Governor Felix and King Herod Agrippa in the days of ancient Rome. It all happened while Paul was under house arrest in the coastal city of Caesarea, where a Roman court of law was convened for him—first with the Roman Governor Felix presiding, and later for the sake of Herod Agrippa.

The city of Caesarea at that time was flush with the burgeoning lifestyle of the Roman Empire. If you were a Roman in the Palestine of those days, you wanted to live in Caesarea. The climate was mild, and the view was terrific—right on the Mediterranean. Options for entertainment and holiday festivals were almost unlimited in the city. And business was booming with the economics of sea trade filling the coffers of merchants and politicians alike. The city had been rebuilt and refurbished with pagan temples, gymnasiums, amphitheaters, gardens, and the famous hippodrome designed especially for horse racing. Also constructed was an aqueduct ten kilometers long to bring vast supplies of water for fountains, swimming pools, and public baths. And Caesarea had some of the best cultural arts of any city during that era—theater, philosophical debates, and architecture.

Into such an arena went Paul to make his stand for God, but it wasn't easy. Governor Felix, whose family had close ties to Rome, was in power. His brother served in the emperor's court in Rome, and his first wife was a grand-daughter of Antony and Cleopatra. Felix was well-known for practicing every kind of cruelty and lust he could imagine. He was an accomplice in the murder of the high priest in Jerusalem, but helped suppress rebellions of the zealous Jews during his reign.

He would have released Paul from prison, but was hoping the Apostle would pay him a bribe. Paul sternly warned Felix of a coming judgment, and Felix trembled knowing it was the truth. However, he finally told Paul, "That's enough for now! You may leave. When I find it convenient, I will send for you." Acts 24:25. But that's as far as he got. He never followed through with his promise and disappeared into the mists of time, his opportunity squandered.

King Agrippa, though an orthodox Jew by profession, was born and educated in Rome, and lived a very secular life. He and his family line, beginning with Herod the Great, had done great things for the Jews, but when the Jews revolted against Rome a few years later, he took the side of Rome. The emperor Nero was impressed with Agrippa and awarded him additional territories to rule in Galilee and Perea.

When Agrippa met Paul in Caesarea, he was fascinated with the Apostle. Paul gave his own personal testimony in the Caesarea court, claiming that Jesus' resurrection from the dead was a reality, giving Christianity its real purpose and power. The other authorities in the courtroom thought Paul was a lunatic, but Agrippa wanted to hear more.

"You think that being in chains is a disgrace for me," Paul added, "but I count it an honor to suffer for the cause of Christ." Acts 26:2. Then he drove the point home. "I know you believe in God's Word, King Agrippa. Why wait further to surrender to Jesus?" Acts 26:27. We can almost see the King leaning forward on his throne as he uttered those celebrated words, "Do you think that in such a short time you can persuade me to be a Christian?" Acts 26:28.

A sad line, quite frankly, for a man who could not seem to make up his mind.

The question still remains for all Christians today, "Why put off 'til tomorrow what you can do today?" Now while the offer is still good, why not claim that promise today? *"Behold, now is the accepted time; … now is the day of salvation."* 2 Corinthians 6:2.

There's a line that is drawn by rejecting our Lord
    Where the call of His Spirit is lost
And you hurry along with the pleasure-mad throng
    Have you counted, have you counted the cost?

Have you counted the cost if your soul should be lost
    Tho' you gain the whole world for your own?
Even now it may be that the line you have crossed
    Have you counted, have you counted the cost?

You may barter your hope of eternity's morn
    For a moment of joy at the most
For the glitter of sin and the things it will win
    Have you counted, have you counted the cost?

While the door of His mercy is open to you
  Ere the depth of His love you exhaust
Won't you come and be healed, won't you whisper, "I yield
  I have counted, I have counted the cost."

Have you counted the cost if your soul should be lost
  Tho' you gain the whole world for your own?
Even now it may be that the line you have crossed
  Have you counted, have you counted the cost?

—A.J. Hodge, "Have You Counted the Cost?"

**Don't Be a Fool—Reading #7**
  "Adam and Eve persuaded themselves that in so small a matter as eating of the forbidden fruit there could not result such terrible consequences as God had declared. But this small matter was the transgression of God's immutable and holy law, and it separated man from God and opened the floodgates of death and untold woe upon our world. Age after age there has gone up from our earth a continual cry of mourning, and the whole creation groaneth and travaileth together in pain as a consequence of man's disobedience. Heaven itself has felt the effects of his rebellion against God. Calvary stands as a memorial of the amazing sacrifice required to atone for the transgression of the divine law. Let us not regard sin as a trivial thing.
  "Every act of transgression, every neglect or rejection of the grace of Christ, is reacting upon yourself; it is hardening the heart, depraving the will, benumbing the understanding, and not only making you less inclined to yield, but less capable of yielding, to the tender pleading of God's Holy Spirit.
  "Many are quieting a troubled conscience with the thought that they can change a course of evil when they choose; that they can trifle with the invitations of mercy, and yet be again and again impressed. They think that after doing despite to the Spirit of grace, after casting their influence on the side of Satan, in a moment of terrible extremity

they can change their course. But this is not so easily done. The experience, the education, of a lifetime, has so thoroughly molded the character that few then desire to receive the image of Jesus.

"Even one wrong trait of character, one sinful desire, persistently cherished, will eventually neutralize all the power of the gospel. Every sinful indulgence strengthens the soul's aversion to God. The man who manifests an infidel hardihood, or a stolid indifference to divine truth, is but reaping the harvest of that which he has himself sown. In all the Bible there is not a more fearful warning against trifling with evil than the words of the wise man that the sinner *"is caught in the cords of his sin." Proverbs 5:22.*

"Christ is ready to set us free from sin, but He does not force the will; and if by persistent transgression the will itself is wholly bent on evil, and we do not desire to be set free, if we will not accept His grace, what more can He do? We have destroyed ourselves by our determined rejection of His love. *"'Behold, now is the accepted time; behold, now is the day of salvation.'" "Today if you will hear His voice, do not harden your hearts.'" 2 Corinthians 6:2; Hebrews 3:7, 8."*[31]

**Illustrative Sketch:**
Many years ago in the heartland of Africa there lived two famous kings. One ruled an expansive kingdom on the plains to the west, and the other lived in a jungle valley to the east. Between them stretched a chain of mountains long and tall and wide.

One day the king on the east decided he would go to the kingdom in the West to conquer and divide its spoil. "And what shall I do with the king of the west?" the king of the east asked his counselors.

"You shall kill the old king of the west," said his advisors. "It is the wisest thing to do, and will show that you are the strongest man in all of Africa."

"Maybe, but perhaps I shall capture him instead and bring him back as a trophy of my power to conquer!" said the king of the east, and all his counselors said that it was good.

And so the king of the east gathered his warriors together, tall and fierce and strong. And he did in fact conquer the king in the west. In great triumph they marched back over the mountains with a wealth

31  White, 33.

of spoils, and behind them all came the conquered king of the west. Humbled now, he was, walking barefoot in the heat and cold, over thorns and thistles on the stony path.

And when the triumphant army reached home, the king of the east paraded his brave warriors up and down the wide streets of the royal city. High on the trailing ox carts came the spoils of war, the gold and silver, the captured cattle, and last of all, limping from the long journey, hobbled the king of the west dressed in tattered rags. The king of the east made a great spectacle of his new prisoner. With great pomp and ceremony he declared himself to be the undisputed ruler of both east and west.

"But I will be benevolent on this day of victory!" the king of the east smiled with satisfaction. "I will let the king of the west live! He shall sleep in my streets, and beg for his meals, but I shall bind him with a chain about his ankle, fastened to a ponderous ball of iron."

So it was that the king of the west came to live in the east, and great was his shame as he walked those streets. The iron ball was heavy and his ankle chafed from the band fastened tightly upon him. If he wanted to eat he had to beg for his food, and at night he slept wherever he could find shelter. It wasn't easy living with his enemies. People laughed and pointed to his shame. Old women shook their walking sticks at him, and children threw stones. Truly, he was the most humbled of kings in his misery.

The days and weeks turned into months and years. The citizens in the streets of the eastern kingdom no longer took notice of the king from the west. Then one day a visiting missionary from Europe came through the village. The king of the east showed him his sumptuous palace, the flourishing economy filled with lively trade, and wide verdant farms, and great herds of cattle.

He even introduced the missionary to the king from the west where he sat begging. "Take note," said the king of the east in triumph, "It is the greatness of my wisdom and power that has reduced this man to what he is today!"

"I should like to offer the prisoner a gift," said the missionary as he bowed to the king of the east. "A Bible, perhaps?"

"It can do no harm," laughed the king of the east. "Maybe it will help him pass the time of day."

As the missionary left town, he stopped to see the beggar king. "What do I want with a Bible!" said the old king from the west. "Why haven't you given me something good, like a choice morsel of food to cheer me, or a warm coat for chilly nights?" and he threw the black book into the corner of his tumbled-down hut.

Time passed. The king of the west grew more and more despondent that he was chained in such shame and dishonor. One rainy day after much time had passed, the forlorn king of the west chanced to see the Bible lying in the corner of the hut where he had thrown it so long ago. He picked it up to examine its contents. "Perhaps I was hasty in rejecting the comfort it might have brought me, if just to pass the time in reading its pages," the king of the west lamented.

As he took the old book in his hands, he felt a ridge inside the back cover. To both his delight and dismay he found a metal file. No doubt the missionary had felt pity for the king of the west and had offered him a means of escape. He held in his hands the key to his freedom, but in horror and disgust he realized he could have had it long ago. "If I had accepted the gift with gratefulness when it was first given me, even now I might be at home free from this dreadful ball and chain!" the king of the west mourned.

Now he earnestly put the tool to work. At night he worked relentlessly on the thick iron chain. The work was slow, and his hands grew tired. By day he read the words from the good old book, and discovered principles of life that would make him a better king when he returned home to rule his subjects.

No one noticed that the old king of the west seemed more content. Slowly, the king of the west made progress on the iron chain. By the time he managed to file through it, he had also read most of the black book.

One evening just after sunset, he made the final cut through the dreadful chain and then planned his escape. Taking only the Bible that had now become so precious to him, he disappeared down a jungle road into the darkness. It was quite dangerous to travel by night, but he had no other choice. The light of the moon shone his way, and God was good.

Within a few weeks he was back home again in his own kingdom in the west, a much wiser man. "I am grateful for my freedom," said the king, as he gathered his subjects around him, "For several years I had exactly what I needed to free myself from that wretched ball and chain, but I despised it! What a fool I've been!"[32]

From that day forward the king declared his Bible to be a symbol of freedom for his people, freedom over the old ways of superstition, and freedom from sin.

> *"And you shall know the truth, and the truth shall make you free."* John 8:32.

## God Sees the Heart—Reading #8

"'*Man looks at the outward appearance, but the Lord looks at the heart.*'"—the human heart, with its conflicting emotions of joy and sorrow; the wandering, wayward heart, which is the abode of so much impurity and deceit. *1 Samuel 16:7.* He knows its motives, its very intents and purposes. Go to Him with your soul all stained as it is. Like the psalmist, throw its chambers open to the all-seeing eye, exclaiming, "'*Search me, O God, and know my heart: try me, and know my anxieties: and see if there is any wicked way in me, and lead me in the way everlasting.*'" Psalm 139: 23, 24.

"Many accept an intellectual religion, a form of godliness, when the heart is not cleansed. Let it be your prayer, *"Create in me a clean heart, O God; and renew a steadfast spirit within me."* Psalm 51:10. Deal truly with your own soul. Be as earnest, as persistent, as you would be if your mortal life were at stake. This is a matter to be settled between God and your own soul, settled for eternity. A supposed hope, and nothing more, will prove your ruin.

"Study God's word prayerfully. That word presents before you, in the law of God and the life of Christ, the great principles of holiness, *"without which no one will see the Lord."* Hebrews 12:14. It convinces of sin; it plainly reveals the way of salvation. Give heed to it as the voice of God speaking to your soul.

"As you see the enormity of sin, as you see yourself as you really are, do not give up to despair. It was sinners that Christ came to save.

---

32  Eric B. Hare (Nampa, ID: Chapel Records Recording).

We have not to reconcile God to us, but—O wondrous love!—God in Christ is *"reconciling the world to Himself."* *2 Corinthians 5:19.* He is wooing by His tender love the hearts of His erring children. No earthly parent could be as patient with the faults and mistakes of his children, as is God with those He seeks to save. No one could plead more tenderly with the transgressor. No human lips ever poured out more tender entreaties to the wanderer than does He. All His promises, His warnings, are but the breathing of unutterable love.

"When Satan comes to tell you that you are a great sinner, look up to your Redeemer and talk of His merits. That which will help you is to look to His light. Acknowledge your sin, but tell the enemy that *"Christ Jesus came into the world to save sinners"* and that you may be saved by His matchless love. *1 Timothy 1:15.* Jesus asked Simon a question in regard to two debtors. One owed his lord a small sum, and the other owed him a very large sum; but he forgave them both, and Christ asked Simon which debtor would love his lord most. Simon answered, *"'I suppose the one whom he forgave more.'"* *Luke 7:43.* We have been great sinners, but Christ died that we might be forgiven. The merits of His sacrifice are sufficient to present to the Father in our behalf.

"Those to whom He has forgiven most will love Him most, and will stand nearest to His throne to praise Him for His great love and infinite sacrifice. It is when we most fully comprehend the love of God that we best realize the sinfulness of sin. When we see the length of the chain that was let down for us, when we understand something of the infinite sacrifice that Christ has made in our behalf, the heart is melted with tenderness and contrition." [33]

**Illustrative Sketch:**
She knelt there in the dust of the stony street, terrified, guilty, embarrassed. She had known that such a day must come sooner or later. She had hoped for later. But now her shame was exposed. Her guilt sure. The authorities caught her in the act of selling her body.

She kept her head down, the only safe thing left to do. Her shoulders shook with tremors of the coming judgment, her tears frantic but unnoticed by the growing mob. Around her in the streets screamed the

---

33   White, 34.

howling rabble, their sneers demonic, their fingers already clutching stones. Execution by stoning was her verdict.

From beneath her swollen painted eyelids she glimpsed a Stranger squatting in the street. Her accusers were hovering over Him, hammering Him with the shameful details of her capture. Her eyes flitted from one accuser in the group to the next, and then fell again as these men turned from time to time to point in her direction.

The Stranger seemed detached, almost uninterested in their excited ramblings, and instead bent Himself to toy with the dust at His feet. The temple delegation seemed intent on getting Him to join them in conversation. But He remained ambivalent as he traced something with his finger in the street for them to see, and many crowded close around him to glimpse it for themselves.

"If any one of you is without sin," the Stranger's voice echoed on the street, "let him be the first to throw a stone at her," and then went back to his curious writing. John 8:7.

Slowly there came an unexplainable shift in the crowd as the multitude grew quiet. She noticed the silence, imperceptible at first, then more pronounced. The crowd melted away, first the authorities, and then those standing closest to her. The thud of stones hitting pavement echoed in the street, and finally to her amazement and grateful relief, the street stood empty and silent.

She glanced around her furtively to be sure that it was so, but when the Stranger straightened up and asked, "Woman, where are they? Has no one condemned you?" she knew it was true. John 8:9.

There was a long pause. Her head down, she finally whispered in relief and surprise. "There is no one, Sir!" Still the silence pressed upon her. She glanced once more through strands of uncombed hair, and then it was she saw His eyes upon her, compassionate and loving, with no hint of blame. Never had she seen such eyes. Never had she felt such a warmth of kindness and acceptance.[34]

"'Neither do I condemn you,'" the Stranger declared in tones that touched her deepest heart strings. "'Go and sin no more.'" John 8:11.

---

34  Story based on John 8:1-11.

Oh, now I see the cleansing wave!
The fountain deep and wide;
Jesus, my Lord, mighty to save,
Points to His wounded side.
The cleansing stream I see, I see!
I plunge, and, oh, it cleanseth me!
Oh, praise the Lord, it cleanseth me!
It cleanseth me, yes, cleanseth me.

I see the new creation rise,
I hear the speaking blood;
It speaks, polluted nature dies,
Sinks 'neath the cleansing flood.

I rise to walk in Heaven's own light,
Above the world and sin,
With heart made pure and garments white,
And Christ enthroned within.

Amazing grace! 'tis Heav'n below
To feel the blood applied,
And Jesus, only Jesus know,
My Jesus crucified.

The cleansing stream I see, I see!
I plunge, and, oh, it cleanseth me!
Oh, praise the Lord, it cleanseth me!
It cleanseth me, yes, cleanseth me.

—Phoebe W. Palmer, "The Cleansing Wave"

# CHAPTER 4

# Confession

**Truth or Consequences—Reading #1**

"*H*e *who covers his sins will not prosper: but whoever confesses and forsakes them will have mercy.' Proverbs 28:13.*

"The conditions of obtaining mercy of God are simple and just and reasonable. The Lord does not require us to do some grievous thing in order that we may have the forgiveness of sin. We need not make long and wearisome pilgrimages, or perform painful penances, to commend our souls to the God of heaven or to expiate our transgression; but he that confesseth and forsaketh his sin shall have mercy.

"The apostle says, *"Confess your trespasses to one another, and pray for one another, that you may be healed." James 5:16.* Confess your sins to God, who only can forgive them, and your faults to one another. If you have given offense to your friend or neighbor, you are to acknowledge your wrong, and it is his duty freely to forgive you. Then you are to seek the forgiveness of God, because the brother you have wounded is the property of God, and in injuring him you sinned against his Creator and Redeemer. The case is brought before the only true Mediator, our great High Priest, who *"was in all points tempted like as we are, yet without sin,"* and who... *"sympathize with our weaknesses,"* and is able to cleanse from every stain of iniquity. *Hebrews 4:15.*

"Those who have not humbled their souls before God in acknowledging their guilt, have not yet fulfilled the first condition of acceptance. If we have not experienced that repentance which is not to be repented of, and have not with true humiliation of soul and brokenness of spirit confessed our sins, abhorring our iniquity, we have never truly sought for the forgiveness of sin; and if we have never sought, we have never found the peace of God. The only reason why we do not have remission of sins that are past is that we are not willing to humble our hearts and comply with the conditions of the word of truth.

"Explicit instruction is given concerning this matter. Confession of sin, whether public or private, should be heartfelt and freely expressed. It is not to be urged from the sinner. It is not to be made in a flippant and careless way, or forced from those who have no realizing sense of the abhorrent character of sin. The confession that is the outpouring of the inmost soul finds its way to the God of infinite pity. The psalmist says, *"The Lord is near to those who have a broken heart, and saves such as have a contrite spirit."* Psalm 34:18.

"True confession is always of a specific character, and acknowledges particular sins. They may be of such a nature as to be brought before God only; they may be wrongs that should be confessed to individuals who have suffered injury through them; or they may be of a public character, and should then be as publicly confessed. But all confession should be definite and to the point, acknowledging the very sins of which you are guilty."[35]

### Illustrative Sketch:

Peter and Judas were birds of a different feather. Both were enterprising, both were bold. Both were followers of Jesus. But that's where the similarities end. One loved Jesus, the other loved himself.

Peter was a tough character, uneducated and unsophisticated in the ways of etiquette. Forged in the company of rough fishermen, he was a man who boasted few social graces, living as he did in the blue collar world of upper Galilee. He made his livelihood on the lake, and no class of society was considered more uncouth in speech and manners. And that's how Jesus found Peter, but immediately the Master saw his value. When Jesus promised Peter that he could become a fisher of men, not fish, he left his nets and followed the Man from Nazareth.

But, too much of the time Peter was brash and impatient. It appears that he saw himself as more of a bodyguard than a childlike student at the Teacher's feet. When mothers brought their children to see Jesus, Peter turned rudely them away. When temple authorities asked Peter if Jesus could pay the temple tax, Peter was annoyed. "Of course He can!"

---

35   White, 37.

he answered indignantly. When Peter saw Jesus talking with glorified heavenly messengers on the Mount of Transfiguration, he wanted to build monuments in memory of the occasion.

And when Jesus asked the disciples, "Who do you say that I am?" Peter was the first to boldly assert that Jesus was the Christ, the Son of the living God. He may have been impetuous and uncultured, but he was genuine. What you saw was what you got.

Jesus knew Peter was sincere in his devotion to God, but He also knew Peter was weak. Peter promised he would be faithful to the death, but on the early morning of Jesus' trial, he caved and swore that he had never even met "the Man." By the time the rooster crowed the third time, Peter had denied His Lord three times just as Jesus predicted he would.

And when Peter caught sight of Jesus looking at him across the courtyard in that moment of truth, it humbled him inside and out. In shame he ran from the courtroom, overwhelmed by his sin.

Little wonder then that he was grieved when a few weeks later Jesus asked him, "'Do you love me ... , Peter?'" John 21:15. Jesus had endured the mockery of a trial, the cruel scourging, and an unthinkable death on a cross. He had risen glorified, returned to his Father for the approval of His sacrifice, and was now encouraging His followers in Galilee.

"'Yes, Lord,'" was all Peter could say. "'You know I love You!'" John 21:16.

Twice more Jesus asked the question as if to prick Peter's conscience and test his durability as a disciple. Twice more a confession of truest devotion was wrung from Peter, and with pathos of regret he exclaimed, "'Lord! You know all things!'" John 21:17.

And then Jesus did something very unusual. He opened the doors to the future to give Peter a glimpse of what this new-found devotion would cost him. Death on a cruel cross as Jesus Himself had suffered. But by now, Peter was undeterred—unrelenting—adamant! By God's grace he would remain faithful to Jesus no matter what the cost! Even if it should be death!

Judas' story took quite another turn. He was a gifted man, a born leader, and somewhat of a financial wizard. But he had real character issues. He was by nature dishonest, self-serving and a scheming young man. Not surprisingly, Judas became the self-appointed treasurer of the disciple group, and though they weren't aware of it, he sometimes helped himself to the money bag.

However, Judas' main concern was Jesus "lack of vision," as he called it. If Jesus really was the Messiah as He claimed He was, why was He waiting so long to set Himself up as King over Israel? All the prophecies pointed to this moment in time. Could Jesus not see it?

Judas hatched a plan to force Jesus' hand. He planned a confrontation between Jesus and the Spiritual leaders of Jerusalem that he thought would thrust Jesus into political and spiritual power. The enterprising Judas considered that he would get all the credit for being the catalyst that launched Jesus into history. Peculiar thought, isn't it? As if the God of the Universe needed Judas' help in marketing Himself to a world He had created and come to die for.

But, Jesus hadn't abandoned Judas yet. On the night of the last supper, the Lord could still see glimmers of hope that Judas desired goodness. Judas felt the Spirit of God calling him to repentance for the inexcusably corrupt deed he was about to commit, but he didn't respond to the call to repentance. Instead he went into the night to finalize his plans with the chief priests, forever removing himself from Jesus voice of forgiveness. A few hours later Judas entered the Garden of Gethsemane leading the temple mafia to betray His Master into their hands with a kiss.

What a sham! How does one betray someone he loves with a kiss? The infamous act has made Judas one of the most notorious characters in history. For over three years He had been with the Son of God walking and talking with Him throughout the length and breadth of Israel! And then he betrayed Him for 30 measly pieces of silver! The price of a slave!

Of course when Jesus was bound and roughly dragged away to trial, Judas saw his plan unravel. But, it was too late. The deed was done. Ashamed and disappointed in his failed promotion of Jesus, Judas saw the part he had played in the shedding of innocent blood. Later that day he hung himself on a tree in an act of desperation. Today, we remember Judas Iscariot simply as the one who betrayed the Son of God.

What a contrast to the life and death of Peter. Peter's experience on the night of Jesus' trial made him legendary, because his repentance accepted the love and sacrifice of his Savior. His repentance changed is life, and he became a great leader of the early church. Eventually, according to Christian history he, too, hung on a tree when he gave himself as a martyr for the gospel of Jesus. However, his dying protest was that he did not deserve to die on a cross in the manner in which his Lord had died. And so they crucified him upside down. *"Do not be deceived, God is not mocked; for whatever a man sows, that he will also reap." Galatians 6:7.*

## Justified—Reading #2

"In the days of Samuel the Israelites wandered from God. They were suffering the consequences of sin; for they had lost their faith in God, lost their discernment of His power and wisdom to rule the nation, lost their confidence in His ability to defend and vindicate His cause. They turned from the great Ruler of the universe and desired to be governed as were the nations around them. Before they found peace they made this definite confession: *"'We have added unto all our sins the evil of asking a king for ourselves.'" 1 Samuel 12:19.* The very sin of which they were convicted had to be confessed. Their ingratitude oppressed their souls and severed them from God.

"Confession will not be acceptable to God without sincere repentance and reformation. There must be decided changes in the life; everything offensive to God must be put away. This will be the result of genuine sorrow for sin. The work that we have to do on our part is plainly set before us: *"'Wash yourselves, make yourselves clean; put away the evil of your doings from before My eyes. Cease to do evil, learn to do good; seek justice, reprove the oppressor; defend the fatherless, plead for the widow.'" Isaiah 1:16, 17. "If the wicked restores the pledge, gives back what he has stolen, and walks in the statutes of life without committing iniquity, he shall surely live; he shall not die.'" Ezekiel 33:15.* Paul says, speaking of the work of repentance: *"You sorrowed in a godly manner: What diligence it produced in you, what clearing of yourselves, what indignation, what fear, what vehement desire, what zeal, what vindication! In all things you proved yourselves to be clear in this matter." 2 Corinthians 7:11.*

"When sin has deadened the moral perceptions, the wrongdoer does not discern the defects of his character nor realize the enormity of the evil he has committed; and unless he yields to the convicting power of the Holy Spirit he remains in partial blindness to his sin. His confessions are not sincere and in earnest. To every acknowledgment of his guilt he adds an apology in excuse of his course, declaring that if it had not been for certain circumstances, he would not have done this or that for which he is reproved.

"After Adam and Eve had eaten of the forbidden fruit, they were filled with a sense of shame and terror. At first their only thought was how to excuse their sin and escape the dreaded sentence of death. When the Lord inquired concerning their sin, Adam replied, laying the guilt partly upon God and partly upon his companion: *'The woman whom You gave to be with me, she gave me of the tree, and I ate.'* The woman put the blame upon the serpent, saying, *'The serpent deceived me, and I ate.'* Genesis 3:12, 13*. Why did You make the serpent? Why did You suffer him to come into Eden? These were the questions implied in her excuse for her sin, thus charging God with the responsibility of their fall. The spirit of self-justification originated in the father of lies and has been exhibited by all the sons and daughters of Adam.

"Confessions of this order are not inspired by the divine Spirit and will not be acceptable to God. True repentance will lead a man to bear his guilt himself and acknowledge it without deception or hypocrisy. Like the poor publican, not lifting up so much as his eyes unto heaven, he will cry, "God be merciful to me a sinner," and those who do acknowledge their guilt will be justified, for Jesus will plead His blood in behalf of the repentant soul."[36]

**Illustrative Sketch:**

Two men went up to the temple to pray, one a Pharisee and the other a publican. The day was young as they wended their way to the holy hill, but even at this hour the street life of Jerusalem stirred at an accelerated pace. Young girls fresh from the city wells were wending their way down the slender streets, and gangling herd boys goaded their unruly flocks of goats and sheep through the city market place. Already old men were sitting together to warm themselves in the morning sunshine, playing their board games, a pastime offering them a chance to sharpen their ailing minds.

36  White, 38.

The morning rush hadn't yet arrived when the Pharisee and Publican entered through the Beautiful Gate, but the temple vendors weren't wasting time waiting. Up went the colorful awnings to block out the sun, and the bright fabrics to attract would-be buyers. Out came the tables of those who could afford a premium on space in the expansive courtyard. A fat merchant with dangling gold earrings sat against the courtyard wall, busily counting out stacks of coins and placing them on a low table in front of him—there were copper ones, and silver, and some even of gold. A small toddler wandered too close to the little stacks of glittering coins, but an angry scowl from the merchant sent the child back to hide in the folds of his mother's garments.

Now the Pharisee was a sanctimonious man, full of self-righteous deeds and meticulous discipline. Of the tribe of Benjamin, a Hebrew of Hebrews in strict obedience to the law, he was devoted to all good works. Long sleeves and tassels and phylacteries garnished the Pharisee's temple robes, and he made sure that everyone saw him as he passed through the crowd untouched.

But the publican was a man of disrepute. Though dressed well, his robes were of a different sort, the kind worn by the rich and famous who have indulged themselves in sumptuous and riotous living. No clothes could hide the fact that the publican was a tax collector, employed by the hated Romans. All things considered, he was a lowlife from the dregs of Jewish society.

The Pharisee crossed the expansive courtyard of the outer temple, and then the marble pavement of the inner Court for the Women, but the publican was careful to follow behind at a respectable distance. Pharisees didn't fraternize with tax collectors. A scowl or a curse was the best they could expect.

The publican walked with shuffling feet, his head down. He had money to give, but knew it would not be accepted. No one would exchange it for temple shekels, the currency needed for offerings. "Your money's no good here!" a money exchanger growled at the publican. In the eyes of a Jew any money the publican might give was as bad as blood money, because it had been earned as a tax collection for the Romans.

His career began shortly after he was 27 when he lost his sight in one eye due to an illness. That was enough to ostracize him from mainstream Jewish life. He kept the eye covered, but no one invited him to betrothals or weddings, or feast day celebrations during Jewish holidays. He had felt rejected by his people, and become bitter in heart. So, when a Roman consul came looking to install a new tax collector in Bethlehem, the publican had signed up.

As usual the Pharisee had come to parade his wealth and affluence in the temple, and his spiritual superiority, of course. With great fanfare he took a bag of copper coins from the folds of his long robes, and dumped them clattering into the ornate, trumpet-shaped contribution boxes. Gold or silver coins would have been worth more, but copper coins made just as much racket, and at a cheaper price. Only other rich folks within sight of his gift would think of that, though.

The Pharisee separated himself from nearby worshipers so that he would be noticed. He stood tall and erect, raised his face to the ceiling far above, and prayed thus with himself, "'I thank you, God, that I am not like other men—extortioners, unjust, adulterers, or even as this tax collector. He gestured absentmindedly in the direction of the publican. I fast twice a week; I give tithes of all that I possess.'" Luke 18:11. The people close by bowed their heads in reverence for the Pharisee as they passed. Here truly must be a holy man, they mused, blessed indeed from heaven above.

The publican stood off to one side and would not so much as raise his eyes to heaven, but struck himself on the chest repeatedly, crying out, "'God, be merciful to me a sinner!'" Luke 18:13. The crowd instinctively, self-righteously separated themselves from the publican too, leaving him and the Pharisee in contrast to one another in the temple court—the haughty arrogance of the one, and the humble, tear-stained face of the other.

Unbeknownst to the watchers this publican went down to his house restored spiritually and vindicated, his treasure in the halls of heaven. The Pharisee received his reward too, but it was in the here-and-now, and not from the Father in heaven.[37]

"This righteousness from God comes through faith in Jesus Christ to all who *believe... for all have sinned and fall short of the glory of God,*

---

37   Story based on Luke 18:9-14 with the characters developed in harmony with the culture of the day.

*and are justified freely by his grace through the redemption that came by Christ Jesus." Romans 3:22-24, NIV.*

Justified, can I be justified,
    With all the load of sin that marks my path?
Crucified, my Lord was crucified,
    'Tis through his death and life we're safe at last.
Wondrous love and grace so full and free,
    Deeds of love he offers you and me.
Satisfied, in Christ I'm satisfied,
    But to be justified how can it be?

Justified, now I am justified?
    My Lord has cleansed my heart of every stain.
Glorified, I shall be glorified,
    When Jesus comes in power and might to reign.
Nevermore shall I in darkness roam,
    Soon the Lord has promised he will come.
Gratified, I am so gratified,
    And since I'm justified, He'll take me home.

—Author Unknown

# CHAPTER 5

# Consecration

**He'll Leave the Light on for You—Reading #1**

"God's promise is, *"You will seek Me, and find Me, when you search for Me with all your heart."* Jeremiah 29:13.

"The whole heart must be yielded to God, or the change can never be wrought in us by which we are to be restored to His likeness. By nature we are alienated from God. The Holy Spirit describes our condition in such words as these: *"Dead in trespasses and sins;" "the whole head is sick, and the whole heart faints;" "no soundness in it."* We are held fast in the snare of Satan, *"taken captive by him to do his will."* Ephesians 2:1; Isaiah 1:5, 6; 2 Timothy 2:26. God desires to heal us, to set us free. But since this requires an entire transformation, a renewing of our whole nature, we must yield ourselves wholly to Him.

"The warfare against self is the greatest battle that was ever fought. The yielding of self, surrendering all to the will of God, requires a struggle; but the soul must submit to God before it can be renewed in holiness.

"The government of God is not, as Satan would make it appear, founded upon a blind submission, an unreasoning control. It appeals to the intellect and the conscience. *"Come now, and let us reason together"* is the Creator's invitation to the beings He has made. Isaiah 1:18. God does not force the will of His creatures. He cannot accept an homage that is not willingly and intelligently given. A mere forced submission would prevent all real development of mind or character; it would make man a mere automaton. Such is not the purpose of the Creator. He desires that man, the crowning work of His creative power, shall reach the highest possible development. He sets before us the height of blessing to which He desires to bring us through His grace. He invites us to give ourselves to Him, that He may work His will in us. It remains for us to choose whether we will be set free from the bondage of sin, to share the glorious liberty of the sons of God." [38]

**Illustrative Sketch:**

Jim Cymbala, pastor of the Brooklyn Tabernacle in New York City, tells this tragic story about someone very dear to him—his daughter. Kristy had wandered spiritually far from home, far from the confines of a mother and father whom she viewed as too restrictive. Why it had to be so for her, she couldn't say. She loved them. She loved who they were. She just couldn't live that lie anymore. She had wanted to shed the facade for years.

And so she drifted away, rather quickly it seemed, out of their home, out of their circle of concern, out of their lives. Where she went and what she did was not information they were always privy to, but rumors found their way to the home altar. Fortunately, the half was not told them, or they would have been basket cases of concern, especially her mother. But parents' intuition and quiet prayer times in the dead of night impressed Pastor Cymbala and his wife with the needs of their daughter. She was into alcohol now, they guessed, and drugs, no doubt. She was into the illicit relationships that almost always come with life-styles of the young and restless.

She never came home to connect with them, and rarely called. The painful ordeal was a tunnel of despair offering them no light at its end. Had she disowned them? Would they ever see her again? Would she die alone in some rundown, god-forsaken tenement of the inner city?

Pastor Cymbala tried his best to carry on his ministry in the church where he was pastor, but it was excruciating at best. Some days he felt like quitting. How could he minister to his flock in good conscience when the one person he should have been able to reach had rejected his values? But people began to read between the lines. The more perceptive parishioners of his church understood, and they rallied to his side.

One evening at his church's weekly prayer meeting, he struggled to present his evening message. His heart just wasn't in it. He continued bravely on, when suddenly a dear soul stood up and said she felt

---

38   White, 43.

impressed they should stop the regular program to pray for Kristy. "I feel we all need to pray for your daughter like we have never prayed before. Kristy's not here tonight," the woman said fervently, "but she should be. The devil man has seen to it that she is kept from us day after day, and night after night. Well, I say it's high time the devil let her go! He's had her long enough, and now it's time to give her back!"

The church resounded with echoes and re-echoes of amen's and hearty halleluiah's, and Pastor Cymbala truly felt the Spirit of the Lord among them. What a prayer session they had with pathos of agony for her soul, and tears of regret that they had somehow failed her, too. Jim was somewhat comforted as he left for home, and slept that night better than he had in a long time.

Two mornings later he was upstairs in the bathroom shaving when his wife came running up the stairs. "Kristy is here!" she stammered excitedly.

He rushed downstairs with his wife, shaving cream still on his face, to find his daughter kneeling on the kitchen floor, weeping as though her heart would break. Jim and his wife knelt on the floor beside Kristy and put their arms around her.

"Who's been praying for me?" Kristy sobbed. "I know someone has been praying for me!"

"How would you know that?" Jim asked her in surprise.

"I know you're a praying man, Daddy, and I know the power of prayer when I see it!" she exclaimed.

Pastor Cymbala listened with bated breath for the story he knew was coming.

"Night before last I felt as if I were at the end of my rope," Kristy gulped through her tears. "I was beyond miserable and felt I had nothing left to live for, but I didn't feel I could come home to you and Mom! I had hurt you too much! I had wandered so far from God and the things you had taught me, and I just wanted to give up and end it all!" Kristy lifted her tearstained face to her father. "I was out of money, out of drugs, and out of hope! Desperation and hopelessness surrounded me, and then suddenly a feeling of warmth and peace came over me like I hadn't felt since I was home here with you and Mom. And I knew that something big had happened. Someone was praying. Who was it Daddy? I don't want to live like this anymore! I want to have that kind of peace in my heart all the time! I want to come back home to Jesus!"[39]

Jesus invites us all to come back home and be free from the bondage of sin. It doesn't matter what we've done. It doesn't matter how far we've wandered from God. There's nothing we can do so bad that will keep our heavenly Father from loving us. He loves us unconditionally and is waiting with open arms for us to come back home.

*"'Turn, turn from your evil ways! For why should you die, O house of Israel?'"Ezekial 33:11.*

Your coat is ragged and your face is so thin
    No way of telling now where you might have been
Your heart is heavy and your pockets are light
    But there's a porch light shining for you tonight.

Porch light shining for you
    And it shines with all the love of a father's heart
Oh how patiently He waits for you
    When you're lost and can't go on
You'll find your way in the dark
    There's a porch light shining for you.

The wind is chilly and it cuts to the bone
    Just down the road someone is calling you home
The room is warm and there's a fire that's bright
    And there's a porch light shining for you tonight.

You're thinking lately that you shouldn't have strayed
    You'd turn around now, but you're really afraid
No need to worry if you're wrong or you're right
    Cause there's a porch light shining for you tonight.

---

39  Jim Cymbala. *Fresh Wind, Fresh Fire* (Grand Rapids: Zondervan, 1997).

You're all alone, so come on home
   There's a porch light shining bright
And it shines with all the love of a father's heart


Oh how patiently He waits for you
   When you're lost and can't go on
You'll find your way in the dark
   There's a porch light shining for you.

—Carm Caponi

**Pilgrim's Progress—Reading #2**
   "In giving ourselves to God, we must necessarily give up all that would separate us from Him. Hence the Savior says, *"'So likewise, whoever of you does not forsake all that he has cannot be My disciple.'"* *Luke 14:33.* Whatever shall draw away the heart from God must be given up. Mammon is the idol of many. The love of money, the desire for wealth, is the golden chain that binds them to Satan. Reputation and worldly honor are worshiped by another class. The life of selfish ease and freedom from responsibility is the idol of others. But these slavish bands must be broken. We cannot be half the Lord's and half the world's. We are not God's children unless we are such entirely.
   "There are those who profess to serve God, while they rely upon their own efforts to obey His law, to form a right character, and secure salvation. Their hearts are not moved by any deep sense of the love of Christ, but they seek to perform the duties of the Christian life as that which God requires of them in order to gain heaven. Such religion is worth nothing. When Christ dwells in the heart, the soul will be so filled with His love, with the joy of communion with Him, that it will cleave to Him; and in the contemplation of Him, self will be forgotten. Love to Christ will be the spring of action. Those who feel the constraining love of God, do not ask how little may be given to meet the requirements of God; they do not ask for the lowest standard, but aim

at perfect conformity to the will of their Redeemer. With earnest desire they yield all and manifest an interest proportionate to the value of the object which they seek. A profession of Christ without this deep love is mere talk, dry formality, and heavy drudgery.

"Do you feel that it is too great a sacrifice to yield all to Christ? Ask yourself the question, "What has Christ given for me?" The Son of God gave all—life and love and suffering—for our redemption. And can it be that we, the unworthy objects of so great love, will withhold our hearts from Him? Every moment of our lives we have been partakers of the blessings of His grace, and for this very reason we cannot fully realize the depths of ignorance and misery from which we have been saved. Can we look upon Him whom our sins have pierced, and yet be willing to do despite to (reject) all His love and sacrifice? In view of the infinite humiliation of the Lord of glory, shall we murmur because we can enter into life only through conflict and self-abasement?"[40]

**Illustrative Sketch:**

John Bunyan, the famous author of the Christian allegory, *Pilgrim's Progress*, was at one time the most celebrated of preachers in all England. He preached from the heart and was a wonderful storyteller. Not surprisingly the common folks loved his style and began deserting the other congregations in Bedford, England to come to his church and hear him preach. In his colorful sermons he "attacked the follies of the time, exposing and condemning heresies without mercy."[41] The priests in the state-run Church of England did not like John's preaching, and eventually they convinced the local magistrate that he was breaking the law and needed to be jailed.

During one of his weekly sermons the constable entered John's church and arrested him. During the next twelve years the Bedford jail became his primary home. John would be kept in prison for three months at a time until the jailer sent him home. The priests and magistrate tried to keep him in prison, but the jailer sympathized with John. "How can a man like Mr. Bunyan be trouble for the law?" the jailer would always say.

---

40    White, 44.

41    George W. Latham, *The Life of John Bunyan*, www.plymouthbrethren. org.

And so the magistrate would tell John he could stay out of jail if only he would stop his preaching. Of course, John would not do this, and sooner or later he was sent to jail again. But that did little good, it seemed, because John preached to audiences of forty and fifty in the jail.

On one occasion when John was sent home "unofficially," a prominent priest happened to walk by his home and saw him through an open window with his family. He knew that John was supposed to be at the Bedford jail, so he sent word to the magistrate that he might want to check the jail to see if John was actually there.

Meanwhile, John was at home eating the evening meal with his family, but was impressed that he should go back to the jail for the evening. When supper was over he headed back to the Bedford jail and locked himself in his cell as he always did, unbeknownst to the jailer.

About an hour later the magistrate showed up with the priest to make an inspection and verify the suspicions of the priest. "Good evening, warden!" they said cheerfully. "Are all your prisoners doing well?"

"Yes," the warden said, wondering what they might be up to.

"Is John Bunyan here as well?"

"Well, yes he is," the jailer lied, knowing he was caught. He had a habit of frequently releasing John.

"Well, let's see him then," the magistrate ordered.

The jailer got his keys, and with bated breath walked the two men to John's cell where to his surprise he found the prisoner reading a book by candlelight.

The priest was stunned and even embarrassed, and the magistrate left quite unimpressed with the credibility of the priest.

After the two visitors left, the jailer stopped by John's cell. "That was a close call," he sighed with relief. "I was shocked to find you in your cell! I thought you were home with your family!"

"I was," John said with a twinkle in his eye, "but for some reason I felt impressed by the Holy Spirit that I should come back tonight."

The jailer could only shake his head in wonder. "Well, John," he finally replied, "I'm not going to tell you when you can go home anymore, or when you should come back to jail. If God speaks to you like that, I'm sure the two of you can manage it much better than I."[42] While in jail John wrote *Pilgrim's Progress*. Published in 1678, today it is among the most widely read books of religious English literature. It has been published in more than 200 languages and has never been out of print.

Today John Bunyan's life and testimony is still one of the greatest stories of self-denial for God and the people of England. No sacrifice was too great for him, a small price to pay for the gift of God's dear Son. His message can be summed up in Ephesians 1:7, 8. "In Him we have redemption through his blood, the forgiveness of sins, *according to the riches of His grace which He made to abound toward us in all wisdom and prudence.*"

> Working, O Christ, with Thee, working with Thee.
>     Unworthy, sinful, weak, though we may be.
> Our all to Thee we give, for Thee alone we live,
>     And by Thy grace achieve, working with Thee.
>
> So let us labor on, working with Thee.
>     'Til earth to Thee is won, from sin set free.
> 'Til men from shore to shore, receive Thee and adore
>     And join us evermore, working with Thee.
>
> —W. A. Ogden, "Working, O Christ, With Thee"

## The Ultimate Sacrifice—Reading #3

"The inquiry of many a proud heart is, "Why need I go in penitence and humiliation before I can have the assurance of my acceptance with God?" I point you to Christ. He was sinless, and, more than this, He was the Prince of heaven; but in man's behalf He became sin for the race. *"He was numbered with the transgressors; and He bore the sin of many, and made intercession for the transgressors."* Isaiah 53:12.

---

42  John Brown, *John Bunyan, His Life, Times, and Work* (London: Isbister and Co., 1902).

"But what do we give up, when we give all? A sin-polluted heart, for Jesus to purify, to cleanse by His own blood, and to save by His matchless love. And yet men think it hard to give up all! I am ashamed to hear it spoken of, ashamed to write it.

"God does not require us to give up anything that it is for our best interest to retain. In all that He does, He has the well-being of His children in view. Would that all who have not chosen Christ might realize that He has something vastly better to offer them than they are seeking for themselves. Man is doing the greatest injury and injustice to his own soul when he thinks and acts contrary to the will of God. No real joy can be found in the path forbidden by Him who knows what is best and who plans for the good of His creatures. The path of transgression is the path of misery and destruction.

"It is a mistake to entertain the thought that God is pleased to see His children suffer. All heaven is interested in the happiness of man. Our heavenly Father does not close the avenues of joy to any of His creatures. The divine requirements call upon us to shun those indulgences that would bring suffering and disappointment, that would close to us the door of happiness and heaven. The world's Redeemer accepts men as they are, with all their wants, imperfections, and weaknesses; and He will not only cleanse from sin and grant redemption through His blood, but will satisfy the heart-longing of all who consent to wear His yoke, to bear His burden. It is His purpose to impart peace and rest to all who come to Him for the bread of life. He requires us to perform only those duties that will lead our steps to heights of bliss to which the disobedient can never attain. The true, joyous life of the soul is to have Christ formed within, the hope of glory."[43]

**Illustrative Sketch:**

Many of us would like to believe that God is asking us to do the impossible! That if we sacrifice all for Him, we'll regret the decision the rest of our lives! Not likely. To the contrary, those who turn down an opportunity to live a life of self-denial for Jesus, almost always regret it in the end. The story of the rich young ruler who came to Jesus is a classic example.

43   White, 45.

*Now as (Jesus) was going out on the road, one came running, knelt before Him, and asked Him, "Good Teacher, what shall I do that I may inherit eternal life?"*

*So Jesus said to him,....."You know the commandments: 'Do not commit adultery,' 'Do not murder,' 'Do not steal,' 'Do not bear false witness,' 'Do not defraud,' 'Honor your father and your mother.'"*

*And he answered and said to Him, "Teacher, all these things I have kept from my youth."*

*Then Jesus, looking at him, loved him, and said to him, "One thing you lack: Go your way, sell whatever you have and give to the poor, and you will have treasure in heaven; and come, take up the cross, and follow Me."*

*But he was sad at this word, and went away sorrowful, for he had great possessions. Mark 10:17-22.*

But which was the greater loss to the rich young ruler—his riches, or service with the Savior of the world? Many, many servants of God have given up everything for Jesus, and been eternally grateful for the opportunity to do so. David Livingston was one such man.

While only ten years-of-age David began working in the cotton mills of England, but spent his evenings in night school, and after much hard work became a doctor. He had his heart set on being a missionary doctor in China, but when he heard Robert Moffat speak about "the smoke of a thousand villages where no one had yet heard the gospel story," David decided to give his life for Africa.

David arrived in Africa when he was 25, but found that being a missionary to the interior of Africa in the usual sense would be almost impossible. There were no maps of the area, and he had to fight enemies of every kind. David's life was made miserable by blood-sucking mosquitoes, flies, and lions. The insects transmitted malaria and sleeping sickness, and he feared for his life with the wild lions. One day a wounded lion attacked Livingstone, ripping his arm open with one bite, and breaking the bone. David almost died from the infection.

Ignorance, superstition, and man's inhumanity to man were the worst of Africa's horrors, and it was these that David spent most of his time battling. He witnessed the curse of polygamy, cannibalism, and slavery, seeing families broken up as slave gangs were chained together. He saw the bodies of unfortunate slaves who died, their bodies lying by the wayside, hung in trees, or floating in rivers. As he fought ignorance and superstition, he suffered from debilitating, life-threatening diseases. During one seven-month journey into the interior to help break the slave trade, David endured 31 attacks of fever and dysentery.

David's fight against the Dutch Boers who were enslaving the Africans was a nightmare. The Boers didn't like David interfering with their prolific slave trade, and they made him pay for it. They robbed him, destroyed his home, and many times threatened his life.

David Livingston's desire to be a missionary came from his love for the gospel, and his hope to one day see Africa free from the grip of slavery. At 60 years of age on one of his trips to the interior, he finally died after repeated malaria attacks and internal bleeding caused by dysentery. Chuma and Susi, his faithful African attendants who had been won to the gospel by Livingston's missionary efforts, found him kneeling at his bedside praying. With great sadness they cut out his heart and buried it under a Mvula tree near the spot where he died. Then they carried Livingston's body on their shoulders a thousand miles to the coast where it was loaded on a British ship and taken back to England for burial at West Minster Abbey.[44]

David Livingston responded to Jesus' call to preach the gospel to the entire world, and in the end he gladly gave his very life for it. *"Greater love has no one than this, than to lay down one's life for his friends." John 15:13.*

So send I you to labor unrewarded,
    To serve unpaid, unloved, unsought, unknown,
To bear rebuke, to suffer scorn and scoffing,
    So send I you to toil for Me alone.

---

44  Eugene Myers Harrison, "David Livinstone: The Pathfinder of Africa," in *Giants of the Missionary Trail* (Wheaton, IL: Scripture Press Book Division, 1954).

So send I you to bind the bruised and broken,
    Over wandering souls to work, to weep, to wake,
To bear the burdens of a world a-weary,
    So send I you to suffer for My sake.

So send I you to leave your life's ambition,
    To die to dear desire, self-will resign,
To labor long, and love where men revile you,
    So send I you to lose your life in Mine.

So send I you to hearts made hard by hatred,
    To eyes made blind because they will not see,
To spend, though it be blood to spend and spare not,
    So send I you to taste of Calvary.
As the Father hath sent me, so send I you.

—E. Margaret Clarkston, "So Send I You"

## All to Jesus I Surrender—Reading #4

"Many are inquiring, "How am I to make the surrender of myself to God?" You desire to give yourself to Him, but you are weak in moral power, in slavery to doubt, and controlled by the habits of your life of sin. Your promises and resolutions are like ropes of sand. You cannot control your thoughts, your impulses, your affections. The knowledge of your broken promises and forfeited pledges weakens your confidence in your own sincerity, and causes you to feel that God cannot accept you; but you need not despair. What you need to understand is the true force of the will. This is the governing power in the nature of man, the power of decision, or of choice.

"Everything depends on the right action of the will. The power of choice God has given to men; it is theirs to exercise. You cannot change your heart, you cannot of yourself give to God its affections; but you can choose to serve Him. You can give Him your will; He will then work in you to will and to do according to His good pleasure. Thus your whole nature will be brought under the control of the Spirit of

Christ; your affections will be centered upon Him, your thoughts will be in harmony with Him.

"Desires for goodness and holiness are right as far as they go; but if you stop here, they will avail nothing. Many will be lost while hoping and desiring to be Christians. They do not come to the point of yielding the will to God. They do not now choose to be Christians.

"Through the right exercise of the will, an entire change may be made in your life. By yielding up your will to Christ, you ally yourself with the power that is above all principalities and powers. You will have strength from above to hold you steadfast, and thus through constant surrender to God you will be enabled to live the new life, even the life of faith." [45]

**Illustrative Sketch:**

The Holy Spirit is the driving force in this life-change, and when we have the fire, it is almost impossible to quench. Hezekiah felt such a call to revival and reformation, not only in his own life, but also for the nation of Judah. His story, beginning about 715 BC, is an example of what God can do through us if we will surrender our time, talents and energy to Him.

Hezekiah's father, King Ahaz, was a wicked man, who walked in all the ways of the evil kings before him. He honored the loathsome gods of the nations around him, and especially Molech, a popular deity of the day. The worship of Molech required its subjects to offer their children as fiery sacrifices on bronze statues built in his honor. Fortunately, Hezekiah himself escaped the heathen practice. When King Ahaz died prematurely at the young age of 36, he was succeeded by his son Hezekiah who removed these heathen rites from the land.

King Hezekiah had a good mother who raised him to reverence God. As a result, Hezekiah lead one of the most remarkable time periods of spiritual revival and reformation in the history of Judah. During his first year as king, Hezekiah "removed the high places [of worship] and broke the sacred pillars, cut down the wooden images, and broke in pieces the bronze serpent that Moses had made; for until those days the children of Israel burned incense to it, and called it Nehushtan." 2 Kings 18:4.

---

45   White, 47.

Then he repaired and cleansed Solomon's temple which had suffered years of neglect and misuse since the days of King Jehoram and his wicked wife, Athaliah, daughter of the infamous Jezebel in Israel to the north. Next, he reinstated the religions services and began celebrating the Passover again with his people. He even invited the ten tribes of Israel from the north to join them in Jerusalem for the holy festival. The people had such a good time celebrating the Passover that they decided to stay on for a second week of festivities.

With religious rejuvenation in Judah came a time of peace and prosperity. The Lord was with Hezekiah and blessed him so that he "prospered wherever he went." 2 Kings 18:7. King Hezekiah's militarily strength repelled the Assyrians and Philistines. He increased the numbers of weapons in his armory, fortified his garrisons, and built watchtowers throughout the country. This allowed him to reclaim territory that his father and grandfather had lost to foreign nations. He made Judah extremely wealthy by all standards of the day, increasing commerce with the surrounding nations. He traded in commodities like silver, gold, precious stones, and spices. He built storehouses for massive harvests of grain, wine, and oil, built extensive folds for the royal flocks and stalls for horses and other livestock. Hezekiah also engineered an underground tunnel through rock from the spring of Gihon outside the city wall so that Jerusalem could have plenty of water during times of war and siege.

But the ultimate test for Hezekiah came in the 14th year of his reign. Sennacherib, General of the Assyrian army, came to besiege and overthrow Jerusalem. Thanks to the moral support given him by Isaiah the prophet and Hezekiah's total reliance on God, the nation of Judah weathered the Assyrian siege. In the end, 185,000 of Sennacherib's forces died from a mysterious plague that ravaged his army in one single night. 2 Kings 19:35.

Hezekiah remains one of the giants in Judean history, a man whose faith in God became a beacon to surrounding nations. There was no God like Jehovah. Hezekiah "trusted in the Lord God of Israel, so that after him was none like him among all the kings of Judah, nor who were before him. For he held fast to the Lord; he did not depart from following Him, but kept His commandments, which the Lord had commanded Moses." 2 Kings 18:5, 6. What a lesson for us all! Let us pray that we can follow Hezekiah's example in glorifying and honoring the God of heaven!

All to Jesus I surrender,
 All to Him I freely give;
I will ever love and trust Him,
 In His presence daily live.

I surrender all,
 I surrender all.
All to Thee, my blessed Savior,
 I surrender all.
All to Jesus I surrender,
 Humbly at His feet I bow,
Worldly pleasures all forsaken;
 Take me, Jesus, take me now.

All to Jesus I surrender,
 Make me, Savior, wholly Thine;
Let me feel Thy Holy Spirit,
 Truly know that Thou art mine.

All to Jesus I surrender,
 Lord, I give myself to Thee;
Fill me with Thy love and power,
 Let Thy blessing fall on me.

All to Jesus I surrender,
 Now I feel the sacred flame.
Oh, the joy of full salvation!
 Glory, glory to His name!

I surrender all,
 I surrender all.
All to Thee, my blessed Savior,
 I surrender all.

   —Judson W. Van DeVenter, "I Surrender All"

# CHAPTER 6

# Faith and Acceptance

**The Greatest Gift—Reading #1**

"As your conscience has been quickened by the Holy Spirit, you have seen something of the evil of sin, of its power, its guilt, its woe; and you look upon it with abhorrence. You feel that sin has separated you from God that you are in bondage to the power of evil. The more you struggle to escape, the more you realize your helplessness. Your motives are impure; your heart is unclean. You see that your life has been filled with selfishness and sin. You long to be forgiven, to be cleansed, to be set free. Harmony with God, likeness to Him—what can you do to obtain it?

"It is peace that you need—Heaven's forgiveness and peace and love in the soul. Money cannot buy it, intellect cannot procure it, wisdom cannot attain to it; you can never hope, by your own efforts, to secure it. But God offers it to you as a gift, *without money and without price.* Isaiah 55:1. It is yours if you will but reach out your hand and grasp it. The Lord says, *'Though your sins are like scarlet, they shall be as white as snow; though they are red like crimson, they shall be as wool.'* Isaiah 1:18. *'I will give you a new heart and put a new spirit within you.'* Ezekiel 36:26.

"You have confessed your sins, and in heart put them away. You have resolved to give yourself to God. Now go to Him, and ask that He will wash away your sins and give you a new heart. Then believe that He does this because He has promised. This is the lesson which Jesus taught while He was on earth, that the gift which God promises us, we must believe we do receive, and it is ours. Jesus healed the people of their diseases when they had faith in His power; He helped them in the things which they could see, thus inspiring them with confidence in Him concerning things which they could not see—leading them to believe in His power to forgive sins. This He plainly stated in the healing of the man sick with palsy: *"'That you may know that the Son of Man has power on earth to forgive sins'—then He said to the paralytic, 'Arise, take up your bed, and go to your house.'"* Matthew 9:6. So also John the evangelist says, speaking of the miracles of Christ, *"these are written that you may believe that Jesus is the Christ, the Son of God, and that believing you may have life in His name." John 20:31".* [46]

**Illustrative Sketch:**

It was a hot day in Capernaum and the dog days of summer had come. The crowd sat fanning themselves inside Simon Peter's house, wishing they could be in the out-of-doors, but today that was an impossibility. It was hotter outside than in. Rivulets of sweat drizzled their way down the faces of the crowd, body odor filled the room, and an occasional fly buzzed through.

The local fisherman had been kind enough to allow the crowd to enter his home. Standing room only, of course, and by now there wasn't even that. There was hardly breathing room. The house wasn't a large one, but already an estimated 150 people were crammed inside and more were trying to get in. And why not? Rabbi Jared and his cronies from the local synagogue were there seated in a half circle, and one or two members of the Sanhedrin in Jerusalem were present, too. More importantly, Jesus of Nazareth was there with his disciples.

The word was out. A showdown was imminent today. For weeks the Pharisees and scribes from Jerusalem had been eager to engage Jesus in some sort of ethical quandary to incriminate Him religiously. All they needed now was a question he couldn't answer, or an argument he couldn't defend. Some were saying that then the religious leaders would be free from His influence in both Galilee and Judea. Planning such a thing was one thing. Getting it done was quite another. Many, many times already Jesus had beaten them at their own game, the game they should easily have won since they were the master debaters of the law and the prophets.

The crowd sat listening, waiting for the next confrontation between Jesus and the wisest of the visiting temple doctors. The stifling heat inside the house increased the tensions of the moment.

---

46  White, 49.

Suddenly a sound above them caught their attention. It sounded like footsteps on the roof. Could it be that workmen were on the roof on a day like this? The people tried to focus on what Jesus was saying, but soon even He and his disciples were looking upward, too. A trickle of dust filtered its way down from the ceiling, and then suddenly a beam of light poked its way through.

A gasp went up from the watching crowd, and the Pharisees sitting there drew their robes tightly around their ankles as if to avoid contamination from the dust. Simon Peter stood to his feet in anger and muttered an oath under his breath. A few more thuds from a blunt instrument above sent a piece of clay roofing tile to the floor near Jesus. Peter lifted his arm to protest. "What's the meaning of this!" he demanded, and the rest of the disciples tried to pull Jesus aside, but the Man from Nazareth seemed unconcerned.

And then the space of light above widened, as more chunks of matted clay and straw fell into the room. "You're breaking up my house!" Simon Peter stepped into the patch of sunlight.

There was no answer from above, but the hole was now big enough so all could see the faces of men standing on the roof. Simon was too stunned to say more. He found himself staring upward at the corner of a hammock held by several cords of rope being lowered through the gaping hole. Its cargo was an invalid.

Everyone was too shocked to say much of anything, but explanations of disgust from the Jewish authorities and clucking tongues in the crowd revealed what everyone was thinking. This was a very sick man, obviously paralyzed by some disease or accident, and his friends on the roof were desperate. Jesus was a very popular Man, and from far and wide the sick and decrepit came to be healed by Him.

As the body in its hammock finally settled on the open space now widening in the middle of the floor, the Man from Nazareth squatted on his heels by the poor man's side. He stared at the invalid for several long moments and caught the look in his tired eyes. Jesus' words were soul searching, but tender. "Don't worry, my son, your sins are forgiven." In that moment a look of peace came over the sick man, and his whole body seemed to relax where he lay on the floor.

The small room erupted with gasps and exclamations of righteous indignation. "This Man is a blasphemer!" several scribes scowled. "In the Law and the Prophets such a thing is forbidden!"

Jesus turned upon the religious leaders almost indignantly. "Why are you thinking such evil thoughts?" he said with spiritual confidence in his voice. "Which is easier for me to say, '*Your* sins are forgiven you,' or 'get up and walk?'" Matthew 9:5.

No one moved. Everyone strained to hear what the Pharisees and scribes would respond, but stillness filled the room.

Turning to the paralyzed man on the floor Jesus said firmly, "What is done here today is for the benefit of this son of Abraham, but it is also done so you may know I have power on earth to forgive sins." He reached out his hand to the invalid, "Stand up, take your bed and go home."

Instantly the sick man's eyes lit up, and he leaned forward as if to take Jesus at His word. Suddenly he was jumping to his feet, a look of astonishment on his face. The crowd reacted too, with ohh's and ahh's, and words of praise to God.

The man, once an invalid, now knelt at Jesus feet and took the Healer's hand in his. "Thank you Master for cleansing me from my burden of sin!" he choked out the words. "The half was not told me, but I now know You are indeed the Son of God!" [47]

## He Came to Set Us Free—Reading #2

"From the simple Bible account of how Jesus healed the sick, we may learn something about how to believe in Him for the forgiveness of sins. Let us turn to the story of the paralytic at Bethesda. The poor sufferer was helpless; he had not used his limbs for thirty-eight years. Yet Jesus bade him, "Rise, take up thy bed, and walk." The sick man might have said, "Lord, if Thou wilt make me whole, I will obey Thy word." But, no, he believed Christ's word, believed that he was made whole, and he made the effort at once; he willed to walk, and he did walk. He acted on the word of Christ, and God gave the power. He was made whole.

---

47   The story is based on Luke 5:17-26 and includes conversation representing Biblical culture.

---

"In like manner you are a sinner. You cannot atone for your past sins; you cannot change your heart and make yourself holy. But God promises to do all this for you through Christ. You believe that promise. You confess your sins and give yourself to God. You will to serve Him. Just as surely as you do this, God will fulfill His word to you. If you believe the promise,—believe that you are forgiven and cleansed,—God supplies the fact; you are made whole, just as Christ gave the paralytic power to walk when the man believed that he was healed. It is so if you believe it.

"Do not wait to feel that you are made whole, but say, "I believe it; it is so, not because I feel it, but because God has promised."

"Jesus says, "*Whatever things you ask when you pray, believe that you receive them, and you will have them.*" *Mark 11:24*. There is a condition to this promise—that we pray according to the will of God. But it is the will of God to cleanse us from sin, to make us His children, and to enable us to live a holy life. So we may ask for these blessings, and believe that we receive them, and thank God that we have received them. It is our privilege to go to Jesus and be cleansed, and to stand before the law without shame or remorse. "*There is therefore now no condemnation to those who are in Christ Jesus, who do not walk according to the flesh, but according to the Spirit.*" *Romans 8:1.*

"Henceforth you are not your own; you are bought with a price. "*You were not redeemed with corruptible things, like silver or gold, …but with the precious blood of Christ, as of a lamb without blemish and without spot.*" *1 Peter 1:18, 19.* Through this simple act of believing God, the Holy Spirit has begotten a new life in your heart. You are as a child born into the family of God, and He loves you as He loves His Son." [48]

### Illustrative Sketch:

According to a legendary story from the days of slavery in the United States, the bidding was brisk one spring morning in Sandersville, Georgia. A dozen slaves stood waiting to walk up the steps to the auction block. Half a dozen plantation owners stood in the street, watching the bidding process, some more interested than others.

One particularly strapping young man was up next, but the scowl on his face told the bidders exactly what he was thinking. *No one had*

---

48  White, 50.

*the right to own another man! The United States of America; it was to this great country that folks came to stake out a new life for themselves and their families, not to be enslaved.*

But such was not the case for Amos, as they called him, nor for the other men and women being sold that morning. The slave master pushed Amos up the steps, Amos resisting all the way, though his hands were bound with manacles. When he felt the butt of a horse whip in the small of his back, he went without further prodding.

But he stood proudly on the block, his eyes on the line of trees near the end of the street. The frown on his forehead was determined and resolute. His fists were clenched, and he seemed to be muttering something to himself under his breath.

Elias Hamilton, a local plantation owner from the next county, watched young Amos with interest. There was something appealing about this slave. He had an intelligent look in his eye, and seemed to have more spirit in him than the other slaves at the auction block.

"What am I bid for this strong young man, not a day over twenty?" the auctioneer shouted. "He's got a good back and is as stout as an ox. You can't go wrong with Amos, here. He'll repay you many times over with the years of work you'll get from him." Elias noticed Amos muttering those same words over and over, but the auctioneer didn't hear him, or maybe it was he didn't care.

"Let's start the bidding at twelve hundred dollars," the auctioneer shouted, "and not a penny less!" but when he saw looks of hesitation on several of the plantation owners' faces, he quickly added, "You're getting a great bargain! He's got a stubborn streak in him, but the boy can work!"

"I won't work!" Amos finally growled loud enough for the owners to hear where they stood near the auction block, and several of them raised their eyebrows. But the bidding kept going higher and still higher. Amos knew slave prices and was surprised that he could bring this much money at an auction. He glanced at the auctioneer from the corner of his eye, but this was no joke. The price now stood at twenty-seven hundred dollars. There were only two owners left doing the bidding, and Elias was one of them.

Finally the gavel fell at twenty-eight hundred dollars, and Elias came with his bill of sale to lead Amos away. "You can't make me work!" Amos glared at Elias as the owner took him to a fine looking buggy sitting in the holding yard of a church nearby.

But Elias said nothing and proceeded to take the manacles off Amos' wrists. "I said I won't work!" Amos raised his voice, thinking perhaps Elias hadn't heard him clearly.

"I heard you," Elias said simply as he got into the buggy. He then beckoned for Amos to get up on the seat beside him, but Amos only glanced at him and the black leather seats in surprise. Slaves didn't ride in buggies. They rode in the backs of wagons. Or better, they often walked. This was the strangest experience Amos had ever had. He had been to an auction twice before in his life—once when he and his mother were sold, separated from Amos' father, and just two years previous when he was sold to an adjoining plantation across the Oconee River. But he had been stubborn—too stubborn for his own good, as many of the other slaves had said. After many whippings by the plantation foreman, and many arguments with an old slave who tried to talk some sense into him, the owner finally sold Amos.

"Get in," Elias patted the seat beside him and waited for Amos to accept the invitation.

"I'll walk!" Amos glowered at his new owner, and then walked to the back of the buggy where he belonged.

"It's twelve miles," Elias said. "That's a long way to walk for someone who's been standing in the sun all morning.

But Amos ignored his warning and stood quietly. Elias realized Amos wasn't comfortable with such an offer and pulled away.

"Aren't you going to tie me behind the buggy?" Amos called out in surprise, knowing full well he could make a break for it and run into the forest of the Georgia countryside.

"No, I can see you'll walk just as well without it," Elias called over his shoulder, but Amos frowned at the plantation owner's simple comment. Who was this man fooling? If he thought being kind to Amos was going to make him want to work, Elias was in for a surprise.

"I won't work!" Amos mumbled to himself again, but Elias acted as if he hadn't heard him, and lightly snapped the reins over the horse's back.

The trip home to the Hamilton plantation was a long one, but Amos walked proudly the whole way, continuing to mutter the words, "I won't work! I won't work!"

When they finally pulled up to the gate at the plantation gate, and then down the long lane to the slave quarters, Elias drove the carriage around to the back and stopped at a small white cottage. Amos looked at the neat little building with boxes of germaniums on the window sills. "What is this?" he asked suspiciously.

"This is your new home," Elias said with a charitable smile.

"My new home?" Amos stared at Elias, clearly confused. Is this some kind of a joke! I told you I won't work, and nothing you can do will make me change my mind!"

"That's alright," Elias replied. "I didn't buy you to make you work. I bought you to give you your freedom!"

A look of shock crossed Amos' face as he suddenly realized what was happening here. He swallowed hard, but could say nothing at first, and then as the tears slowly trickled down his face, he knelt beside the carriage. "Oh, Master Elias," he stammered with his head down. "I'll be your humble servant for the rest of my life."[49]

"For you were bought *at a price; therefore glorify God in your body and in your spirit, which are God's." 1 Corinthians 6:20.*

### Whiter Than Snow—Reading #3

"Now that you have given yourself to Jesus, do not draw back, do not take yourself away from Him, but day by day say, "I am Christ's; I have given myself to Him;" and ask Him to give you His Spirit and keep you by His grace. As it is by giving yourself to God, and believing Him, that you become His child, so you are to live in Him. The apostle says, *"As you therefore have received Christ Jesus the Lord, so walk in Him." Colossians 2:6.*

"Some seem to feel that they must be on probation, and must prove to the Lord that they are reformed, before they can claim His blessing. But they may claim the blessing of God even now. They must have His grace, the Spirit of Christ, to help their infirmities, or they cannot resist evil. Jesus loves to have us come to Him just as we are, sinful, helpless, dependent. We may come with all our weakness, our folly, our

---

49    Nyree Thompkins, "What's In a Name?" *Signs of the Times Magazine,* Australia New Zealand edition, December, 2010.

sinfulness, and fall at His feet in penitence. It is His glory to encircle us in the arms of His love and to bind up our wounds, to cleanse us from all impurity.

"Here is where thousands fail; they do not believe that Jesus pardons them personally, individually. They do not take God at His word. It is the privilege of all who comply with the conditions to know for themselves that pardon is freely extended for every sin. Put away the suspicion that God's promises are not meant for you. They are for every repentant transgressor. Strength and grace have been provided through Christ to be brought by ministering angels to every believing soul. None are so sinful that they cannot find strength, purity, and righteousness in Jesus, who died for them. He is waiting to strip them of their garments stained and polluted with sin, and to put upon them the white robes of righteousness; He bids them live and not die.

"God does not deal with us as finite men deal with one another. His thoughts are thoughts of mercy, love, and tenderest compassion. He says, *"Let the wicked forsake his way, and the unrighteous man his thoughts; let him return to the Lord, and He will have mercy on him; and to our God, for He will abundantly pardon."" "I have blotted out, like a thick cloud, your transgressions, and like a cloud, your sins."* Isaiah 55:7; 44:22."* [50]

**Illustrative Sketch:**

In the 1st year of King Jehoiachin, King Nebuchadnezzar came up against Jerusalem, and his armies surrounded the city. King Jehoiachin had refused to pay tribute to the foreign monarch, but now he wisely surrendered the city, knowing what the king of Babylon was capable of doing. Nebuchadnezzar had laid waste the cities of the coastal plain, the Judean Shephelah, and now all the city states of the highlands.

And King Nebuchadnezzar deposed Jehoaichin and took him away in chains to Babylon along with other members of the royal family. And he put Zedekiah, Jehoiachin's uncle on the throne and made Judah a vassal of the kingdom of Babylon. But Zedekiah did evil in the sight of the Lord and did not obey the Divine commands as written in the Law and the prophets. 2 Chronicles 36:12.

---

50    White, 52.

Now the Word of the Lord came to Jeremiah in those days. Over and over again he sent Zedekiah warnings which he wrote on scrolls of parchment, by the hand of Baruch. "'Will you steal, murder, commit adultery, perjury, burn incense to Baal and walk after other gods whom you do not know?' This is what the Lord says, 'If you thoroughly amend your ways and your doings, if you thoroughly execute judgment between a man and his neighbor, if you do not oppress the stranger, the fatherless, and the widow, and do not shed innocent blood in this place, or walk after other gods to your hurt, then I will cause you to dwell in this place, in the land that I gave to your fathers forever and ever.' Then your soul shall live; this city shall not be burned with fie, and you and your house shall live.'" Jeremiah 7:9, 5-7, 38:17.

But King Zedekiah was a weak man and ill advised by his young friends at court. They despised Jeremiah's messages from God and tempted King Zedekiah to disregard the divine warnings too. And so it was that openly, in the presence of his advisors, Zedekiah ignored the Word of the Lord, but he called for Jeremiah secretly from time to time hoping for better news.

"Yes," said Jeremiah. "Behold, Nebuchadnezzar will come against this place, and 'You shall be delivered into the hand of the king of Babylon!' Jeremiah 37:17. Surrender the city of Jerusalem to King Nebuchadnezzar. Pay your tribute taxes and he will not come up to destroy Mount Zion." God was giving Zedekiah one last chance to save Jerusalem. "Come now, while there is still hope!" Jeremiah begged the king. "'Bring your necks under the yoke of the king of Babylon, and serve him and his people, and live! Why will you die, you and your people?'" Jeremiah 27:12, 13.

Zedekiah promised to consider the words of Jeremiah, but the prophet knew the king would do no such thing. He was too dependent on the whims of his supporters at the royal court. And from there things went from bad to worse.

When the false prophets of Judah visited the king, they also turned the heart of Zedekiah against Jeremiah. "The City of David is the flower of Judah, the chosen seat of the Lord our God," they crooned. "How can Jehovah suffer this city to be overrun by pagan armies? Do not listen to Jeremiah. His message will only stir up the hearts of the people against you.

And it worked. King Zedekiah's courtiers and advisors were allowed to arrest Jeremiah. Angrily they took the prophet and threw him into the deepest darkest place they could find, an old pit with mud and water at the bottom.

What a sight! The pitiful plight of God's people was hanging in the balance, and the only man that could really help them through the horrible days ahead, was in a dungeon, out of sight, and out of mind.

But God did not forsake the man of God. Plagued by guilt and the memory of the fearful prophecies given by Jeremiah, King Zedekiah finally did the right thing and brought Jeremiah out of that despicable pit. But it was too little and too late. With the city under siege by Nebuchadnezzar's army, Zedekiah knew all hope was gone.

And still he followed the ill-timed counsel of his courtiers. When the battering rams finally broke through the city wall, instead of surrendering to the king of Babylon as Jeremiah had advised, Zedekiah fled by night toward Jericho, hoping to escape across the Jordan. But Nebuchadnezzar's warriors pursued him and caught him when it was daylight. And King Nebuchadnezzar killed the sons of Zedekiah in his presence, and put out Zedekiah's eyes, and then took him away in chains to Babylon.

Thus ended the sad career of a man who had all the help he needed in choosing which path he should take. God wanted to save Zedekiah and his people, but it was not to be. Faced with warnings from the pen of inspiration, Zedekiah chose instead to follow the crowd.

Let us not be like the Judean king, expecting the blessings of God, while ignoring our responsibilities to Him. Jesus calls us today asking that we give him our sin-hardened hearts, our weak wills, our idols and pet desires that have taken first place in our lives.

Why not surrender to Him? Why not accept his offer of salvation and let His blood cover the filthy rags of our unrighteousness?[51] [52]

Lord Jesus, I long to be perfectly whole;
   I want Thee forever to live in my soul.
Break down every idol, cast out every foe;
   Now wash me, and I shall be whiter than snow.

---

51  Excepts from Ellen G. White, Chapters 34-36, in *Prophets and Kings*, Mountain View, CA: Pacific Press Publishing, 1943).

52  Based on 2 Kings 24, 25; 2 Chronicles 36.

Lord Jesus, let nothing unholy remain,
　　Apply Thine own blood and extract every stain;
To get this blest cleansing, I all things forego—
　　Now wash me, and I shall be whiter than snow.

Lord Jesus, look down from Thy throne in the skies,
　　And help me to make a complete sacrifice.
I give up myself, and whatever I know,
　　Now wash me, and I shall be whiter than snow.

Lord Jesus, for this I most humbly entreat,
　　I wait, blessed Lord, at Thy crucified feet.
By faith, for my cleansing, I see Thy blood flow,
　　Now wash me, and I shall be whiter than snow.

Lord Jesus, Thou seest I patiently wait,
　　Come now, and within me a new heart create;
To those who have sought Thee, Thou never saidst "No,"
　　Now wash me, and I shall be whiter than snow.

The blessing by faith, I receive from above;
　　O glory! my soul is made perfect in love;
My prayer has prevailed, and this moment I know,
　　The blood is applied, I am whiter than snow.

Chorus:
Whiter than snow, yes, whiter than snow.
　　Now wash me, and I shall be whiter than snow.

　　　　—James L. Nicholson, "Whiter Than Snow"

## Coming Home—Reading #4

　　*"'For I have no pleasure in the death of one who dies,'" says the Lord God. "'Therefore turn and live!'" Ezekiel 18:32.* Satan is ready to steal away the blessed assurances of God. He desires to take every glimmer

of hope and every ray of light from the soul; but you must not permit him to do this. Do not give ear to the tempter, but say, "Jesus has died that I might live. He loves me, and wills not that I should perish. I have a compassionate heavenly Father; and although I have abused His love, though the blessings He has given me have been squandered, I will arise, and go to my Father, and say, *"I have sinned against heaven and before you, and I am no longer worthy to be called your son. Make me like one of your hired servants.""* The parable tells you how the wanderer will be received: *"When he was still a great way off, his father saw him and had compassion, and ran and fell on his neck and kissed him."* Luke 15:18-20.

"But even this parable, tender and touching as it is, comes short of expressing the infinite compassion of the heavenly Father. The Lord declares by His prophet, *"I have loved you with an everlasting love; therefore with loving kindness I have drawn you."* Jeremiah 31:3. While the sinner is yet far from the Father's house, wasting his substance in a strange country, the Father's heart is yearning over him; and every longing awakened in the soul to return to God is but the tender pleading of His Spirit, wooing, entreating, drawing the wanderer to his Father's heart of love.

"With the rich promises of the Bible before you, can you give place to doubt? Can you believe that when the poor sinner longs to return, longs to forsake his sins, the Lord sternly withholds him from coming to His feet in repentance? Away with such thoughts! Nothing can hurt your own soul more than to entertain such a conception of our heavenly Father. He hates sin, but He loves the sinner, and He gave Himself in the person of Christ, that all who would might be saved and have eternal blessedness in the kingdom of glory. What stronger or more tender language could have been employed than He has chosen in which to express His love toward us? He declares, *"'Can a woman forget her nursing child, and not have compassion on the son of her womb? Surely they may forget, yet I will not forget you.'"* Isaiah 49:15.

"Look up, you that are doubting and trembling; for Jesus lives to make intercession for us. Thank God for the gift of His dear Son and pray that He may not have died for you in vain. The Spirit invites you today. Come with your whole heart to Jesus, and you may claim His blessing.

"As you read the promises, remember they are the expression of unutterable love and pity. The great heart of Infinite Love is drawn toward the sinner with boundless compassion. *"We have redemption through His blood, the forgiveness of sins." Ephesians 1:7.* Yes, only believe that God is your helper. He wants to restore His moral image in man. As you draw near to Him with confession and repentance, He will draw near to you with mercy and forgiveness." [53]

**Illustrative Sketch:**

*If we confess our sins, He is faithful and just to forgive us our sins and to cleanse us from all unrighteousness. 1 John 1:9.*

The cool of the day had come, and sunset with it. Swallows dipped their wings on the evening air, and a hoot owl could already be heard calling to its mate. Jacob could hear his flocks of sheep and goats milling about and bleating as they settled in for the night across the winding Jabbok River.

From where he knelt on an outcropping of rock, he could see the clusters of family tents already pitched. The smoke of evening fires was rising into the deep purple of evening stretching away from the crimson skies in the west. It should have been a peaceful scene with his extensive herds of cattle, donkeys, and camels browsing on the twilight grasses in the hills of Gilead, but it wasn't. Jacob was in anguish. He should have been with his family tonight. He had sent them over the Jabbok ahead of him in anticipation of what must come in the morning, and now he had chosen to stay behind to wrestle with God in prayer.

Wrestling with God in prayer! Must he really contend with God to get the blessings and protection he needed? Hadn't Jehovah always provided for him? Hadn't God always kept him from sickness and harm? Hadn't He blessed Jacob beyond everyone's wildest expectations for over twenty years, even in a foreign land? Jacob was now a rich man, with vast wealth in gold and silver and sheep and cattle. He had numerous servants to tend his holdings, and eleven sons to make any father proud!

However, all had not been a bed of aloes and frankincense for Jacob, a fact he had accepted long ago. Jacob had been swindled by

---

53   White, 53.

his father-in-law Laban. Wasn't this a fitting payback for his treachery back home? Deceiving his father and stealing Esau's birthright were no small crimes! Not surprisingly, he had fled from home, unable to take with him his dowry for a future wife. Then Laban had schemed to give him Leah as his wife instead of Rachel. After hiring Jacob to work for him, the conniving, grasping father-in-law had changed his wages ten times. What else could be expected of the man? Knowing Laban, he wanted to capitalize on the blessings Jacob was receiving from God. His only problem was he couldn't figure out how Jacob grew wealthier every day.

When Jacob had had enough of Laban's shenanigans, he had taken all that was his and fled like a refugee from Padan Aram to return home to the hills of Canaan. Of course, Laban pursued, but the angel of the Lord sent Laban a dream in the night, warning him not to harm even a hair on Jacob's head.

Now, the worst kind of trouble was on its way. Esau was on the warpath, headed for Jacob in the hills of Gilead, and he was surely out for blood. But again, Jacob wasn't surprised. If trouble was to come from his brother Esau after all these years, he knew he deserved it, and it was long overdue.

"Please, Lord!" Jacob prayed, as he bowed his face to the ground under the light of the rising moon. "I just wanted to come home to the land of promise and my father. But now I must face this new danger! Save my family, Lord! I ask little for myself, but spare my children! Protect my wives! They are good women and don't deserve this kind of treatment! It wasn't them that brought this danger upon us! Esau wants revenge, and with good reason! I behaved like a child and stole something that only You can give!"

Somewhere during the night Jacob must have dozed as he prayed on the stony ledge. He didn't know how long it was, but suddenly he was awake again, alert to the crunch of gravel as if something or someone were lurking nearby. Jacob struck out instinctively, in desperation, and caught the corner of a man's cloak. Together they fell from the rocky ledge. It wasn't far, but the fall stunned Jacob. Still he struggled, trying to get a foothold in the damp night soil, hoping to gain an advantage over his enemy. Was it his brother? Not a chance—he would know his brother anywhere, wouldn't he? Was it an assassin sent by Esau to kill him here and now? "Help me, Lord!" Jacob cried out in anguish, but heaven seemed far away. The sins of his past loomed up before him and pressed out any hopes he felt he might have for deliverance.

Jacob struggled with the Stranger, sometimes gaining ground, but the enemy could not be beaten, nor would he leave! As the gentle light of dawn began to swell the eastern sky, the enemy finally broke free and headed for the Jabbok valley below. Jacob suddenly remembered his family was there, and with a new burst of energy, he snatched at the Stranger's cloak, pulling him to the ground again. The Stranger reached back and in that instant a terrible pain shot through Jacob's hip.

At that moment Jacob sensed an overpowering force of something supernatural, and the pit of his stomach told him this was no ordinary Stranger. He had been grappling with a heavenly Messenger, and it humbled him to think that he had been in the presence of the Almighty God. A wave of emotion swept over him like a warm spring breeze. He had wrestled with God and was alive.

"Oh, Lord," Jacob wept, his face now salty with tears, "thank You for bringing me back to the land of my fathers. My sins are many, but I pray that You will forgive me for a life of transgression! Bless me that I may find favor in Your eyes!"

"Your prayer has been heard," said the Stranger. "From this day forward you shall no longer be called Jacob, but Israel, for you have wrestled with God and prevailed," and then He vanished in the mists of growing morning light.[54]

I've wandered far away from God,
Now I'm coming home;
The paths of sin too long I've trod,
Lord, I'm coming home.

I've wasted many precious years,
Now I'm coming home;
I now repent with bitter tears,
Lord, I'm coming home.

54  Based on Genesis 32.

I need His cleansing blood I know,
    Now I'm coming home;
Oh, wash me whiter than the snow,
    Lord, I'm coming home.

Coming home, coming home,
    Nevermore to roam;
Open wide Thine arms of love,
    Lord, I'm coming home.

—William J. Kirkpatrick, "Lord, I'm Coming Home"

---⟨⬥⟩---

# CHAPTER 7

# The Test of Discipleship

**I'll Be True—Reading #1**

"*I* *f anyone is in Christ, he is a new creation; old things have passed away; behold, all things have become new.*" *2 Corinthians 5:17.*

"A person may not be able to tell the exact time or place, or trace all the chain of circumstances in the process of conversion; but this does not prove him to be unconverted. Christ said to Nicodemus, "*The wind blows where it wishes, and you hear the sound of it, but cannot tell where it comes from and where it goes. So is everyone who is born of the Spirit.*" *John 3:8.* Like the wind, which is invisible, yet the effects of which are plainly seen and felt, is the Spirit of God in its work upon the human heart. That regenerating power, which no human eye can see, begets a new life in the soul; it creates a new being in the image of God.

"While the work of the Spirit is silent and imperceptible, its effects are manifest. If the heart has been renewed by the Spirit of God, the life will bear witness to the fact. While we cannot do anything to change our hearts or to bring ourselves into harmony with God; while we must not trust at all to ourselves or our good works, our lives will reveal whether the grace of God is dwelling within us. A change will be seen in the character, the habits, the pursuits. The contrast will be clear and decided between what they have been and what they are. The character is revealed, not by occasional good deeds and occasional misdeeds, but by the tendency of the habitual words and acts.

"It is true that there may be an outward correctness of deportment without the renewing power of Christ. The love of influence and the desire for the esteem of others may produce a well-ordered life. Self-respect may lead us to avoid the appearance of evil. A selfish heart may perform generous actions. By what means, then, shall we determine whose side we are on?

Who has the heart? With whom are our thoughts? Of whom do we love to converse? Who has our warmest affections and our best energies? If we are Christ's, our thoughts are with Him, and our sweetest thoughts are of Him. All we have and are is consecrated to Him. We long to bear His image, breathe His spirit, do His will, and please Him in all things." [55]

## Illustrative Sketch:

Years ago during the height of the Cultural Revolution in China there lived a Chinese man named Glorious Country Wong. A very patriotic man, he was known to be a tough, macho cop with a violent nature.

One day, a co-worker thought it would be a good practical joke to register Mr. Wong for a Bible correspondence course. When the lessons came in the mail, Mr. Wong did not take them seriously. However, he did read them and soon found himself believing more and more of what he was reading about Christianity and God. The Chinese government did not allow these beliefs, but Mr. Wong knew what he had discovered in the Bible was truth, and finally decided he could no longer go on living as he had been. He gave up his job and changed other areas of his life to become a Christian. Most important of all, Mr. Wong now felt compelled to preach and share his new love for Jesus, though he knew what would happen if he did.

Before long he was arrested. After being interrogated and brutally beaten, he was sent to a hard labor camp high in the desert of eastern China where he spent the next twenty years. His crime? He was a Christian who loved to speak of his best friend Jesus, and of God's "Ten Regulations."

But if the prison authorities thought they would "reeducate" Mr. Wong with the principles of communistic Red China, they were in for a surprise. Even in prison Mr. Wong was not afraid to tell others of his friend Jesus because he believed that God would protect him through anything. This led to more beatings from his persecutors with sticks and whips and chains, sometimes for days at a time!

---

55 White, 57.

It was here that Mr. Wong got his nickname, "The Man Who Couldn't Be Killed." Guards inflicted the worst kinds of torture on Mr. Wong, but his faith in God kept him strong. They tried to starve him. They tied heavy weights to his body and hung him up for days at a time. They even broke both his legs once and threw him on the prison garbage dump to die. But to everyone's shock, Mr. Wong got up off the garbage heap the next morning and walked back into camp completely healed.

Once he was tied to a pole with his arms bound behind his back for an entire night in sub-zero temperatures. Amazingly an angel untied the knot so Mr. Wong could move about and keep warm. Miraculously he survived the night, but with his hands untied it occurred to him that someone in camp would be accused of helping him escape. So before the guard returned the next morning, Mr. Wong put his hands behind the pole and tried to retie the knot. To his astonishment he felt an unseen hand tightening the ropes around his hands, and soon his hands were once again tied. When the guard returned a few minutes later, Mr. Wong greeted him cheerfully, but the guard gasped and turned white. "This can't be," he stammered when he saw that Mr. Wong was alive and warm. "You should be frozen to death by now!"

Of the five thousand prisoners sent with Mr. Wong to the prison camp in 1948, only 18 survived the twenty-year term, and only one was released to his family again—the "man who couldn't be killed." His unforgettable story of faith and miraculous deliverance reminds us to be courageous for Jesus, no matter what the cost. [56]

The Eleventh Chapter of Hebrews has been called the Hall of Faith because of the illustrious members of Bible lore registered there. And what can we say? It's a pretty impressive list!

For the time would fail me to tell of Gideon and Barak and Samson and Jephthah, also of David and Samuel and the prophets, who through faith subdued kingdoms, worked righteousness, obtained promises, stopped the mouths of lions, quenched the violence of fire, escaped the edge of the sword, out of weakness were made strong, became valiant in battle,

---

56 Stanley Maxwell, *The Man Who Couldn't Be Killed* (Boise: Pacific Press Publishing Association, 1995).

turned to flight the armies of the aliens. Women received their dead raised to life again. And others were tortured, not accepting deliverance, that they might obtain a better resurrection. Still others had trial of mockings and scourgings, yes, and of chains and imprisonment. They were stoned, they were sawn in two, were tempted, were slain with the sword. They wandered about in sheepskins and goatskins, being destitute, afflicted, tormented—of whom the world was not worthy. They wandered in deserts and mountains, in dens and caves of the earth.

These all died in faith, not having received the promises, but having seen them afar off were assured of them, embraced them and confessed that they were strangers and pilgrims on the earth... They desire a better, that is, a heavenly country. Therefore God is not ashamed to be called their God, for He has prepared a city for them. Hebrews 11:32-38, 13, 16.

These Bible heroes were faithful to God despite the odds against them, and Mr. Wong has joined them to become one of the elite, a faithful servant in God's hall of faith. Like the Bible characters of the past, Mr. Wong surrendered himself to the cause of the gospel, regardless of the price. Their lives and sufferings are a testimony to all who choose to follow Jesus.

I'll be true precious Jesus, I'll be true,
    I'll be true precious Jesus, I'll be true.
There's a race to be run,
    There's a victory to be won.
Every hour, by Thy power I'll be true.

I love You precious Jesus, I love You,
    I love You precious Jesus, I love You.
You have paid my sinful debt
    And I never will forget,
Every moment, this my token, I love You.

I choose You precious Jesus, I choose You,
    I choose You precious Jesus, I choose You.
You're the Father's only Son,
    And for me you are the One.
    Every minute, 'til life's finished,
I choose You.

—Unknown, "I'll Be True"

———— ✣ ————

## A New Creation—Reading #2

"Those who become new creatures in Christ Jesus will bring forth the fruits of the Spirit, *"love, joy, peace, longsuffering, kindness, goodness, faithfulness, gentleness, self-control."* Galatians 5:22, 23. They will no longer fashion themselves according to the former lusts, but by the faith of the Son of God they will follow in His steps, reflect His character, and purify themselves even as He is pure. The things they once hated they now love, and the things they once loved they hate. The proud and self-assertive become meek and lowly in heart. The vain and supercilious become serious and unobtrusive. The drunken become sober, and the profligate pure. The vain customs and fashions of the world are laid aside. Christians will seek not the *"outward adorning,"* but *"... the hidden person of the heart, with the incorruptible beauty of a gentle and quiet spirit."* 1 Peter 3:3, 4.

"There is no evidence of genuine repentance unless it works reformation. If he restore the pledge, give again that he had robbed, confess his sins, and love God and his fellow men, the sinner may be sure that he has passed from death unto life.

"When, as erring, sinful beings, we come to Christ and become partakers of His pardoning grace, love springs up in the heart. Every burden is light, for the yoke that Christ imposes is easy. Duty becomes a delight, and sacrifice a pleasure. The path that before seemed shrouded in darkness, becomes bright with beams from the Sun of Righteousness.

"The loveliness of the character of Christ will be seen in His followers. It was His delight to do the will of God. Love to God, zeal for

His glory, was the controlling power in our Savior's life. Love beautified and ennobled all His actions. Love is of God. The unconsecrated heart cannot originate or produce it. It is found only in the heart where Jesus reigns. *"We love Him because He first loved us." 1 John 4:19.* In the heart renewed by divine grace, love is the principle of action. It modifies the character, governs the impulses, controls the passions, subdues enmity, and ennobles the affections. This love, cherished in the soul, sweetens the life and sheds a refining influence on all around." [57]

### Illustrative Sketch:

The afternoon sun was well past its zenith when Lysias turned the busy street corner at the western Jericho gate. Shimmering heat waves rose from the cobblestone pavement in the warmth of an afternoon spring day. Sun-bronzed faces in the streets trickled with sweat, and little gray lizards skittered to get out of the way. Lysias paused to duck under a roll of carpet being hoisted onto the shoulder of a passing vendor, and then sidestepped a camel loaded high with market goods.

The trip from Jerusalem had been a rugged one with its steep canyon road, but to Lysias the resort town of Jericho was usually worth the effort. The city boasted swimming pools and the best food in Judea. Here on business for the governor as centurion of the Praetorian Guard, Lysias hoped to also make contact with one called Zacchaeus, a man now famous among Christians for his curious encounter with Jesus of Nazareth. He had a story to tell, no doubt, and the centurion wanted to hear it.

The last few months had been trying ones for Lysias. Since witnessing the death of Jesus on the cross at Golgotha, nothing about working at the Antonia fortress in Jerusalem felt right anymore. He had felt a sense of despair as he watched them lay the body of Jesus in a tomb, but took courage a few days later when the story broke, announcing He had risen from the dead. Lysias believed every word of it, even the part about Jesus ascending to heaven.

His whole focus in life was different now. He wanted to become part of the new Christian movement in Jerusalem. Like Jesus 'other followers Lysias wanted to tell the good news that the Man from Galilee would be coming back soon to set up His Kingdom of righteousness. Unfortunately, he didn't know Jesus well, and he felt bad about that. He

---

57  White, 58.

had seen Jesus around Jerusalem countless times, but had never fathomed that the celebrated Healer was the Son of God, at least not until His infamous crucifixion on Golgotha. And now the tax commissioner would be able to help him make up for lost time. After all, like the centurion, the tax man's encounter with Jesus had changed his life, they said.

Finding the commissioner was as easy as Lysias had thought it would be. But where he found him was the shock. Surprisingly, faces on the street brightened when he mentioned the commissioner's name. That's was a bit odd. Commoners usually had nothing but disgust for the rich, and Zacchaeus was definitely rich. Without a word, an old woman took Lysias by the hand and led him down a narrow alley to the doorway of a broken down lean-to that butted up against the city wall. An open sewer ran past the doorway of the little hut, and Lysias had to hold his nose at the stench. The interior of the shanty was dark and rags had been stuffed into crevices of the roof and walls where the weather had taken its toll. The feeble light of a flickering oil lamp revealed an elderly man on a dirty floor pallet, and Lysias had to squint to adjust to the darkness.

The old man was very sick, it appeared, and kneeling beside him was the man Lysias had been searching for. It could be no other. The tax man's distinguished robes betrayed him, but his bedside manner told a different story. "How are you feeling, my friend?" The commissioner was gentle and kind as though he really cared about the plight of the sick man. Could it be possible? Rich folks did not fraternize with the destitute and diseased.

"I've been worried about you," the commissioner continued. "This is no place for an elderly man." His voice nearly broke with emotion. "I've brought you medicine and some food, but I'm not sure that's enough, now that I see your condition. We need to get you out of here for some real help. I wish Jesus were here," he added sadly. "He would have you well in a jiffy."

Zacchaeus suddenly saw Lysias. "Welcome to Jericho," he said as he stood to his feet, and the Roman officer had to smile as he looked down into the little man's face. Zacchaeus was every bit as short as all the stories declared him to be.

"I can't believe I left this poor man here so long," the tax man turned again sadly to stare at the invalid lying on his pallet. "Can you help me get him up to my house? I'll send for a doctor as soon as we get him settled in." They carried the poor man in a hammock up the narrow street, across the marketplace, and into the affluent district where Zacchaeus lived. Strange looks followed them as they neared Zacchaeus' front gate.

"No one seems to care about the plight of the poor," the commissioner frowned, "and we're all worse off because of it. The poor can't improve their lives. A few might prefer it that way, but most would give anything to be better off. It's a vicious cycle!" The commissioner appeared angry at such sentiments. "You know, I always fancied myself a financial wizard of sorts, but the idea of us all prospering if the poor had enough, was a new thought to me when I met Jesus."

Servants came running to help carry the old man to the servant's quarters in the back, and Zacchaeus welcomed Lysias for a cool drink and an evening meal. They visited amiably as more servants washed their tired feet in basins of water. The centurion felt strangely drawn to this man in fine robes. Zacchaeus was surprisingly friendly for one of such high rank. Usually the rich were painfully snobbish. This one was charming, almost childlike with his magnetic ways. There was something extraordinary here, the Roman officer mused. It was almost as if the tax commissioner had a direct connection with heaven.

"You certainly do have a special touch with the common folks," the Centurion announced. "I'm impressed, and I wish to hear more about how you came to know Jesus."

Zacchaeus smiled at the Centurion's eager eyes. "Of course, I'm always glad to share the story of the Master, and tell you of my conversion—not that there is much to tell. If you knew Jesus personally, you would know that He transforms lives simply by looking into the life. In a moment, in the twinkling of an eye, He takes the old, and makes it new. Corruption makes way for a new heart—a heart of flesh." The commissioner pointed to his own chest for emphasis.

He loosened his tunic belt and sighed contentedly. "I knew I would meet the Man of Galilee someday," he continued. "It was inevitable— He often came this way. The question was, did I really want to meet Him? I knew Jesus had a reputation for changing people's lives in dramatic ways, and that scared me." The commissioner smiled sheepishly. "And then one day He came to town, as I knew He must. It was as if He came to Jericho just for me."

The shadows of evening were beginning to fall, and heaven seemed very near in the elegance of the tax commissioner's home. Zacchaeus' eyes reflected a feeling of peace that filled his home. It was as if nothing could shake his confidence in the goodness of God.

"Jesus changed my life forever the day he found me in the sycamore tree on Market Street," Zacchaeus said quietly. "If He could make me a new man, then he can do it for anyone. I was the lowest of the low. I was financially blind, spiritually poor. I was wretched in spirit and so far from the God of heaven, that everyone in these parts had already consigned my soul to the fires of hell. But Jesus took this miserable piece of humanity and made me whole."

*"My cup runs over. Surely goodness and mercy shall follow me all the days of my life; and I will dwell in the house of the Lord forever." Psalm 23:5, 6.*

**Trust and Obey—Reading #3**

"There are two errors against which the children of God—particularly those who have just come to trust in His grace—especially need to guard. The first, already dwelt upon, is that of looking to their own works, trusting to anything they can do, to bring themselves into harmony with God. He who is trying to become holy by his own works in keeping the law, is attempting impossibility. All that man can do without Christ is polluted with selfishness and sin. It is the grace of Christ alone, through faith, that can make us holy.

"The opposite and no less dangerous error is that belief in Christ releases men from keeping the law of God; that since by faith alone we become partakers of the grace of Christ, our works have nothing to do with our redemption.

"But notice here that obedience is not a mere outward compliance, but the service of love. The law of God is an expression of His very nature; it is an embodiment of the great principle of love, and hence is the foundation of His government in heaven and earth. If our hearts are renewed in the likeness of God, if the divine love is implanted in the soul, will not the law of God be carried out in the life? When the principle of love is implanted in the heart, when man is renewed after the image of Him that created him, the new-covenant promise is fulfilled, *"'I will put My laws into their hearts, and in their minds I will write them.'" Hebrews 10:16.*

"And if the law is written in the heart, will it not shape the life? Obedience—the service and allegiance of love—is the true sign of discipleship. Thus the scripture says, *"This is the love of God, that we keep His commandments." "He who says, 'I know Him,' and does not keep His commandments, is a liar, and the truth is not in him." 1 John 5:3; 2:4.* Instead of releasing man from obedience, it is faith, and faith only, that makes us partakers of the grace of Christ, which enables us to render obedience.

"We do not earn salvation by our obedience; for salvation is the free gift of God, to be received by faith. But obedience is the fruit of faith. *"And you know that He was manifested to take away our sins, and in Him there is no sin. Whoever abides in Him does not sin. Whoever sins has neither seen Him nor known Him." 1 John 3:5,6.* Here is the true test. If we abide in Christ, if the love of God dwells in us, our feelings, our thoughts, our purposes, our actions, will be in harmony with the will of God as expressed in the precepts of His holy law. *"Little children, let no one deceive you. He who practices righteousness is righteous, just as He is righteous." 1 John 3:7.* Righteousness is defined by the standard of God's holy law, as expressed in the ten precepts given on Sinai."[58]

**Illustrative Sketch:**

An amazing miracle story comes to us from Leningrad, Russia where communism flourished for over seven decades. During these years of domination and repression of religious freedom God's people kept the light of the gospel burning, though it cost them life, liberty, and what many of us have come to call "the pursuit of happiness." Of course, happiness is a relative concept, and faithful Christians in the Soviet Union were "happy" to stand up for the gospel of Jesus. Pastor Sergei was just such a man.

Because Sergei had refused to reveal the location of his church to the communist authorities, one dark night the KGB came knocking. Knowing the charges were serious and that he might never return home again, he still refused to comply with their orders.

---

58   White, 59.

Sergei's wife was frantic, but Sergei reminded her that all Christians must be willing to suffer for Jesus. He promised her that if they should not see each other again on earth, they would certainly meet in heaven. Sergei was taken to headquarters, cruelly beaten, and then brought before the director of KGB operations. After repeated interrogations, he still refused to talk, so they finally sentenced him to prison far, far away. Sergei had no Bible to read, but he didn't allow himself to become discouraged. He kept his faith strong by reciting texts of Scripture that he had been memorizing for years. There was too much at stake here, and he gratefully anticipated God's call to be a witness in the prison to which he was headed.

For two days Sergei rode a train, and although under guard, he conducted Bible studies with other travelers on the train. The light of hope in the eyes of the travelers was truly rewarding, and the guards even listened as he shared the gospel story.

When Sergei finally arrived in the prison, he was turned over to the warden who taunted him for his belief in God. He confined Sergei to a maximum-security cell and threatened that there would be no food until he learned to cooperate with the government.

Sergei bravely accepted the sentence, but assured the warden that God would care for his every need. The warden laughed at the idea of God providing food for Sergei in his prison cell. If God existed at all, why had He allowed Sergei to be locked up in prison in the first place?

The prison cell was quite small, containing only a bed, chair, and chamber pot. There was a small window in the cell door, and a larger window high in the cell wall above his bed. Sergei felt discouraged and alone in his surroundings, but claimed God's promises as he fell asleep in the cold, dark cell, wondering what God would do for Him next. "My God shall supply all [my] need according to His riches in glory by Christ Jesus," Sergei kept reminding himself. Philippians 4:19. God could supply his every need, and with that he was satisfied.

The next morning he awoke to a scratching sound at the window, and when he stood up on his bed, he found a slice of Russian black bread on the windowsill. He could hardly believe it. Who had brought the bread? A prison guard? Sergei wanted to eat the bread, but decided to save it and show it to the warden to prove that God had provided for him. When evening came another slice of bread appeared on the windowsill, and the next morning the same thing happened again. Sergei was very hungry but decided not to eat any of it. If one slice of bread was living proof of God's watch care, then more slices of bread would be even better. One by one he hid them all under his mattress.

By now Sergei was thinking of all the stories in the Bible where God's people had been miraculously fed. Could it be ravens that were feeding him, as in the story of Elijah? Or was it possibly an angel?

On the morning of the fifth day the warden came to visit Sergei and taunted him once again. Was Sergei now ready to renounce his belief in God and give up his foolish ways? Sergei smiled bravely and told the warden that God had indeed provided him with food. Then he lifted the mattress where he had been hiding the bread and showed the warden six whole slices of Russian bread. The warden was furious, thinking that someone had been feeding Sergei, and he threatened to punish the culprit when he discovered who it was.

However, just at that moment they heard a scratching sound at the window. Suddenly, there on the window ledge was a cat with a slice of bread in its mouth. The warden was dumbfounded. The cat was his daughter's cat. The bread in its mouth was fresh from the warden's own kitchen table. The warden was amazed that God would do such a thing for Sergei. What a testimony to Sergei's faith under trial and persecution. May God's grace help us all stand for Jesus under similar circumstances.[59]

> When we walk with the Lord in the light of His Word,
>    What a glory He sheds on our way!
> While we do His good will, He abides with us still,
>    And with all who will trust and obey.
>
> Not a shadow can rise, not a cloud in the skies,
>    But His smile quickly drives it away;
> Not a doubt or a fear, not a sigh or a tear,
>    Can abide while we trust and obey.
>
> Not a burden we bear, not a sorrow we share,
>    But our toil He doth richly repay;
> Not a grief or a loss, not a frown or a cross,
>    But is blessed if we trust and obey.

59   John McGhee, conversation with author, 1994.

Then in fellowship sweet we will sit at His feet,
   Or we'll walk by His side in the way;
What He says we will do, where He sends we will go;
   Never fear, only trust and obey.

Trust and obey, for there's no other way
   To be happy in Jesus, but to trust and obey.

—J. H. Sammis, "Trust and Obey"

## Do Unto Others—Reading #4

"That so-called faith in Christ which professes to release men from the obligation of obedience to God, is not faith, but presumption. *"For by grace you have been saved through faith."* But *"... faith by itself, if it does not have works, is dead." Ephesians 2:8; James 2:17.* Jesus said of Himself before He came to earth, *"I delight to do Your will, O my God, and Your law is within my heart." Psalm 40:8.* And just before He ascended again to heaven He declared, *"'I have kept My Father's commandments, and abide in His love.'" John 15:10.* The scripture says, *"Now by this we know that we know Him, if we keep His commandments. ... He who says he abides in Him ought himself also to walk just as He walked." 1 John 2:3-6. "Because Christ also suffered for us, leaving us an example, that you should follow His steps." 1 Peter 2:21.*

"The condition of eternal life is now just what it always has been—just what it was in Paradise before the fall of our first parents—perfect obedience to the law of God, perfect righteousness. If eternal life were granted on any condition short of this, then the happiness of the whole universe would be imperiled. The way would be open for sin, with all its train of woe and misery, to be immortalized.

"It was possible for Adam, before the fall, to form a righteous character by obedience to God's law. But he failed to do this, and because of his sin our natures are fallen and we cannot make ourselves righteous. Since we are sinful, unholy, we cannot perfectly obey the holy law. We have no righteousness of our own with which to meet the claims of the law of God. But Christ has made a way of escape for us. He lived on earth amid trials and temptations such as we have to meet. He lived a sinless life. He died for us, and now He offers to take our sins and give us His righteousness. If you give yourself to Him, and accept Him as your Savior, then, sinful as your life may have been, for His sake you are accounted righteous. Christ's character stands in place of your character, and you are accepted before God just as if you had not sinned.

"More than this, Christ changes the heart. He abides in your heart by faith. You are to maintain this connection with Christ by faith and the continual surrender of your will to Him; and so long as you do this, He will work in you to will and to do according to His good pleasure. So you may say, *"The life which I now live in the flesh I live by the faith of the Son of God, who loved me, and gave Himself for me." Galatians 2:20.* So Jesus said to His disciples, *"'It is not you that speak, but the Spirit of your Father who speaks in you.'" Matthew 10:20.* Then with Christ working in you, you will manifest the same spirit and do the same good works—works of righteousness, obedience.

"So we have nothing in ourselves of which to boast. We have no ground for self-exaltation. Our only ground of hope is in the righteousness of Christ imputed to us, and in that wrought by His Spirit working in and through us."[60]

**Illustrative Sketch:**
Many years ago on the fringes of an American colonial settlement, lived a pioneer couple, William and Mary Sullivan. Their home was a neat cottage on a homestead they had built scratch. The place was ideal with wide open fields, rising hills, and a small, clear stream that turned a large sawmill for business. Maize, beans, and pumpkins grew in their garden, and sweet cherry trees in their orchard. Beyond all this was a pine forest and fine hunting-grounds where the men folk of the settlement gathered in late fall for their annual hunting trips.

Generally, relations between the whites and Indians were not friendly, but the Minateree Indian tribes near the settlement were not hostile; although settlers in this part of the country were few in number, and many feared the harm such Indians might do. But Sullivan

60  White, 61.

despised all Indians and made this clear on many occasions to the other farmers in the settlement.

On a warm evening in July, the tall, muscular William was on his doorstep at twilight, sharpening a scythe in preparation for the soon-coming grain harvest. A pale moon was just rising and he failed to notice a tall Indian stranger approach the house.

"Can you give an unfortunate hunter some supper, and a place to sleep for the night?" the tired Indian asked.

William glanced up and immediately a sneer curled his lip. "Heathen Indian dog!" he snarled, "I'll give you nothing!" and he sent him away empty handed!

The proud Indian hesitated and then in discouragement retreated to the clear river running some distance away. He sank to the ground wearily, took a long drink, and then rested a bit before going on. Suddenly, he turned to see the graceful figure of William's wife coming toward him, a pitcher of cold milk in one hand, and a loaf of warm bread in the other. She apologized for her husband's mean spirit, and offered the food to the hungry Indian. Then she watched him eat until it was all gone.

"Thank you," he said softly with a light of gratitude shining from his eyes. He then pulled a white feather from a bundle on his back and offered it to Mary with these words, "This feather is a sign between Carcoochee and the white dove for the kindness she has shown him today. You and your young ones shall remain unharmed, and if your mate will wear this feather when he flies over the Indian's hunting-grounds during his autumn hunt, for your sake Carcoochee will not seek revenge." Then he disappeared into the woods and was gone.

William knew nothing of this, else he might have protested such kindness to the Indian, though in his heart he would have known his wife was right.

The summer passed with the harvest of wheat and maize and golden pumpkins. The cool days of autumn were upon them, and soon preparations were made for the annual hunt. Strangely, William did not find himself looking forward to the hunt as he always had, and his wife wondered if he was remembering his rude treatment to Carcoochee.

On the eve of the hunt Mary brought out the white feather and told her husband the story. He hung his head fearfully. "An Indian never forgives an insult."

"Nor does he forget a kindness," added Mary hopefully. "Let me sew this feather into your hunting-cap and trust you to God's keeping." And then, wonderfully they were kneeling in prayer, something they had not done together for quite some time.

The next morning the lively troop of men was off to the hunt beyond the river and into the pine forests of the hills beyond. William was a skilled hunter, an expert in the use of his rifle and woodman's ax, and along with the other men he had good success those first few days. Things were looking good for the winter's meat supply as they managed to kill several deer and a moose.

On the morning of the third day William somehow got separated from the others. The woods were expansive and the chase swift, and before he knew it, he was alone. He tried to retrace his steps, but to no avail. By noon he was hopelessly lost. Near sunset he came into an open field, and headed for a nearby river to quench his thirst. On the banks of the river he was suddenly startled by the snort of an enormous bull bison! The beast charged, and William fired his rifle, but his aim was off! The animal was only wounded. On came the brute, and William managed to sidestep him and plunge his hunting knife into the side of the beast! This seemed to have no effect either, and the buffalo charged again. William realized that he had no defense. Suddenly, he heard the crack of another rifle, and saw the buffalo topple over and lay dead at his side.

Then he saw in the evening shadows the dark form of an Indian glide out of the forest . "I've lost my way," William said with some embarrassment. "Would you be so kind as to direct me to the nearest white settlement?"

"We must rest tonight," the Indian said, "and tomorrow I will show you." Sullivan followed the Indian to a camp deep in the forest where he was given some hominy and venison to eat. Then the Indian spread animal skins on the ground, and they slept. Before dawn they ate briefly and departed, the Indian leading the way through the dim forest. They rested only briefly during the day for the journey was long. That evening before the golden sun sank behind him in the mountains to the west, William stood once again overlooking the valley of his beloved home.

Only then did the Indian allow his face to be fully seen in the light of the setting sun, and it was with dismay that William recognized Carcoochee. "Four moons ago you called me 'Indian dog,' and drove me away," Carcoochee said. "I might have avenged myself of you last night, but your white dove fed me, and for her sake I have spared you. Remember this lesson, and from this day forward treat all Red Men with kindness. Do for others as has been done for you," and with that he disappeared into the forest.

But that's not the end of the story. Carcoochee returned often, now a welcome guest at William Sullivan's table, and what a change came over both of them. In fact, eventually Carcoochee himself became a Christian, the first Indian baptized in that colonial settlement, and all because of the kindness shown him by White Dove.[61]

**Safe in the Arms of Jesus—Reading #5**

"When we speak of faith, there is a distinction that should be borne in mind. There is a kind of belief that is wholly distinct from faith. The existence and power of God, the truth of His word, are facts that even Satan and his hosts cannot at heart deny. The Bible says that *"the devils also believe, and tremble,"* but this is not faith. James 2:19. Where there is not only a belief in God's word, but a submission of the will to Him; where the heart is yielded to Him, the affections fixed upon Him, there is faith—faith that works by love and purifies the soul. Through this faith the heart is renewed in the image of God. And the heart that in its unrenewed state is not subject to the law of God, neither indeed can be, now delights in its holy precepts, exclaiming with the psalmist, *"O how I love Your law! It is my meditation all the day." Psalm 119:97.* And the righteousness of the law is fulfilled in us, *"who do not walk according to the flesh, but according to the Spirit." Romans 8:1.*

"There are those who have known the pardoning love of Christ and who really desire to be children of God, yet they realize that their character is imperfect, their life faulty, and they are ready to doubt whether their hearts have been renewed by the Holy Spirit. To such

---

61   *Sabbath Readings for the Home Circle,* (Ithaca, MI: A. B. Publishing, 1905).

I would say, Do not draw back in despair. We shall often have to bow down and weep at the feet of Jesus because of our shortcomings and mistakes, but we are not to be discouraged. Even if we are overcome by the enemy, we are not cast off, not forsaken and rejected of God. No; Christ is at the right hand of God, who also makes intercession for us.

"Said the beloved John, *"These things I write to you, so that you may not sin. And if anyone sins, we have an Advocate with the Father, Jesus Christ the righteous." 1 John 2:1.* And do not forget the words of Christ, *"'The Father Himself loves you.'" John 16:27.* He desires to restore you to Himself, to see His own purity and holiness reflected in you. And if you will but yield yourself to Him, He that hath begun a good work in you will carry it forward to the day of Jesus Christ. Pray more fervently; believe more fully. As we come to distrust our own power, let us trust the power of our Redeemer, and we shall praise Him who is the health of our countenance.

"The closer you come to Jesus, the more faulty you will appear in your own eyes; for your vision will be clearer, and your imperfections will be seen in broad and distinct contrast to His perfect nature. This is evidence that Satan's delusions have lost their power; that the vivifying influence of the Spirit of God is arousing you.

"No deep-seated love for Jesus can dwell in the heart that does not realize its own sinfulness. The soul that is transformed by the grace of Christ will admire His divine character; but if we do not see our own moral deformity, it is unmistakable evidence that we have not had a view of the beauty and excellence of Christ.

"The less we see to esteem in ourselves, the more we shall see to esteem in the infinite purity and loveliness of our Savior. A view of our sinfulness drives us to Him who can pardon; and when the soul, realizing its helplessness, reaches out after Christ, He will reveal Himself in power. The more our sense of need drives us to Him and to the word of God, the more exalted views we shall have of His character, and the more fully we shall reflect His image."[62]

**Illustrative Sketch:**

Fanny Crosby is considered one of the most beloved Christian songwriters of all time. She didn't begin writing hymns until her 40s,

62   White, 63.

but she lived to be 95, producing over 8,000 hymns in her lifetime. At least 50 of her songs are still sung as favorites in churches across the United States, among them "Blessed Assurance," "To God Be the Glory," and "Redeemed!"

That Fanny could become such a prolific songwriter is amazing, and that she accomplished it in spite of being blind is astounding! At just six weeks of age, Fanny had an infection in her eyes that caused her to eventually lose her sight. Crosby was never bitter about being blind. In fact, when she was only eight years of age she wrote these verses about her condition:

"Oh what a happy soul I am,
    Although I cannot see;
I am resolved that in this world,
    Contented I will be.
How many blessings I enjoy,
    That other people don't;
To weep and sigh because I'm blind,
    I cannot, and I won't."[63]

Fanny was deeply spiritual and a humble servant of Jesus, something quite evident in the sacred quality of her hymns. Her willingness to accept her limitations helped her be content, and gave her a healthy perspective on eternal things. "It seemed intended by the blessed providence of God that I should be blind all my life," she once said, "and I thank Him for the dispensation. If perfect earthly sight were offered me tomorrow, I would not accept it. I might not have sung hymns to the praise of God if I had been distracted by the beautiful and interesting things about me."[64] Her premise in life was to "be content with such things as you have. For He… has said, 'I will never leave you nor forsake you.'" Hebrews 13:5.

63  Jacob H. Hall, "Miss Fanny J. Crosby: Hymn Writer and Poetess," (online: Wholesome Words, 2011) in Christian Biography Resources, http://www.wholesomewords.org/biography/bcrosby5.html (accessed November 15, 2010)

64  Fanny Crosby, in Wikipedia, http://en.wikipedia.org/wiki/Fanny_Crosby (Accessed November 15, 2010)

A fascinating fact about Ms. Crosby's talent was that she composed not only the lyrics, but also the music to some of her poems. Sometimes she composed as many as 12 hymns in her mind before having her secretary copy them down.

Because of her unusual gifts, she became an international celebrity during her lifetime, meeting with presidents, generals, and other important dignitaries. She was often invited to the White House, and when President Ulysses Grant died, she was asked to play at his funeral.

One of Fanny's most famous lines is timeless in its message. "When I get to heaven, the first face that shall ever gladden my sight will be that of my Savior!"[65] What a testimony for a woman who learned to trust Jesus completely, and live her whole life for Him! The lyrics of her song "Safe in the Arms of Jesus" convey that sentiment well. It was her prayer that those who listened to these words would experience a closer walk with Jesus.

> Safe in the arms of Jesus,
>> Safe on His gentle breast;
> There by His love o'ershaded,
>> Sweetly my soul shall rest.
> Hark! 'tis the voice of angels
>> Borne in a song to me,
> Over the fields of glory,
>> Over the jasper sea.
>
> Safe in the arms of Jesus,
>> Safe from corroding care,
> Safe from the world's temptations;
>> Sin cannot harm me there.
> Free from the blight of sorrow,
>> Free from my doubts and fears;
> Only a few more trials,
>> Only a few more tears!

---

65  Retrieved November 15, 2010 from http://homesteadblogger.com/
treasurebox/139719/

Jesus, my heart's dear Refuge,
    Jesus has died for me;
Firm on the Rock of Ages
    Ever my trust shall be.
Here let me wait with patience,
    Wait till the night is o'er;
Wait till I see the morning
    Break on the golden shore.

Safe in the arms of Jesus,
    Safe on His gentle breast;
There by His love o'ershaded,
    Sweetly my soul shall rest.

—Fanny J. Crosby, "Safe in the Arms of Jesus"

# CHAPTER 8

## Growing Up Into Christ

**The Breath of Life—Reading #1**

"The change of heart by which we become children of God is in the Bible spoken of as birth. Again, it is compared to the germination of the good seed sown by the husbandman. In like manner those who are just converted to Christ are, *"as newborn babes,"* to *"grow up"* to the stature of men and women in Christ Jesus. *1 Peter 2:2; Ephesians 4:15.* Or like the good seed sown in the field, they are to grow up and bring forth fruit. Isaiah says that they shall *"be called trees of righteousness, the planting of the Lord, that He might be glorified." Isaiah 61:3.* So from natural life, illustrations are drawn, to help us better to understand the mysterious truths of spiritual life.

"Not all the wisdom and skill of man can produce life in the smallest object in nature. It is only through the life which God Himself has imparted, that either plant or animal can live. So it is only through the life from God that spiritual life is begotten in the hearts of men. Unless a man is *"born again,"* he cannot become a partaker of the life which Christ came to give. *John 3:3.*

"As with life, so it is with growth. It is God who brings the bud to bloom and the flower to *fruit. It is by His power that the seed develops, "first the blade, then the head, after that the full grain in the head." Mark 4:28.* And the prophet Hosea says of Israel, that *"he shall grow like the lily." "They shall be revived like grain, and grow like a vine." Hosea 14:5, 7.* And Jesus bids us *"'consider the lilies how they grow.'" Luke 12:27.* The plants and flowers grow not by their own care or anxiety or effort, but by receiving that which God has furnished to minister to their life.

"The child cannot, by any anxiety or power of its own, add to its stature. No more can you, by anxiety or effort of yourself, secure spiritual growth. The plant, the child, grows by receiving from its surroundings that which ministers to its life—air, sunshine, and food. What these gifts of nature are to animal and plant, such is Christ to those who trust in Him. He is their *"everlasting light," "a sun and shield."* Isaiah 60:19; Psalm 84:11. He shall be as *"the dew to Israel." "He shall come down like rain upon the grass before mowing."* Hosea 14:5; Psalm 72:6. He is the living water, *"the bread of God … who comes down from heaven and gives life to the world."* John 6:33.

"In the matchless gift of His Son, God has encircled the whole world with an atmosphere of grace as real as the air which circulates around the globe. All who choose to breathe this life-giving atmosphere will live and grow up to the stature of men and women in Christ Jesus."[66]

**Illustrative Sketch:**

Oxygen is one of the most important elements in creation. Our planet needs oxygen to live. Our earth's atmosphere is approximately 21% oxygen in content, and the world's oceans are almost 90% oxygen. Surprisingly enough, the third most abundant chemical element in the universe is oxygen.

About two thirds of the human body is made of oxygen, and all animals require oxygen for respiration. Animals inhale oxygen, and plants exhale it. The process of photosynthesis in plants releases oxygen into the atmosphere for all living creatures to breathe.

Oxygen is colorless, odorless, and tasteless, is necessary for fires, can be used in acetylene torches to make flames hotter for cutting metal, helps heal wounds, is magnetic in nature, and is responsible for the bright red, yellow, and green colors of the northern lights in our night sky. It can be pressurized to be used in space suits, spaceships, and jet aircraft. Football players and mountain climbers also use oxygen at higher altitudes, making them better able to perform. Scuba tanks and submarines take pressurized oxygen below water for humans to breathe. Hospitals use pressured oxygen in medical treatments for patients.

In the very beginning God saw fit to design oxygen as one of the wonder elements. "By the word of the Lord were the heavens made; and all the host of them by the breath of his mouth." Psalm 33:6. When God made Adam He breathed into his nostrils and "man became a

---

66   White, 67.

living soul." Genesis 2:7. Now whether God breathes oxygen is probably not the point, but that He created us with an ability to use it to maintain life and health is important. If we die, on the other hand, that life-giving oxygen leaves our body, we return to the earth, and all life as we know it stops. "Our plans perish." Psalm 146:4.

Oxygen is important to us, and is vital for the ecological balance of life on earth. God's grace is the vital force of our spiritual life. He offers us salvation and forgiveness, a blanket of benevolent mercy from heaven through God's only Son. It is a marvelous gift, given without money and without price, and we will spiritually die without it. If we ignore it, postpone it, sideline it, or reject it, we will regret it. As oxygen is to our bodies, so grace is to our souls.

> Marvelous grace of our loving Lord,
>     Grace that exceeds our sin and our guilt!
> Yonder on Calvary's mount outpoured,
>     There where the blood of the Lamb was spilled.
>
> Sin and despair, like the sea waves cold,
>     Threaten the soul with infinite loss;
> Grace that is greater, yes, grace untold,
>     Points to the refuge, the mighty cross.
>
> Dark is the stain that we cannot hide.
>     What can avail to wash it away?
> Look! There is flowing a crimson tide,
>     Brighter than snow you may be today.
>
> Marvelous, infinite, matchless grace,
>     Freely bestowed on all who believe!
> You that are longing to see His face,
>     Will you this moment His grace receive?
>
> Grace, grace, God's grace,
>     Grace that will pardon and cleanse within;
> Grace, grace, God's grace,
>     Grace that is greater than all our sin.
>
> —Julia H. Johnston, "Grace Greater Than Our Sin"

**In the Potter's Hand—Reading #2**

"As the flower turns to the sun, that the bright beams may aid in perfecting its beauty and symmetry, so should we turn to the Sun of Righteousness, that heaven's light may shine upon us, that our character may be developed into the likeness of Christ.

"Jesus teaches the same thing when He says, '*Abide in Me, and I in you. As the branch cannot bear fruit of itself, unless it abides in the vine, neither can you, unless you abide in Me. ... Without Me you can do nothing.*' *John 15:4, 5.* You are just as dependent upon Christ, in order to live a holy life, as is the branch upon the parent stock for growth and fruitfulness. Apart from Him you have no life. You have no power to resist temptation or to grow in grace and holiness. Abiding in Him, you may flourish. Drawing your life from Him, you will not wither nor be fruitless. You will be like a tree planted by the rivers of water.

"Many have an idea that they must do some part of the work alone. They have trusted in Christ for the forgiveness of sin, but now they seek by their own efforts to live aright. But every such effort must fail. Jesus says, '*Without Me you can do nothing.*' *John 15:15.* Our growth in grace, our joy, our usefulness—all depend upon our union with Christ. It is by communion with Him, daily, hourly—by abiding in Him—that we are to grow in grace. He is not only the Author, but the Finisher of our faith. It is Christ first and last and always. He is to be with us, not only at the beginning and the end of our course, but at every step of the way. David says, '*I have set the Lord always before me: because He is at my right hand, I shall not be moved.*' *Psalm 16:8.*

"Do you ask, "How am I to abide in Christ?" In the same way as you received Him at first. *"As you have therefore received Christ Jesus the Lord, so walk in Him." "The just shall live by faith." Colossians 2:6; Hebrews 10:38.* You gave yourself to God, to be His wholly, to serve and obey Him, and you took Christ as your Savior. You could not yourself atone for your sins or change your heart; but having given yourself to God, you believe that He for Christ's sake did all this for you. By faith you became Christ's, and by faith you are to grow up in Him—by giving and taking. You are to give all—your heart, your will, your service—give yourself to

Him to obey all His requirements; and you must take all—Christ, the fullness of all blessing, to abide in your heart, to be your strength, your righteousness, your everlasting helper—to give you power to obey.

"Consecrate yourself to God in the morning; make this your very first work. Let your prayer be, "Take me, O Lord, as wholly Thine. I lay all my plans at Thy feet. Use me today in Thy service. Abide with me, and let all my work be wrought in Thee." This is a daily matter. Each morning consecrate yourself to God for that day. Surrender all your plans to Him, to be carried out or given up as His providence shall indicate. Thus day by day you may be giving your life into the hands of God, and thus your life will be molded more and more after the life of Christ." [67]

**Illustrative Sketch:**

Adoniram Judson was one of the first successful missionaries of the modern era. However, from the moment he decided to be a missionary for God his life was marked with hardship and sacrifice. But God could not have had a more faithful worker than Adoniram.

The day after he and his fiancée Ann were married, they were ordained as missionaries in Salem, Massachusetts, and their honeymoon was an ocean voyage to Burma. When they finally reached their destination in Burma, they were told by the Baptists in the area that evangelism would be impossible in a Buddhist country. But Judson set out to prove them wrong. He already knew Latin, Greek, and Hebrew, and now set out to learn Burmese. He hired a tutor to work with him for 12 hours a day, but even so it took him over three years to successfully learn the language. In 1819 he baptized his first Burmese convert. The most difficult task Adoniram had was convincing Buddhists that there is only one living God, so he had very few conversions during those first years. In fact, it took him 12 years to make 18 converts to Christianity.

During a war between England and Burma, Adoniram was imprisoned for 17 months at the famous "death prison" in Ava. While he was gone, his wife Ann worked tirelessly to get him released from prison, and all alone managed to give birth to her third child. However, when Adoniram finally returned, she died, worn out from the long months of stress and hardship apart from him. But, God sustained Adoniram

---

67  White, 68.

so he could continue his work in Burma where he helped spread the gospel for 40 years.

One of Adoniram's goals was to translate the Bible into the Myanmar language, and another was to raise up a church with at least 100 members. By the time he died in 1850, he left a complete translation of the Bible, 100 churches, and over 8,000 believers. To this day his Bible translation still remains the most popular version in the Myanmar language. His work had been overwhelming, but he always felt that no sacrifice was too great for God. Adoniram's one prayer was that he could be a humble servant of Jesus, laboring for the Master as long as there was life in his veins.

Adoniram considered himself as clay in the Divine Potter's hands, ready and willing to be used wherever God should call him. He understood that being a pioneer missionary for God in Burma required prayer, sacrifice, and humble submission.[68]

God has had his missionaries like Mr. Judson in every age. Abraham was the first one mentioned in Scripture to travel to a new land. His job? To establish a culture of people in the land of Canaan that would worship the One True God. And then there was Joseph, sold into Egyptian slavery so he could witness for God in that Pagan land and prepare them for a coming crisis. Jonah was asked by God to go to Nineveh and preach a message of repentance. Daniel and his three friends were sent to Babylon where they witnessed to Nebuchadnezzar about the Jehovah God. Led by Paul, the early Christian missionaries took the gospel across the Roman Empire and evangelized the then-known world.

In the modern era, thanks to the Spirit of God and dedicated, willing missionaries like Adoniram, the gospel message has spread to the corners of the globe. Today Christianity has missionaries in every country of the world, and the Scriptures are everywhere—in print, in audio format, and online. Led by the power of God, we can become like clay in the Divine Potter's hands, prayerfully submit our lives to Him, and say, "Your will be done." In this way we can all be His missionaries.

*"As the clay is in the potter's hand, so are you in My hand."*
*Jeremiah 18:6.*

68    Clifford G. Howell, *Pioneer American Missionaries to Burma, The Advanced Guard of Missions* (Mountain View, CA: Pacific Press Publishing, 1912).

Have Thine own way, Lord! Have Thine own way!
Thou art the Potter, I am the clay.
Mold me and make me after Thy will,
While I am waiting, yielded and still.

Have Thine own way, Lord! Have Thine own way!
Search me and try me, Master, today!
Whiter than snow, Lord, wash me just now,
As in Thy presence humbly I bow.

Have Thine own way, Lord! Have Thine own way!
Wounded and weary, help me, I pray!
Power, all power, surely is Thine!
Touch me and heal me, Savior divine.

Have Thine own way, Lord! Have Thine own way!
Hold o'er my being absolute sway!
Fill with Thy Spirit till all shall see
Christ only, always, living in me.

—Adelaide A. Pollard, "Have Thine Own Way, Lord"

## Do Not Be Afraid—Reading #3

"A life in Christ is a life of restfulness. There may be no ecstasy of feeling, but there should be an abiding, peaceful trust. Your hope is not in yourself; it is in Christ. Your weakness is united to His strength, your ignorance to His wisdom, your frailty to His enduring might. So you are not to look to yourself, not to let the mind dwell upon self, but look to Christ. Let the mind dwell upon His love, upon the beauty, the perfection, of His character. Christ in His self-denial, Christ in His humiliation, Christ in His purity and holiness, Christ in His matchless love—this is the subject for the soul's contemplation. It is by loving Him, copying Him, depending wholly upon Him, that you are to be transformed into His likeness.

"Jesus says, '*Abide in Me.*' " These words convey the idea of rest, stability, confidence. Again He invites, "*Come to Me, … and I will give you rest.'" Matthew 11:28.* The words of the psalmist express the same thought: *"Rest in the Lord, and wait patiently for Him."* And Isaiah gives the assurance, *"In quietness and in confidence shall be your strength." Psalm 37:7; Isaiah 30:15.* This rest is not found in inactivity; for in the Savior's invitation the promise of rest is united with the call to labor: *"'Take My yoke upon you: ... and you shall find rest.'" Matthew 11:29.* The heart that rests most fully upon Christ will be most earnest and active in labor for Him.

"When the mind dwells upon self, it is turned away from Christ, the source of strength and life. Hence it is Satan's constant effort to keep the attention diverted from the Savior and thus prevent the union and communion of the soul with Christ. The pleasures of the world, life's cares and perplexities and sorrows, the faults of others, or your own faults and imperfections—to any or all of these he will seek to divert the mind. Do not be misled by his devices. Many who are really conscientious, and who desire to live for God, he too often leads to dwell upon their own faults and weaknesses, and thus by separating them from Christ he hopes to gain the victory.

"We should not make self the center and indulge anxiety and fear as to whether we shall be saved. All this turns the soul away from the Source of our strength. Commit the keeping of your soul to God, and trust in Him. Talk and think of Jesus. Let self be lost in Him. Put away all doubt; dismiss your fears. Say with the apostle Paul, *"It is no longer I who live, but Christ lives in me; and the life which I now live in the flesh I live by faith in the Son of God, who loved me and gave Himself for me." Galatians 2:20.* Rest in God. He is able to keep that which you have committed to Him. If you will leave yourself in His hands, He will bring you off more than conqueror through Him that has loved you." [69]

### Illustrative Sketch:

If you couldn't see, life would be very hard. You could see where you were going. No chance for you to ride your bike in the park, or take a computer graphics class. No chance of going to a football stadium to "watch" a game. On top of that, what if you couldn't hear? Besides not being able to see a Fourth of July parade you wouldn't be able to hear it

---

69 White, 70.

either. Most activities in society would be unavailable to you. It would be hard to trust people around you if you had no sight and no hearing.

But there are people who have lived that life. Helen Keller was one of them, blind and deaf almost all her life, she became one of the most famous girls in American history. By the time she was an adult, she was a celebrity. Known for many things that she could do, it is what she could not do that made her a legend.

Born a normal child in 1880, she got a bad fever before she was two years old and lost her sight and hearing. Because she couldn't see or hear, she couldn't learn to talk either. That is, until she met Alexander Graham Bell. In addition to his invention of the telephone, Mr. Bell studied ways to teach deaf people how to talk.

Helen was six years old when Mr. Bell arranged to have Annie Sullivan, a partially blind woman, come to live with her. Annie had attended a special school where she learned how to use sign language to teach blind and deaf students to communicate. Because Helen couldn't see or hear, she was a very frustrated little girl, but eventually learned to trust Annie. Helen learned to spell her first word, "water", by feeling cool water run over her hand and associating it with the signs Annie made in her hand.

Helen attended schools in Boston and New York City and learned to speak by putting her fingers on her teacher's lips and throat. After learning braille, she went to college and later wrote several books. She became a famous speaker and traveled all over the world. Helen Keller once wrote, "I seldom think about my limitations, and they never make me sad."[70]

God promises that with His help we can accomplish the work He has for us to do. Like Helen we should never let bad experiences keep us from being happy in Jesus and "successful" in the life He has planned for us. If we give Jesus a chance to help us, we can turn our troubles into stepping stones for our future. "'Fear not, for I am with you; Be not dismayed, for I am your God. I will strengthen you, Yes, I will help you, I will uphold you with My righteous right hand." Isaiah 41:10.

---

70  Royal National Institute of Blind People, "The Life of Helen Keller," www.rnib.org.uk/xpedio/groups/public/documents/publicwebsite/public_keller.hcsp

When Israel was finally ready to enter the Promised Land, perched on its very borders, the Lord appeared to Joshua to encourage him. God reminded Joshua that He would be with him every step of the way to lead and direct him as Israel's newly appointed leader. "'I will not leave you nor forsake you...'" God promised Joshua. "'Be strong and of good courage; do not be afraid, nor be dismayed, for the Lord your God is with you wherever you go.'" Joshua 1:5, 9.

These words are just as much for us today as they were for God's people at the Canaan border. Whenever you are tempted to give way to fear, remember the experiences of God's people in the past. Faith in God carried them through, and confidence in His promises will be the life-blood of our spiritual walk. Like Joshua and Jeremiah and the chosen ones in every age, we must say with confidence, "*I can do all things through Christ who strengthens me.*" *Philippians 4:13.*

Moses led his band to the promised land
    Everyone was scared that there'd be a fight
So he sent some men to see if they would win
    If they tried to challenge the Canaanites
Ten of the men were afraid of that land
    Thinking they would be better off dead
Caleb and Joshua had different thoughts
    And this is what they said
Do not be afraid, for God is with you
    Do not be afraid, declares the Lord
Do not be afraid, for God is with you
    And will rescue you forever more

Jeremiah bowed himself before the Lord
    God had told him that he was set apart
He would be God's hand, a prophet to the land
    He should do all that the Lord commands
Jeremiah said "I am only a boy
    And I don't even know the right words"
The Lord reached down and touched his mouth
    And this is what he heard
Do not be afraid, for God is with you
    Do not be afraid, declares the Lord

Do not be afraid, for God is with you
    And will rescue you forever more

I can't see far ahead of me
    Dark storms cloud my view
Take courage and you will see
    Give it to God and he will rescue you

Do not be afraid, for God is with you
    Do not be afraid, declares the Lord
Do not be afraid, for God is with you
    And will rescue you forever more

—Keith Lancaster, Acapella, (1995). *Beyond a Doubt.*

**Love One Another—Reading #4**

"When Christ took human nature upon Himself, He bound humanity to Himself by a tie of love that can never be broken by any power save the choice of man himself. Satan will constantly present allurements to induce us to break this tie—to choose to separate ourselves from Christ. Here is where we need to watch, to strive, to pray, that nothing may entice us to choose another master; for we are always free to do this. But let us keep our eyes fixed upon Christ, and He will preserve us. Looking unto Jesus, we are safe. Nothing can pluck us out of His hand. In constantly beholding Him, we *"are being transformed into the same image from glory to glory, just as by the Spirit of the Lord."* 2 Corinthians 3:18.

"It was thus that the early disciples gained their likeness to the dear Savior. When those disciples heard the words of Jesus, they felt their need of Him. They sought, they found, they followed Him. They were with Him in the house, at the table, in the closet, in the field. They were with Him as pupils with a teacher, daily receiving from His lips lessons of holy truth. They looked to Him, as servants to their master, to learn their duty. Those disciples were men *"with a nature like ours."* James 5:17. They had the same battle with sin to fight. They needed the same grace, in order to live a holy life.

"Even John, the beloved disciple, the one who most fully reflected the likeness of the Savior, did not naturally possess that loveliness of character. He was not only self-assertive and ambitious for honor, but impetuous, and resentful under injuries. But as the character of the Divine One was manifested to him, he saw his own deficiency and was humbled by the knowledge. The strength and patience, the power and tenderness, the majesty and meekness, that he beheld in the daily life of the Son of God, filled his soul with admiration and love.

"Day by day his heart was drawn out toward Christ, until he lost sight of self in love for his Master. His resentful, ambitious temper was yielded to the molding power of Christ. The regenerating influence of the Holy Spirit renewed his heart. The power of the love of Christ wrought a transformation of character. This is the sure result of union with Jesus. When Christ abides in the heart, the whole nature is transformed. Christ's Spirit, His love, softens the heart, subdues the soul, and raises the thoughts and desires toward God and heaven." [71]

**Illustrative Sketch:**

John the beloved was quite young when he first met Jesus. Born in Galilee a fisherman by trade, John became interested in Jesus when John the Baptist appeared at the Jordan announcing the coming of the Messiah. When John the Baptist baptized Jesus, he declared Him to be "'the Lamb of God that takes away the sins of the world,'" John 1:29. John the beloved left all and followed Jesus to become his most ardent disciple. He soon became known as Jesus' closest companion and was rarely absent from his side.

For over three years John walked the roads of Galilee and Judea, witnessing Jesus' amazing rise to fame. He heard Jesus message of peace and hope, that forgiveness is a hallmark of godliness and love for others is the guiding principle of the New Gospel. He was astonished at the simplicity of Jesus' words, and the authority with which he preached. He saw the Master perform amazing miracles as he healed the lame, the blind and the deaf. He watched Jesus cast out demons and cleanse lepers. John was in Bethany to witness Jesus raise a man to life who had been dead for four days. Surely this Man from Galilee was indeed the Son of God!

---

71   White, 72.

John witnessed Jesus' transfiguration with Moses and Elijah, and Jesus' superhuman struggle with demons in the Garden of Gethsemane. No doubt, John was stunned as he watched the trial of Jesus and His crucifixion on Golgotha. True to character, John stayed with Jesus to the Savior's last breath, and it was to John that Jesus entrusted the care of His mother. Like the rest of the disciples, he thought that Jesus' unusual powers would propel Him to greatness, that He was destined to overthrow the Romans and set up an earthly kingdom in Jerusalem.

After Jesus' resurrection and ascension to heaven, John remained in Jerusalem for over ten years to evangelize Jerusalem. When persecution from Herod Agrippa made it impossible to preach the gospel in Judea any longer, John fled with Peter to Samaria, and then Asia Minor where he helped build up the early Christian church.

Throughout his lifetime John endured much for the sake of the gospel. He suffered cruel beatings and imprisonment, and even escaped from prison with the help of angels. According to tradition he witnessed the destruction of Jerusalem, and later was arrested and brought to Rome during the reign of the Emperor Domitian. The cruel emperor ordered John's execution by immersion in a vat of boiling oil, but miraculously he was preserved unharmed. The Beloved Disciple was then banished to the Greek island of Patmos where Jesus came from heaven to meet him personally and encourage him to be faithful.

John later returned to Ephesus where he became a pillar of the Church. It is said that in his waning years his fellow believers carried him to gatherings, but because of his old age he gave only very short sermons. His theme centered on the love Christian brothers and sisters should have for one another. "My little children, let us not love in word or in tongue, but in deed and in truth" 1 John 3:18.

Tradition says that John lived in Ephesus, Asia Minor, where he died and was buried in AD 100. He was the only one of the original twelve disciples to die a natural death. One day soon Jesus will come again and reward John the Beloved for his faithful years of service. What a day that will be!

This most beloved of the Apostles left behind five books that can be found in the New Testament: the Gospel of John, three Epistles to the early Church, and the book of Revelation. John's overwhelming devotion to the Savior and His gospel led him to pen these famous words: "And we know that His testimony is true. And there are also many other things that Jesus did, which if they were written one by one, I suppose that even the world itself could not contain the books that would be written...." John 21:24, 25.

The love of God is greater far
    Than tongue or pen can ever tell;
It goes beyond the highest star,
    And reaches to the lowest hell;
The guilty pair, bowed down with care,
    God gave His Son to win;
His erring child He reconciled,
    And pardoned from his sin.

When hoary time shall pass away,
    And earthly thrones and kingdoms fall,
When men who here refuse to pray,
    On rocks and hills and mountains call,
God's love so sure, shall still endure,
    All measureless and strong;
Redeeming grace to Adam's race—
    The saints' and angels' song.

Could we with ink the ocean fill,
    And were the skies of parchment made,
Were every stalk on earth a quill,
    And every man a scribe by trade;
To write the love of God above
    Would drain the ocean dry;
Nor could the scroll contain the whole,
    Though stretched from sky to sky.

Oh, love of God, how rich and pure!
    How measureless and strong!
It shall forevermore endure—
    The saints' and angels' song.

—Frederick M. Lehman, "The Love of God"

**I Will Come Again—Reading #5**

"When Christ ascended to heaven, the sense of His presence was still with His followers. It was a personal presence, full of love and light. Jesus, the Savior, who had walked and talked and prayed with them, who had spoken hope and comfort to their hearts, had, while the message of peace was still upon His lips, been taken up from them into heaven, and the tones of His voice had come back to them, as the cloud of angels received Him—*"Lo, I am with you always, even to the end of the age." Matthew 28:20.*

"He had ascended to heaven in the form of humanity. They knew that He was before the throne of God, their Friend and Savior still; that His sympathies were unchanged; that He was still identified with suffering humanity. He was presenting before God the merits of His own precious blood, showing His wounded hands and feet, in remembrance of the price He had paid for His redeemed. They knew that He had ascended to heaven to prepare places for them, and that He would come again and take them to Himself.

"As they met together after the ascension they were eager to present their requests to the Father in the name of Jesus. In solemn awe they bowed in prayer, repeating the assurance, *"Whatever you ask the Father in My name He will give you. Until now you have asked nothing in My name. Ask, and you will receive, that your joy may be full." John 16:23, 24.* They extended the hand of faith higher and higher with the mighty argument, *"It is Christ who died, and furthermore is also risen, who is even at the right hand of God, who also makes intercession for us." Romans 8:34.*

"And Pentecost brought them the presence of the Comforter, of whom Christ had said, He *"'will be in you.'"* And He had further said, *"'It is to your advantage that I go away; for if I do not go away, the Helper will not come to you; but if I depart, I will send Him to you.'" John 14:17; 16:7.* Henceforth through the Spirit, Christ was to abide continually in the hearts of His children. Their union with Him was closer than when He was personally with them. The light, and love, and power of the indwelling Christ shone out through them, so that men, beholding, *"marveled, and they realized that they had been with Jesus." Acts 4:13.*

"All that Christ was to the disciples, He desires to be to His children today; for in that last prayer, with the little band of disciples gathered about Him, He said, *'I do not pray for these alone, but also for those who will believe in Me through their word.'" John 17:20.* Jesus prayed for us, and He asked that we might be one with Him, even as He is one with the Father. What a union is this! The Savior has said of Himself, *"'The Son can do nothing of Himself,'" "'the Father who dwells in Me does the works.'" John 5:19; 14:10.* Then if Christ is dwelling in our hearts, He will work in us *"both to will and to do for His good pleasure." Philippians 2:13.* We shall work as He worked; we shall manifest the same spirit. And thus, loving Him and abiding in Him, we shall *"grow up in all things into Him who is the head—Christ." Ephesians 4:15."*[72]

## Illustrative Sketch:

"I must go now," Aniam said with a tone of sadness that betrayed his hidden feelings. He pushed a stray lock of dark hair from his sun-bronzed face. "I will prepare a place for us to live. In my father's house are many rooms, but I must add one more for you and me."

He stared intently into Sheerah's beautiful eyes, to whom he had so recently been betrothed. "But don't worry!"he took her hands in his, and then hurried on excitedly. "I will come again for you, that where I live, there you may also live."

And so he journeyed to Ophrah in the hill country of Ephraim, to fulfill the days of his betrothal—almost a year to the day would need to pass before she could become his own. In the little mountain village he worked in his father's carpenter shop making wheels for carts and yokes for oxen and tables for the wealthy in town. He was proud to help provide a living for his family, but often on a late afternoon his father would catch him gazing out the window, his mind far away.

In the evenings when the shop work was finished and the sun was setting low on the horizon, Aniam would begin his real work of love. Bending his energy to the project he had been planning for all his life, he applied himself in earnest to the promise he had made his be-trothed. Where he was she must be also, and that meant they needed a

[72] White, 73.

home. His family was to be her family, but a room all their own off the main courtyard was his goal. Maybe two, if he could raise the money and find the space.

He laid the foundation with limestone blocks, and used real mortar to seal the joints. Not mud as many builders were accustomed to doing. Next came the mud bricks needed to build stout walls a cubit's width in thickness. Cold nights and hot days would be strangers inside these walls. Windows were added, something many of the other rooms in the courtyard did not have, and he even fashioned wooden shutters in his father's shop. And then there was the door. Some of his older brothers had merely hung a blanket over the open doorway to their homes, but not Aniam. Sheerah would have the security of a real door, one of oak, if he could get the wood.

Evening by evening he worked, sometimes long into the night. Holidays were a blur to him as he continued his labor of love, counting the days until the woman of his dreams would become his blushing bride. He could think of nothing he would rather do than prepare the way for the arrival of Sheerah, his betrothed. The weeks and months passed speedily because of the love he had for her. His thoughts were of her continually, and the hours he spent working by the sweat of his brow seemed but a trifle to him.

In the end there was no place for the two rooms he had planned in his house. There just wasn't space enough in the already-crowded courtyard. The only direction to go was up, and when Aniam finally made that decision, he bent all his energies to building a second room over the first, with a stairwell of mud bricks up the back wall of the house. When he finished, the house was a beautiful sight with a mud tiled roof over the finished upper room.

The family watched his progress, asking questions of him now and then about his plans, but he said little. The less he talked of it, the more special it seemed. By now the house had become almost a part of him. And the fact that the home was new and would not be used until the two of them should become one, made the gift seem somehow sacred.

Then the year was up, and it was time for Aniam to bring Sheerah "home." He made the journey himself to escort her personally and arrived on schedule amid much fanfare. "The bridegroom comes!" a village crier announced excitedly, and the message quickly traveled the length of the town. "Let us be glad and rejoice in honor of the happy couple, for the day of their wedding has come!"

She was a beautiful sight dressed in her elaborate wedding garments draped with an ornate veil and a fine headpiece of silver coins. Aniam could not see her smiling face beneath the veil, but he imagined it perfectly, and it gave him a sense of satisfaction like nothing he had ever felt before. For him the promise of seeing that wonderful smile in the years to come was well worth the months of work and waiting.[73]

Someday soon Jesus will come for His bride, the Church. That is one promise we can bank on, and when the day arrives we who have waited so long will be glad and rejoice. *"Let not your heart be troubled,'"* He said,… *"'I go to prepare a place for you. And if I go, I will come again and receive you to Myself that where I am you may be also.'" John 14:1,3.*

The church has one foundation,
    'Tis Jesus Christ her Lord;
She is His new creation,
    Through water by the word.
From heav'n He came and sought her
    To be His holy bride;
With His own blood He bought her,
    And for her life He died.

—Samuel J. Stone, "The Church Has One Foundation"

---

73 Based on John 14 with additional events representing biblical culture.

---
⟨𝔰⟩
---

# CHAPTER 9

# The Work and the Life

---

**Tell Me the Story of Jesus—Reading #1**

"God is the source of life and light and joy to the universe. Like rays of light from the sun, like the streams of water bursting from a living spring, blessings flow out from Him to all His creatures. And wherever the life of God is in the hearts of men, it will flow out to others in love and blessing.

"Our Savior's joy was in the uplifting and redemption of fallen men. For this He counted not His life dear unto Himself, but endured the cross, despising the shame. So angels are ever engaged in working for the happiness of others. This is their joy. That which selfish hearts would regard as humiliating service, ministering to those who are wretched and in every way inferior in character and rank, is the work of sinless angels. The spirit of Christ's self-sacrificing love is the spirit that pervades heaven and is the very essence of its bliss. This is the spirit that Christ's followers will possess, the work that they will do.

"When the love of Christ is enshrined in the heart, like sweet fragrance it cannot be hidden. Its holy influence will be felt by all with whom we come in contact. The spirit of Christ in the heart is like a spring in the desert, flowing to refresh all and making those who are ready to perish, eager to drink of the water of life.

"Love to Jesus will be manifested in a desire to work as He worked for the blessing and uplifting of humanity. It will lead to love, tenderness, and sympathy toward all the creatures of our heavenly Father's care.

"The Savior's life on earth was not a life of ease and devotion to Himself, but He toiled with persistent, earnest, untiring effort for the salvation of lost mankind. From the manger to Calvary He followed the path of self-denial and sought not to be released from arduous

---

tasks, painful travels and exhausting care and labor. He said, "'*the Son of Man did not come to be served, but to serve, and to give His life a ransom for many.*'" *Matthew 20:28.* This was the one great object of His life. Everything else was secondary and subservient. It was His meat and drink to do the will of God and to finish His work. Self and self-interest had no part in His labor."[74]

**Illustrative Sketch:**

The afternoon was a dreary one, cloudy and gray. A cloud of hopelessness settled on the hill town of Nazareth, and none seemed able to shake it. Even the little sparrows flew away to be somewhere else. Death had come to the house of Eliam, son of Zabdi, in the form of the dreaded dysentery. Illness was no stranger to the little hamlet of Nazareth, but most folks didn't know what to do about it. More tragedy would come. Where there was one death by this cursed disease, there would be others.

There were no doctor priests in Nazareth, and the few that came from other towns had no solutions. "God is displeased," said one doctor from Cana, who refused to enter the darkened doorway to the house of death. "And small wonder!" he peered inside at the form of the man lying cold and still on the table in the house. "I liked Eliam. But the rabbi at the synagogue here in Nazareth tells me he failed to go to Mount Zion this year to pay his temple tax!"

"It's the sins of his father Zabdi that finally did him in!" a second doctor pulled his pious robes tighter around him. "Zabdi was the hated tax collector for years over in Cana. He worked most of these hill towns for the Romans, and for that God can never forgive him! His curse will always rest on this family!"

Jesus stood in the doorway of His father's carpenter shop and listened to the sad commentary. "Why do the doctors tell folks such tales?" the young Boy turned His troubled eyes to Joseph.

Joseph set down his wooden mallet, "They don't know the Father of light," he said slowly, shaking his head sadly.

"Then someone should tell them." Jesus turned his gaze back to the forlorn faces of Eliam's family as the doctors strode away taking with them yet another fee in payment for their words of condemnation.

---

74  White, 77.

"You could be the One to do that." Joseph followed the Boy's look of compassion and came to lay a calloused hand on His shoulder. "Remember, Jesus, You must be about Your heavenly Father's business."

Jesus turned to Joseph's eyes again. "Thank you, Papa. If you don't mind, I think I will. I've finished putting pins and braces on the two wood stools. I've cut all the boards for the table you're building, and I've swept the shop twice."

"You've done a good job, Son. I couldn't ask for more."

A short while later the boy was in the poor family's doorway, handing Eliam's wife a small basket of pomegranates. "I'm so sorry for your loss," He said bowing His head. "I know the Father in heaven cares about your husband, and His angels will mark the resting place to which he is gathered. 'Precious in the sight of the Lord is the death of His saints,' and I know your husband did his best to serve the Lord. 'God is our refuge and strength, a very present help in trouble, therefore we will not fear,' Jesus continued quoting Scriptures full of hope. "'I will say of the Lord, He is my refuge and my fortress, my God, in Him I will trust'"... He shall cover you with His feathers, and under His wings you shall take refuge."[75]

"Thank you, Jesus," Eliam's widow was too broken up with emotion to say more. As she bowed her head, the tears fell fast.[76]

The people of Nazareth loved Jesus because through acts of kindness He demonstrated concern for their cares and hardships. He was wise beyond his years, and the grace of God was upon Him. Luke 2:40. There was no place on earth that could not have been honored by His presence even as a Child. Kings and princes would have been privileged to receive Him as a guest. *"And Jesus increased in wisdom and stature, and in favor with God and men." Luke 2:52.*

Tell me the story of Jesus,
    Write on my heart every word;
Tell me the story most precious,
    Sweetest that ever was heard.
Tell how the angels in chorus,
    Sang as they welcomed His birth,

---

75   Psalm 116:15, Psalm 46: 1, 2, Psalm 91:2, 4.

76   Based on Ellen G. White, "Chapter 7," *Desire of Ages,* (Mountain View, CA: Pacific Press Publishing Association, 1943.

"Glory to God in the highest!
    Peace and good tidings to earth."

Fasting alone in the desert,
    Tell of the days that are past,
How for our sins He was tempted,
    Yet was triumphant at last.
Tell of the years of His labor,
    Tell of the sorrow He bore;
He was despised and afflicted,
    Homeless, rejected and poor.

Tell of the cross where they nailed Him,
    Writhing in anguish and pain;
Tell of the grave where they laid Him,
    Tell how He liveth again.
Love in that story so tender,
    Clearer than ever I see;
Stay, let me weep while you whisper,
    "Love paid the ransom for me."

Tell me the story of Jesus,
    Write on my heart every word;
Tell me the story most precious,
    Sweetest that ever was heard.

—Frances J. Crosby, "Tell Me the Story of Jesus"

**Co-workers With Christ—Reading #2**
"Those who are the partakers of the grace of Christ will be ready to make any sacrifice, that others for whom He died may share the heavenly gift. They will do all they can to make the world better for their stay in it. This spirit is the sure outgrowth of a soul truly converted. No sooner does one come to Christ than there is born in his heart a desire to make known to others what a precious friend he has found in Jesus; the saving and sanctifying truth cannot be shut up in his heart.

"If we are clothed with the righteousness of Christ and are filled with the joy of His indwelling Spirit, we shall not be able to hold our peace. If we have tasted and seen that the Lord is good we shall have something to tell. Like Philip when he found the Savior, we shall invite others into His presence. We shall seek to present to them the attractions of Christ and the unseen realities of the world to come. There will be an intensity of desire to follow in the path that Jesus trod. There will be an earnest longing that those around us may behold *"the Lamb of God, who takes away the sin of the world."* John 1:29.

"The effort to bless others will react in blessings upon ourselves. This was the purpose of God in giving us a part to act in the plan of redemption. He has granted men the privilege of becoming partakers of the divine nature and, in their turn, of diffusing blessings to their fellow men. This is the highest honor, the greatest joy, that it is possible for God to bestow upon men. Those who thus become participants in labors of love are brought nearest to their Creator.

"God might have committed the message of the gospel, and all the work of loving ministry, to the heavenly angels. He might have employed other means for accomplishing His purpose. But in His infinite love He chose to make us co-workers with Himself, with Christ and the angels, that we might share the blessing, the joy, the spiritual uplifting, which results from this unselfish ministry."[77]

**Illustrative Sketch:**

Christmas Eve had come, and with it a cold snowy night that threatened to turn even colder. It was the night that everyone in town anticipated all year. It was the night of the Christmas program in the biggest church in the country. Everyone gathered to see the huge Christmas tree decorated with bright, colorful candles, to watch the Christmas pageant with wise men and shepherds, and to hear the choir sing. The king himself would be there, and his royal counselors in their regal clothes. And as usual everyone brought offerings to the great altar at the front of the Church near the nativity scene with its manger and the baby Jesus.

Ronald hurried to dress for the big night. Into his heavy mitten went the few coins for his precious Christmas offering. It wasn't much, but he had scrimped and scraped all year in order to have it ready to

---

77 White, *Steps to Christ*, 78.

give at Christmas Eve. Times were hard now with his father gone, a victim of the war. Ronald had managed to make a Christmas gift for his little brother Eric, and buy something simple for his mother, too, but an offering at the Church seemed almost even more important. It was a longstanding tradition for hundreds of years that everyone come to church on the eve of Christmas and give a gift, their very best gift. Legend had it that someday someone would give an offering so great that the angels would ring the old church bells for sheer joy.

"Do you think the bells will ring tonight?" Ronald asked his mother as he stood waiting for his little brother to get ready.

"The bells?" his mother smiled. "Oh, I don't know. It would probably take a really extraordinary gift for the angels to ring those old bells. Her blue eyes sparkled in the light of their own Christmas candles. "As far as we know there aren't even any bells up in that old steeple anymore. No one in this town has ever heard them ring. If they're there, I imagine the ropes have rotted off long ago."

But her tone changed as she glanced out the window into the darkness. "I don't know if you boys should go out tonight, after all," she frowned. "It's bitterly cold out! The snow is coming down faster now, and it's getting harder to see with every passing minute."

"Please let us go!" Ronald begged. "We've been waiting for this night all year! We'll go straight there and back!"

"Alright," she finally relented, "but don't dawdle on the way!" and with that she sent them on their way, with hugs and promises that they would come home as soon as the program was over.

The boys hurried down the snowy streets toward the church. It wasn't too far, but they didn't want to be late. Ronald wanted to get to the program early so he could get a good seat up near the front, but as usual his little brother Eric was having a hard time keeping up. As they passed a dark alley, they heard a cry for help and discovered, to their surprise, an old man down in the snow. Evidently, he had fallen off his horse and couldn't get up.

Ronald glanced at his little brother, and then at the church with its glowing windows far down the street. "We've got to help the old man!" he told his brother.

"We'll be late for sure if we do," Eric's eyes were big, "and besides, mother said we're not to stop along the way!"

"But we can't just leave the poor man here! He could freeze to death!" Ronald turned down the dark alley. "I've got to help him. You go on ahead, and I'll catch up with you in a bit!"

Ronald rubbed the old man's arms and legs to get the circulation going again, and then helped him to his feet. By the time he had caught the man's horse for him and helped him on his way, the hour was late, and he wondered if it was too late to go to the church. But, he was still responsible for his little brother, and of course, there was the offering to give. He felt for the coins in his mitten to see that they were still there, and then hurried on his way. He was sick at heart that he had missed the blessed night he had anticipated all year.

When he arrived at the church, there was standing room only, and he could barely see over the heads of the watching, waiting crowd. The program was almost over, but the best part had been saved until last—the giving of the offerings. Ronald got in line with the others and watched as the king himself stood and walked to the big old altar to give his offering. What would he give this year? Deeds to land? Treasure ships? They waited with bated breath and then gasped when he took the royal crown off his head and laid it on the altar! Such a gift had never been given! Surely the angels would ring the bells for sheer joy. The waiting congregation looked upward expectantly, but the old bells did not ring.

Now the others began to bring their gifts. The king's courtiers brought golden chalices and jewel encrusted crosses, but nothing compared with the king's amazing gift. The rich merchants came, and the statesmen, laying their bars of silver on the altar, their gifts of ivory, and their expensive wooden chests of polished ebony. And the bells did not ring.

Then the common folks came bringing their gifts. Ronald took his place in the line down the long aisle of the church, and soon realized he was the very last person. The closer he got to the altar, the more nervous he became. He had so little to give and it seemed every eye was on him.

He was right in front of the altar—everyone else had gone, leaving him alone. He fumbled anxiously with his mitten to retrieve the coins. One, two, three pennies. He laid the simple offering on the altar, as near to the king's crown as he could, as near as he dared.

Suddenly, far above him in the steeple of the ancient church the bells sounded their deep, rich tones. It was musical and melodious, and its resonance pealed out over the snowy streets of the windswept city.

"The bells!" people looked up, searching the ceiling of the majestic cathedral as if to find there an explanation for the sudden rolling, tolling clang of the bells. Then in surprise and confusion they glanced around them in the church. The king and his courtiers raised their eyebrows too, and the rich merchants were astounded indeed. "Who has given a gift so great that the angels are ringing the bells?" With wonder they asked in one accord. But all they saw was a little boy hurrying down the aisle, mumbling to himself, "What did I do for God tonight?"[78]

*"'Take heed that you do not do your charitable deeds before men, to be seen by them. Otherwise you have no reward from your Father in heaven. ... But when you do a charitable deed, do not let your left hand know what your right hand is doing, that your charitable deed may be in secret; and your Father who sees in secret will Himself reward you openly.'" Matthew 6:1, 3, 4.*

**Let Us Labor for the Master—Reading #3**

"We are brought into sympathy with Christ through the fellowship of His sufferings. Every act of self-sacrifice for the good of others strengthens the spirit of beneficence in the giver's heart, allying him more closely to the Redeemer of the world, who *"was rich, yet for your sakes... became poor, that you through His poverty might become rich."* *2 Corinthians 8:9.* And it is only as we thus fulfill the divine purpose in our creation that life can be a blessing to us.

"If you will go to work as Christ designs that His disciples shall, and win souls for Him, you will feel the need of a deeper experience and a greater knowledge in divine things, and will hunger and thirst after righteousness. You will plead with God, and your faith will be strengthened, and your soul will drink deeper drafts at the well of salvation. Encountering opposition and trials will drive you to the Bible

78   Arthur Maxwell, "How Ronald Rang the Bells," *The Children's Hour,* vol. 5 (Mountain View, CA: Pacific Press Publishing Association, 1949) 59.

and prayer. You will grow in grace and the knowledge of Christ, and will develop a rich experience.

"The spirit of unselfish labor for others gives depth, stability, and Christ-like loveliness to the character, and brings peace and happiness to its possessor. The aspirations are elevated. There is no room for sloth or selfishness. Those who thus exercise the Christian graces will grow and will become strong to work for God. They will have clear spiritual perceptions, a steady, growing faith, and an increased power in prayer. The Spirit of God, moving upon their spirit, calls forth the sacred harmonies of the soul in answer to the divine touch. Those who thus devote themselves to unselfish effort for the good of others are most surely working out their own salvation.

"The only way to grow in grace is to be disinterestedly doing the very work which Christ has enjoined upon us—to engage, to the extent of our ability, in helping and blessing those who need the help we can give them. Strength comes by exercise; activity is the very condition of life. Those who endeavor to maintain Christian life by passively accepting the blessings that come through the means of grace, and doing nothing for Christ, are simply trying to live by eating without working. And in the spiritual as in the natural world, this always results in degeneration and decay. A man who would refuse to exercise his limbs would soon lose all power to use them. Thus the Christian who will not exercise his God-given powers not only fails to grow up into Christ, but he loses the strength that he already had."[79]

**Illustrative Sketch:**

Hudson Taylor was an unusual man. Driven by divine energy and enthusiasm he became an icon of the Christian missionary movement during the 1800s. While still a young man, he became fascinated with China's great need and decided to go there as a British Protestant missionary. His five-month trip by sea to China was filled with one trial after another, and when he finally arrived in the city of Shanghai, he found the city embroiled in a civil war. Hudson had to fight fires, famine, and fear, but never without prayer, and always God delivered him.

He started the China Inland Mission in 1865, but soon learned a valuable lesson. If he wanted to be effective as a missionary, he would

---

79   White, 79.

have to eat, dress, and travel like the Chinese. Such a thing was rare for missionaries to do at that time. However, he chose wear a queue, or pigtail, and to shave his eyebrows and forehead.

Years passed, and Mr. Taylor seemed to have no success. Confucianism, Buddhism, and Taoism were powerful forces in the Chinese culture, and the Chinese did not readily accept foreigners. It took him several years to learn the Chinese language effectively, and only then was he able to successfully begin a translation of the Chinese Bible.

Hudson spent 51 years in China doing what he loved most: being a witness for Jesus. Hudson Taylor believed that men were moved by God, not by man's preaching. This man of faith and fortitude mastered the ministry of moving men to God by the power of prayer. Empowered by the Holy Spirit, his contagious Christian character helped him become the ultimate evangelist for God and the people of China.

When he died on June 3, 1905, he left behind a great legacy for Christian missions. In his lifetime God helped him start 300 mission stations and 125 schools. He brought 850 missionaries to China, established a network of 125,000 Chinese Christian workers in the mission organization, and was directly responsible for the conversion of 18,000 Chinese to Christianity. Not surprisingly, his mission's active fight against the opium trade made him especially welcome by the Chinese government.

It has been said that no other missionary—in the nineteen centuries since the Apostle Paul—had a wider vision and carried out a more effective plan of evangelism over a larger area than Hudson Taylor. Like Paul, Hudson Taylor was at his best when he was working as a missionary for God. He was willing to work tirelessly, uncomplainingly, to spread the gospel. He was truly a great man, but the thing that made him successful in the eyes of God was his willingness to first become a servant. Because of his humble ways, Hudson won the hearts of the people.[80] *"He who is greatest among you shall be your servant."* *Matthew 23:11.*

---

80   Howard Taylor, *Hudson Taylor's Spiritual Secret* (Chicago: Moody Press, 2009).

When the trumpet of the Lord shall sound,
    And time shall be no more,
And the morning breaks, eternal, bright and fair;
    When the saved of earth shall gather
Over on the other shore,
    And the roll is called up yonder, I'll be there.

On that bright and cloudless morning
    When the dead in Christ shall rise,
And the glory of His resurrection share;
    When His chosen ones shall gather
To their home beyond the skies,
    And the roll is called up yonder, I'll be there.

Let us labor for the Master
    From the dawn till setting sun,
Let us talk of all His wondrous love and care;
    Then when all of life is over,
And our work on earth is done,
    And the roll is called up yonder, I'll be there.

When the roll is called up yonder,
    When the roll is called up yonder,
When the roll is called up yonder,
    When the roll is called up yonder, I'll be there.

—James M. Black, "When the Roll is Called Up Yonder"

**Faithfulness in Little Things—Reading #4**

"The church of Christ is God's appointed agency for the salvation of men. Its mission is to carry the gospel to the world. And the obligation rests upon all Christians. Everyone, to the extent of his talent and opportunity, is to fulfill the Savior's commission. The love of Christ, revealed to us, makes us debtors to all who know Him not. God has given us light, not for ourselves alone, but to shed upon them.

"If the followers of Christ were awake to duty, there would be thousands where there is one today proclaiming the gospel in heathen lands. And all who could not personally engage in the work, would yet sustain it with their means, their sympathy, and their prayers. And there would be far more earnest labor for souls in Christian countries.

"We need not go to heathen lands, or even leave the narrow circle of the home, if it is there that our duty lies, in order to work for Christ. We can do this in the home circle, in the church, among those with whom we associate, and with whom we do business.

"The greater part of our Savior's life on earth was spent in patient toil in the carpenter's shop at Nazareth. Ministering angels attended the Lord of life as He walked side by side with peasants and laborers, unrecognized and unhonored. He was as faithfully fulfilling His mission while working at His humble trade as when He healed the sick or walked upon the storm-tossed waves of Galilee. So in the humblest duties and lowliest positions of life, we may walk and work with Jesus.

"The apostle says, *Let each one remain with God in that state in which he was called.*" 1 Corinthians 7:24. The businessman may conduct his business in a way that will glorify his Master because of his fidelity. If he is a true follower of Christ he will carry his religion into e 'erything that is done and reveal to men the spirit of Christ. The mechanic may be a diligent and faithful representative of Him who toiled in the lowly walks of life among the hills of Galilee. Everyone who r.ames the name of Christ should so work that others, by seeing his g ood works, may be led to glorify their Creator and Redeemer." [81]

**Illustrative Sketch:**
The sign was up in Mr. McGregor's shop window again. This was the third time in one week that Henry had seen it taken down and then put up again. "Help Wanted," it read, and the fact that no one seemed to be able to keep the job, seemed an enticement to Henry. What was so hard about working for the old gentleman? Henry had heard all the rumors, but Mr. McGregor seemed nice enough.

Summer vacation had just begun, so Henry stopped in to check out his prospects for the job, but Blake Davis was there before him, and Henry's heart sank a bit at sight of him. Blake was a showoff and a bully

---

81  White, 81.

sometimes at school. He grinned triumphantly at Henry as though he already had the job

"Well now, son," Mr. McGregor stared at Henry over his wire rims. "I have a young man here who tells me he's ready to take the job. Can you tell me why I should hire you instead of him?"

"No, sir, I can't," Henry admitted honestly. He was not in the habit of selling himself like this, and today seemed no different.

Mr. McGregor glanced at both boys. "Well, I tell you what I'm going to do, then. I'm going to send you both on an errand, and the one that finishes first will get the job. Fair enough?"

The two boys agreed and were sent off in two different directions—Blake to deliver a message to the feed store with a neatly wrapped box in brown paper—Henry to ride his bike to the paper mill with an order for a wagonload of news print. Henry rode as fast as his legs would pedal, but to him the deal didn't seem quite fair. The feed store was much closer, he fumed, so it was likely Blake would win. On the other hand, Henry did have his bike. Maybe that would give him the edge over Blake. The thought gave Henry new energy, and he rode like the wind. By the time he had returned up the street to Mr. McGregor's shop, he could see Blake coming in at a dead run. It would be a close tie.

In fact it was a tie, and when both boys stood panting before the old man, he was at a loss as to how to deal with this new quandary. Both boys had run their errands, and both had come back in record time. Mr. McGregor scratched his chin in his characteristic way, "I guess I'll have to give you both a try. I don't need two errand boys, but we'll see how it goes for a few days."

They both worked the rest of the day, eyeing each other each time one was given a job that seemed especially enviable. The next morning they were both set to work again, taking messages to businesses in town, delivering parcels to the train station, and helping do a hundred and one things needed to run a Wells Fargo office in the 1890s. After lunch Henry was sent to the feed store with a purchase order for 1000 bushels of corn to be delivered to one called Jeb Carter. As he scooted out the front door he heard Mr. McGregor telling Blake to go upstairs to the attic to do some chore.

Henry was next sent off to the town smithy with a wheelbarrow full of horseshoes, and then to Major Burnside with a message that his piano was waiting for him at the railroad depot. The jobs weren't that difficult, but he couldn't take his bike for every errand, and he was getting tired running all over town. However he remembered some choice words of advice his father had often given him, "A job worth doing is a job well done," and they seemed especially fitting now.

The next morning Henry showed up bright and early, only to catch the tale end of a conversation between Blake and Mr. McGregor. "I'll not need your help any more, son. I don't think you're suited for this sort of job." Henry saw a look of surprise on Blake's face. It looked as if he wanted to say something, but then he just turned and walked out the door angrily. Henry didn't ask for an explanation of what had happened, and Mr. McGregor didn't offer one.

All that morning Henry ran more errands, and then in the afternoon was sent up to the attic to "straighten up the big wooden chest in the corner" as Mr. McGregor put it. Henry took an old kerosene lantern with him as he climbed several fights of rickety old steps to the attic. He shivered in the musty shadows of the large garret and wiped the cobwebs away. Sure enough, there was the old wooden chest under the eaves, and Henry wondered what secrets lay hidden in it. The place was creepy and he wondered why this job was so important. "Mr. McGregor must have run out of chores to send me all the way up here," Henry muttered.

He opened the old box and stared at its contents. The box was huge and seemed to be filled with nothing but junk. Old metal hinges, bolts, hooks, nails, strings, pieces of old clocks. Never in his life had he seen such a collection of odds and ends that were so totally unrelated. He pulled a few things out of the box and studied them. The more he looked the contents over, the more he could see that this job was going to be endless, and quite pointless, to be frank.

Then he had a thought. Was this the job Blake had been sent up to do, because if it was, he could see why Blake had quit? Or rather, Mr. McGregor had let him go. Either way the box was filled with useless rubbish, and Henry thought it might be helpful for him to go downstairs and tell his boss what kinds of things were in the old box. Maybe Mr. McGregor didn't actually know. But, he had a second thought. "I wonder what the old boy is up to?" he muttered to himself. He pawed through the junk a few more minutes, and then finally set his mind to the task. If Mr. McGregor thought the box was important enough to clean, then it was worth doing well.

He started right in and worked on through the afternoon, hardly noticing the time. When Mr. McGregor called from the bottom of the stair that it was quittin' time, Henry was surprised. "I'll be down in a minute!" he called. "I'm almost done! Thirty minutes later he came down the stairs, all covered with dust and cobwebs, but with a tired smile on his face. "I've done the best I could, sir. Here's a five dollar gold piece I found at the bottom of the box. Can't tell how such a thing might have gotten there," and with that he headed for home.

After Mr. McGregor closed up shop for the night, he took the lantern and climbed the rickety stairs to the attic. In wonder he stood over the box, admiring the simple, yet orderly work the boy had done. The contents had been completely emptied and then returned to the box, rearranged in little partitions that Henry had made using pieces of old wooden shingles. Into one partition went bolts, into another, screws. There were partitions filled with nails of various sizes, and hinges, and old hooks for heavy drapery. On the top of each partition Henry had laid a piece of scrap paper on which he had scribbled the item which belonged in the little portion.

"Well, well," smiled the old man, "if I don't miss my guess, I think I've found my boy." And indeed, he had. The "help wanted" sign was taken down and never seen in Mr. McGregor's shop window again. In fact, the old businessman made Henry a full partner and eventually gave the shipping company to Henry in his will when he died. All because Henry's motto had been, "A job worth doing is a job well done."[82]

This should be the code of every Christian, and the types of stones we build in the foundation of our characters. Doing our best is a long-lost virtue, but one worth pursuing, and an honest testimony for a Christ-centered life.

*"Whatever your hand finds to do, do it with your might." Ecclesiastes 9:10.*

---

82  Seventh-day Adventist Department of Education, *A Treasury of Devotional Aids for Home and School* (Washington, D.C.: Review and Herald Publishing Association, 1951).

**Be Thou Faithful—Reading #5**

"Many have excused themselves from rendering their gifts to the service of Christ because others were possessed of superior endowments and advantages. The opinion has prevailed that only those who are especially talented are required to consecrate their abilities to the service of God. It has come to be understood by many that talents are given to only a certain favored class to the exclusion of others who of course are not called upon to share in the toils or the rewards. But it is not so represented in the parable. When the master of the house called his servants, he gave to every man his work.

"With a loving spirit we may perform life's humblest duties *"as to the Lord." Colossians 3:23.* If the love of God is in the heart, it will be manifested in the life. The sweet savor of Christ will surround us, and our influence will elevate and bless. You are not to wait for great occasions or to expect extraordinary abilities before you go to work for God. You need not have a thought of what the world will think of you. If your daily life is a testimony to the purity and sincerity of your faith, and others are convinced that you desire to benefit them, your efforts will not be wholly lost.

"The humblest and poorest of the disciples of Jesus can be a blessing to others. They may not realize that they are doing any special good, but by their unconscious influence they may start waves of blessing that will widen and deepen, and the blessed results they may never know until the day of final reward. They do not feel or know that they are doing anything great. They are not required to weary themselves with anxiety about success. They have only to go forward quietly, doing faithfully the work that God's providence assigns, and their life will not be in vain. Their own souls will be growing more and more into the likeness of Christ; they are workers together with God in this life and are thus fitting for the higher work and the unshadowed joy of the life to come." [83]

**Illustrative Sketch:**

Following the death of Jesus, His followers boldly preached the message of His death, resurrection, and second coming. Uneducated

---

83   White, 82.

and ill-prepared as they were, they became eloquent ambassadors for their Savior. The power of the Holy Spirit attended them at every step, and soon the gospel of Jesus was the most popular religion in Palestine. Thousands were converted to the Church in a day.

However, it was not God's plan that the Church should make Jerusalem its long-term headquarters. Jesus Himself had told them, "You shall receive power when the Holy Spirit has come upon you; and you shall be witnesses for Me in Jerusalem, and in all Judea and Samaria, and to the end of the earth." Acts 1:8.

And so it was that Stephen was stoned in AD 34 for daring to confront the Sanhedrin about their murder of Jesus, God's Son. The Christians in Jerusalem were devastated over the loss of one of their greatest champions. Of what value was it to have this man of God die at the hands of corrupt powerful-mongers in the Jewish Sanhedrin. The numbers of Christians in Jerusalem and all Judea had grown remarkably, and they had hoped this would signal the beginning of a new era in Jerusalem.

They remembered Jesus' words. "'You will be brought before governors and kings for My sake, as a testimony to them and to the Gentiles. ... Blessed are those who are persecuted for righteousness' sake, for theirs is the kingdom of heaven. ... Rejoice and be exceedingly glad, for great is your reward in heaven, for so they persecuted the prophets who were before you.'" Matthew 10:18, 5:10, 12. "For this gospel of the kingdom must go to all the world.'" Matthew 24:14.

And indeed the blood of Stephen became the seed of the infant Church. Many witnessed Stephens' shining face at his execution, and desired to have that kind of peace in their hearts. Large numbers of priests were converted to the gospel. "And the Lord added to the church daily those who were being saved." Acts 2:47.

But the Church continued to suffer under the ruling class of priests who jockeyed for power, and after the stoning of Stephen things went for bad to worse. In fact, Stephen's death seemed to be the catalyst for a whole new wave of persecution against the fledgling Church. Saul, a member of the Sanhedrin, and one of the youngest zealots ever to sit on that prestigious governing body, began a campaign of persecution against the Church at this time. He traveled far and wide, and "made havoc of the church, entering every house, and dragging off men and women, committing them to prison." Acts 8:3.

But Saul was unaware of God's plans for him. On a road trip to Damascus to find and ferret out pockets of Christians hiding there, he had an encounter with Jesus Himself, and became a changed man. This began a new life for Paul, in which he now became a missionary for God throughout the nations of the Mediterranean Middle East. Wherever he went he now spoke convincingly of the death and resurrection of Jesus, and the truth which he had worked so hard to suppress.

And conditions for the Christina Church in Jerusalem did not improve. King Herod put James the brother of John in prison, and then had him executed to "please the Jewish leaders." Then he locked Peter up too, and had it not been for a miracle in which his angel released him, the Apostle would no doubt have died a martyr's death at that time too.

By this time there was so much pressure on the Church in Judea that the followers of the "Way" scattered to the far corners of the Mediterranean. All of the Apostles left the vicinity of Jerusalem, some to Samaria, and Antioch, and countries far beyond. Tradition and the writings of early Christian historians tell us that some of the disciples went to Greece, Britain, and even as far away as India. But no matter what the price, their greatest joy was to testify of their love for Jesus. And like James, many even died for the cause.

Peter and Paul both finally died as martyrs in Rome, probably during the infamous reign of Nero. Early Christian historians tell us that Peter died on a cross, but asked that he be crucified upside down because he considered himself unworthy to die in the same manner as Jesus. Paul was beheaded, the only form of execution allowed for Roman citizens.

According to tradition Andrew was also crucified, and Matthew died a martyr in Ethiopia. Thomas is said to have been executed with a lance. Thaddeus preached the gospel in Armenia, and was then martyred in Persia, now the country of modern Iran. James Alpheus was thrown down from the temple in Jerusalem by the scribes and Pharisees, and then stoned to death.

Clearly, it was Satan's intention to stamp out the growing Christian movement. One of the darkest chapters in Church history tells how the Romans persecuted the Christians and tortured them in their sports amphitheaters. They were crucified, burned as torches, and fed to wild beasts. But through it all the Christians maintained their faith in God's promises of eternal life, and the Romans even found themselves admiring them for it.

But the relentless persecutions designed to break the Church were to no avail. The greater the indignities heaped upon Christians, the more steadfast was their allegiance to the gospel mandate. "'Go therefore and make disciples of all the nations, baptizing them in the name of the Father and of the Son and of the Holy Spirit.'" Matthew 28:19.

And the Church continued to grow. In the forty years following the death of Jesus the Church convincingly conquered the then-known world. It is estimated that by the time Peter and Paul were martyred, the number of Christians in the Roman Empire reached 1,000,000.

The sacrifices of Christians in ages past have not been in vain. Today the message of the gospel story is being told in the furthest corners of the world. There are over 6000 languages on earth, and the Bible has been printed in 4000 of them. Within the next few years Bible publishers worldwide have plans to translate the Scriptures into the remaining 2,250 languages that do not now have a Bible. And with the help of radio, satellite TV, and the Internet, the gospel is truly going to every nation, tribe, tongue, and people. Take heart! There can be no doubt that Jesus is coming soon![84]

---

84    Based on Acts 7-9 and *Catholic Encyclopedia*, 1917.

---◎---

# CHAPTER 10

# A Knowledge of God

**Our God Is An Awesome God!—Reading #1**

"Many are the ways in which God is seeking to make Himself known to us and bring us into communion with Him. Nature speaks to our senses without ceasing. The open heart will be impressed with the love and glory of God as revealed through the works of His hands. The listening ear can hear and understand the communications of God through the things of nature. The green fields, the lofty trees, the buds and flowers, the passing cloud, the falling rain, the babbling brook, the glories of the heavens, speak to our hearts, and invite us to become acquainted with Him who made them all.

"Our Savior bound up His precious lessons with the things of nature. The trees, the birds, the flowers of the valleys, the hills, the lakes, and the beautiful heavens, as well as the incidents and surroundings of daily life, were all linked with the words of truth, that His lessons might thus be often recalled to mind, even amid the busy cares of man's life of toil.

"God would have His children appreciate His works and delight in the simple, quiet beauty with which He has adorned our earthly home. He is a lover of the beautiful, and above all that is outwardly attractive He loves beauty of character; He would have us cultivate purity and simplicity, the quiet graces of the flowers.

"If we will but listen, God's created works will teach us precious lessons of obedience and trust. From the stars that in their trackless courses through space follow from age to age their appointed path, down to the minutest atom, the things of nature obey the Creator's will. And God cares for everything and sustains everything that He has created. He who upholds the unnumbered worlds throughout immensity, at the same time cares for the wants of the little brown sparrow that sings its humble song without fear.

"When men go forth to their daily toil, as when they engage in prayer; when they lie down at night, and when they rise in the morning; when the rich man feasts in his palace, or when the poor man gathers his children about the scanty board, each is tenderly watched by the heavenly Father. No tears are shed that God does not notice. There is no smile that He does not mark.

"If we would but fully believe this, all undue anxieties would be dismissed. Our lives would not be so filled with disappointment as now; for everything, whether great or small, would be left in the hands of God, who is not perplexed by the multiplicity of cares, or overwhelmed by their weight. We should then enjoy a rest of soul to which many have long been strangers." [85]

**Illustrative Sketch:**

Jesus sees the burdens we bear. He knows our anxieties, our sorrows, and our pain. He is so completely aware of our every need that He numbers the hairs of our head. Matthew 10:30. He is our personal Savior, and our God, too, capable of running the Universe. By faith we understand that the Universe was formed at God's command, so that what is seen was not made out of what was visible. Hebrews 11:3 NIV. What an awesome God! With omnipotence He hangs the worlds and puts the stars in their place.

Our sun, the single greatest source of energy in our solar system, is one of those stars. Hot beyond imagination, it has energy to burn for millions of years to come, and is so important to life as we know. It warms our earth and atmosphere, keeps our plants green, and helps our bodies stay healthy.

The sun may look comparatively small in the sky, but that's only because it's so far away—93 million miles to be exact. Think of driving that distance in your car. If you could drive at a modest 60 miles per hour, 24/7, 365 days a year, it would take you 176 years to reach the sun.

Compared to our earth, the sun is astronomically larger. The earth is approximately 8000 miles in diameter, while the sun is roughly

---

85  White, 85.

900,000 miles across. One hundred earths lined up side-by-side still wouldn't span the width of the sun. With those proportions it would take 1,000,000 earths to reach across the sun.

Yet, our sun is just one tiny speck in the Universe, much smaller than the huge star giants Arcturus, Betelgeuse, and Mu Cephei. The largest star known in the universe—Canis Majoris, or more commonly called the Big Dog Star—is about 1.7 billion miles in diameter. In fact, if our sun were replaced by Canis Majoris, the radius of this giant star would probably extend beyond the orbit of Saturn.

In the known universe our solar system is comparatively small— about 7 billion miles across. And we smile because as big as our solar system seems to us, for God it is a simple cog in the machinery of the night skies. Not only must He manage our solar system with its sun, nine planets, and extensive asteroid belt, He must also oversee the mechanics of the Milky Way, the galaxy where we live.

To put things in perspective, consider this. If our solar system were the size of a quarter, the Milky Way galaxy would be about the size of the United States. The Milky Way is about six quadrillion miles across, or about 100,000 light years. It has approximately 200 billion stars, each one possibly representing a solar system of its own. Such numbers are mind-boggling!

Our galaxy is quite small when we consider the size of the universe, and the number of other galaxies it includes. Such mental gymnastics weary the mind! How many galaxies are we talking about? Not too many decades ago astronomers thought there might be about 1000. Then they upped that figure to 100,000, and then to the tens of millions. Today, using the latest technology with our most powerful telescopes, experts now estimate there are at least 100 billion galaxies, maybe more. They come in spiral shapes, elliptical patterns, and even in clusters. The far reaches of space are full of them, and God manages them all!

"The heavens declare the glory of God," for God "has stretched out the heavens at His discretion." Psalm 19:1, Jeremiah 10:12. Our God designed the universe, and knows no margin of error. He placed the earth in the precise location needed for sustaining life. Not too close to our sun, or we would boil, and not too far, or we would freeze. This same God who called forth the Milky Way galaxy, who created light that travels 186,000 miles per second, who constructed the Big Dog

Star, cares about you and your simplest needs. Most importantly, while we were yet sinners, He died for us. He rose again, claimed victory over the grave, intercedes for us in the heavenly sanctuary, and is coming soon to take us to our heavenly home beyond the stars! What an awesome God we serve!

> Oh Lord my God, when I in awesome wonder,
>     Consider all the worlds Thy Hands have made;
> I see the stars, I hear the rolling thunder,
>     Thy power throughout the universe displayed.
>
> When through the woods, and forest glades I wander,
>     And hear the birds sing sweetly in the trees.
> When I look down, from lofty mountain grandeur
>     And see the brook, and feel the gentle breeze.
>
> And when I think, that God, His Son not sparing;
>     Sent Him to die, I scarce can take it in;
> That on the Cross, my burden gladly bearing,
>     He bled and died to take away my sin.
>
> When Christ shall come, with shout of acclamation,
>     And take me home, what joy shall fill my heart.
> Then I shall bow, in humble adoration,
>     And then proclaim: "My God, how great Thou art!"
>
> Then sings my soul, My Savior God, to Thee,
>     How great Thou art, How great Thou art.
> Then sings my soul, My Savior God, to Thee,
>     How great Thou art, How great Thou art!
>
> —Stuart K. Hine, "How Great Thou Art"

## Let Me Walk With Thee—Reading #2

"As your senses delight in the attractive loveliness of the earth, think of the world that is to come, that shall never know the blight of sin and death; where the face of nature will no more wear the shadow of the curse. Let your imagination picture the home of the saved, and remember that it will be more glorious than your brightest imagination can portray. In the varied gifts of God in nature we see but the faintest gleaming of His glory. *"It is written, 'Eye has not seen, nor ear heard, nor have entered into the heart of man the things which God has prepared for those who love Him.'"* 1 Corinthians 2:9.

"The poet and the naturalist have many things to say about nature, but it is the Christian who enjoys the beauty of the earth with the highest appreciation, because he recognizes his Father's handiwork and perceives His love in flower and shrub and tree. No one can fully appreciate the significance of hill and vale, river and sea, who does not look upon them as an expression of God's love to man.

"God speaks to us through His providential workings and through the influence of His Spirit upon the heart. In our circumstances and surroundings, in the changes daily taking place around us, we may find precious lessons if our hearts are but open to discern them. The psalmist, tracing the work of God's providence, says, *"The earth is full of the goodness of the Lord."* *"Whoever is wise will observe these things, and they will understand the loving kindness of the Lord."* Psalm 33:5; 107:43.

"God speaks to us in His word. Here we have in clearer lines the revelation of His character, of His dealings with men, and the great work of redemption. Here is open before us the history of patriarchs and prophets and other holy men of old. They were men *"with a nature like ours."* James 5:17. We see how they struggled through discouragements like our own, how they fell under temptation as we have done, and yet took heart again and conquered through the grace of God; and, beholding, we are encouraged in our striving after righteousness. As we read of the precious experiences granted them, of the light and love and blessing it was theirs to enjoy, and of the work they wrought through the grace given them, the spirit that inspired them kindles a flame of holy emulation in our hearts and a desire to be like them in character—like them to walk with God." [86]

**Illustrative Sketch:**
Noah was a great champion of truth, perhaps the greatest in world history. He was an unusual man in his day, and because he stood tall for God in a godless generation, he found grace in the eyes of the Lord.

---

86   White, 86.

Like the legendary patriarchs before him, Noah walked with God and was the last of the antediluvians dedicated to the covenant of the one true God.

Called by God to build an ark for the saving of all mankind and to preach a message of coming disaster, Noah courageously answered the call. During the first stages of its planning and construction, the ship received little attention from the outside world. However, as the ribs of the vessel began to reach to the sky, the public became more interested. The coming years were ones of tremendous excitement and often great disappointment. Few people really believed Noah's message of doom. Even his extended family failed to support him sufficiently in his efforts to build the ark. Noah's faith was tested again and again as the ark took shape. A project of this size was a financial burden of astronomical proportions, and before long he became a pauper. With little money on hand, construction was sometimes painfully slow.

To Noah's dismay the wickedness of coastal cities now crept inland. Everywhere evil was increasing, even in the rural area where Noah was building the ark. It seemed all mankind was now suffering from unchecked greed for power and wealth. In the local towns and villages violence reached a new peak, with indescribable crimes becoming more and more common. There seemed nothing to stem the tide of evil overtaking the world as the last vestiges of God's Spirit were being withdrawn from the world.

Both Lamech and Methuselah died within five years of the coming flood, leaving Noah and his sons alone to finish the project. But Noah remained faithful to the end, warning everyone that only those who entered the ark would be safe from destruction.

Then one momentous day thousands of animals and birds miraculously paraded toward the ark. The local folks were astonished! It was obvious that a supernatural hand was at work. Still, no one took Noah's offer of salvation seriously. However, when a bright flash of light descended from the sky and mysteriously closed the ark's massive door, panic gripped the onlookers. The gigantic door was now shut, and no one could open it. They watched and waited breathlessly, but when nothing further developed, their fears subsided. When the sun rose the next morning as usual and all things appeared normal, most grew complacent again.

For several days the watching crowd around the ark increased in size until it grew to mob-like proportions. A few folks in the drunken throng were genuinely worried, but most were simply curious about what Noah and his family might be doing inside the ark. Others were angry that Noah would "shut them out," and before long Satan took possession of the doomed watchers. Scores of onlookers grew bold with a desire for demonic vengeance and became violent. Some tried to break into the ark, and others tried setting it on fire.

However, on the eighth day flashes of light on the horizon coupled with sonic booms, high winds, and dark clouds sent the crowds screaming in every direction. An earthquake split cracks into crevices, and geysers erupted into the sky. As lightning and thunder brought rain and hail, streams and rivers rose over their banks. People and animals stampeded for the hills, frantically competing for a place on high ground. In shock and horror the terrified crowds watched as tsunamis rolled through the land sweeping away their homes and temples. Eventually, even the highest hills were covered, and one by one man and beast lost their fragile foothold. In desperation a few clung to the ark until the violent turbulence of the waters swept them away to their death.

So ended the last days of the primeval world given to mankind. Antediluvian times were a thing of the past, and Noah rode his ark across the stormy waves to a new world order. He was a man out of time and place, an example of what we should be for God.

In these last days of earth's history, like Noah we must stand for the right though the heaven's fall, "… though the mountains be carried into the midst of the sea, though its waters roar and be troubled." Psalm 46:2, 3. We must be willing to be witnesses for God in a perverse generation, to warn the world of the crisis soon to break on the unsuspecting crowds. If we walk with God as Noah did, we will be empowered to share salvation's message of hope that Jesus alone is the answer for a lost world. *"For there is no other name under heaven given among men by which we must be saved."* Acts 4:12.

O Master, let me walk with Thee,
In lowly paths of service free;
Tell me Thy secret; help me to bear
The strain of toil, the fret of care.

Help me the slow of heart to move
    By some clear, winning word of love;
Teach me the wayward feet to stay,
    And guide them in the homeward way.

O Master, let me walk with Thee,
    Before the taunting Pharisee;
Help me to bear the sting of spite,
    The hate of men who hide Thy light.

The sore distrust of souls sincere
    Who cannot read Thy judgments clear,
The dullness of the multitude,
    Who dimly guess that Thou art good.

Teach me Thy patience; still with Thee
    In closer, dearer, company,
In work that keeps faith sweet and strong,
    In trust that triumphs over wrong.

In hope that sends a shining ray
    Far down the future's broadening way,
In peace that only Thou canst give,
    With Thee, O Master, let me live.

—Washington Gladden, "O Master, let Me Walk With Thee"

**Give Me the Bible—Reading #3**

"Jesus said of the Old Testament Scriptures—and how much more is it true of the New—"*These are they which testify of Me,*'" the Redeemer, Him in whom our hopes of eternal life are centered. *John 5:39.* Yes, the whole Bible tells of Christ. From the first record of creation—for *"without Him nothing was made that was made"*—to the closing promise, "*Behold, I am coming quickly,*'" we are reading of His works and listening to His voice. *John 1:3; Revelation 22:12.* If you would become acquainted with the Savior, study the Holy Scriptures.

"Fill the whole heart with the Words of God. They are the living water, quenching your burning thirst. They are the living bread from heaven. Jesus declares, *'Unless you eat the flesh of the Son of man, and drink His blood, you have no life in you.'* And He explains Himself by saying, *'The words that I speak to you, they are spirit, and they are life.'* John 6:53, 63.* Our bodies are built up from what we eat and drink; and as in the natural economy, so in the spiritual economy: it is what we meditate upon that will give tone and strength to our spiritual nature.

"The theme of redemption is one that the angels desire to look into; it will be the science and the song of the redeemed throughout the ceaseless ages of eternity. Is it not worthy of careful thought and study now? The infinite mercy and love of Jesus, the sacrifice made in our be-half, call for the most serious and solemn reflection. We should dwell upon the character of our dear Redeemer and Intercessor. We should meditate upon the mission of Him who came to save His people from their sins. As we thus contemplate heavenly themes, our faith and love will grow stronger, and our prayers will be more and more acceptable to God, because they will be more and more mixed with faith and love. They will be intelligent and fervent. There will be more constant con-fidence in Jesus, and a daily, living experience in His power to save to the uttermost all that come unto God by Him." [87]

## Illustrative Sketch:

Sometimes we get so used to something that we don't really think much about it. The Bible, for example. We may take it for granted be-cause we think we'll always have it. Or, we think that if we had to, we could get along without it. But could we really, now? Perhaps a better question to ask ourselves is, "How much do we read our Bibles, and what would we do if we couldn't get one?" We have to be honest with ourselves when we wonder, "would we really miss it that much? Would life be that much different without one?"

During the Dark Ages most people in Europe couldn't read or write, so biblical knowledge among the common people was limited. People hungered for God's Word, but it just wasn't available. Those were times of great spiritual darkness, and it seemed the whole world

---

87  White, 88.

had fallen asleep spiritually. But God wasn't asleep, and He kept a close watch over the copies of His Sacred Writings.

Then came the great leaders of the Protestant Reformation. William Tyndale, one of the outstanding characters of the European religious renaissance during the 1500s, became interested in the work of Erasmus and Martin Luther, both of whom were reformers in the translation of the Scriptures. A few Bibles had been printed in Europe, but most copies of the Bible were still in Latin, a dead language that only the priests, monks, and bishops of the Catholic Church could read.

More than anything, Tyndale wanted the common people to have the Bible to read in their own language. And so, after studying Hebrew, Greek, and German, he went to work translating the Bible into English. On one of his trips to smuggle Bibles into England via a merchant ship, Tyndale was betrayed by a so-called friend. Because of his work in translating the scriptures, the authorities threw Tyndale in prison where he endured the most inhuman treatment.

When the church finally gave him a trial 500 days later, it was a ridiculous charade. Tyndale was tried and convicted by the Church for heresy and sentenced to be executed in the prison yard on October 6, 1536. William Tyndale burned at the stake for his work in translating Bibles and smuggling them into England. Can you believe it?

Unfortunately, King Henry VIII, a Christian himself, did nothing to stop Tyndale from being executed. Tyndale's last words as he died were, "Lord, open the eyes of the King of England." Three years later the reformer's prayer was answered when King Henry VIII began to initiate reforms in his country.

Today, William Tyndale is considered the father of the English reformation, the apostle of England, and a brilliant scholar who was used by God to change the history of the Protestant Reformation. He bravely led the way so that other reformers could follow. God has always had His champions to shed eternal light on the pathway to heaven. Time and again when the road has seemed darkest, the light of truth has broken forth to illuminate the way.

So now, in retrospect, how much value can you place on that personal copy of the Bible sitting on your shelf? Is it worth more than the hours you spend watching TV? Is it worth as much as the music you listen to incessantly, or the sports you watch? How about that bank account? Is your desire to get Bibles to the Chinese greater than your need for a new car? Or, maybe it's your house? When Jesus comes again will you be wishing you had spent more money maintaining a classy home, or will you regret neglecting an offering to finance a shipment of Bibles to Africa?

If we truly value God's Word, we will be willing to spend more time with it, and we will sacrifice some of our earthly dreams and possessions in order to share His Word with others. Don't fool yourself. If Jesus mentioned it in several of His parables, the Bible must be worth a spiritual fortune! "The *Words of the Lord are pure words: as silver tried in a furnace of earth, purified seven times." Psalm 12:6. "Your Word is a lamp to my feet, and a light to my Path." Psalm 119:105.*

Give me the Bible, star of gladness gleaming,
    To cheer the wanderer lone and tempest tossed;
No storm can hide that radiance peaceful beaming,
    Since Jesus came to seek and save the lost.

Give me the Bible, when my heart is broken,
    When sin and grief have filled my soul with fear;
Give me the precious words by Jesus spoken,
    Hold up faith's lamp to show my Savior near.

Give me the Bible, all my steps enlighten,
    Teach me the danger of these realms below;
That lamp of safety o'er the gloom shall brighten,
    That light alone the path of peace can show.

Give me the Bible, lamp of life immortal,
    Hold up that splendor by the open grave;
Show me the light from Heaven's shining portal,
    Show me the glory gilding Jordan's wave.

Give me the Bible, holy message shining;
    Thy light shall guide me in the narrow way;
Precept and promise, law and love combining,
    Till night shall vanish in eternal day.

—Priscilla Jane Owens, "Give Me The Bible"

## More Precious Than Gold—Reading #4

"As we meditate upon the perfections of the Savior, we shall desire to be wholly transformed and renewed in the image of His purity. There will be a hungering and thirsting of soul to become like Him whom we adore. The more our thoughts are upon Christ, the more we shall speak of Him to others and represent Him to the world.

"The Bible was not written for the scholar alone; on the contrary, it was designed for the common people. The great truths necessary for salvation are made as clear as noonday; and none will mistake and lose their way except those who follow their own judgment instead of the plainly revealed will of God.

"We should not take the testimony of any man as to what the Scriptures teach, but should study the words of God for ourselves. If we allow others to do our thinking, we shall have crippled energies and contracted abilities. The noble powers of the mind may be so dwarfed by lack of exercise on themes worthy of their concentration as to lose their ability to grasp the deep meaning of the word of God. The mind will enlarge if it is employed in tracing out the relation of the subjects of the Bible, comparing scripture with scripture and spiritual things with spiritual.

"There is nothing more calculated to strengthen the intellect than the study of the Scriptures. No other book is so potent to elevate the thoughts, to give vigor to the faculties, as the broad, ennobling truths of the Bible. If God's word were studied as it should be, men would have a breadth of mind, a nobility of character, and a stability of purpose rarely seen in these times.

"But there is but little benefit derived from a hasty reading of the Scriptures. One may read the whole Bible through and yet fail to see its beauty or comprehend its deep and hidden meaning. One passage studied until its significance is clear to the mind and its relation to the plan of salvation is evident, is of more value than the perusal of many chapters with no definite purpose in view and no positive instruction gained. Keep your Bible with you. As you have opportunity, read it; fix the texts in your memory. Even while you are walking the streets you may read a passage and meditate upon it, thus fixing it in the mind." [88]

**Illustrative Sketch:**
The Bible is the oldest book in the world, written by different kinds of people over a span of 1,500 years. Farmers, fishermen, shepherds, prophets, generals, preachers, and kings contributed to this project inspired by the Holy Spirit. It has weathered the storms of time, suffering censor and incrimination by kings and emperors, fire and persecution, the sword, and even logic and science.

During the last 200 years the validity and authenticity of the Bible has come under intense scrutiny. Is it accurate after all these years, scholars began asking? How can it possibly be free from error after centuries of change and translation? Surely, much has been lost! However, God has always had a plan for preserving His Written Word. Through the darkest of times He has raised up special people who searched for the oldest copies of the Bible to validate the Scripture record. Constantin von Tischendorf was that kind of man.

During the mid-1800s Tischendorf became a biblical scholar and traveled the world as an archaeologist trying to prove that the Bible was still the Word of God. He wanted to prove God's Word is genuinely reliable, and that it is the same document God inspired men of old to write.

Tischendorf is best known for his discovery of one of the oldest known manuscripts of the Greek Bible. He made his big find while digging in a trash pile at a monastery near the legendary Mount Sinai. The manuscript was 44 pages of the New Testament, called the Sinaiticus, and was written in the Fourth Century A.D. It's now considered one of the most valuable biblical manuscripts anywhere in the world.

Tischendorf was a man for his time. A new age of science and enlightenment had arrived. The world was in the heart of the Industrial Revolution, a period of powerful change in the ways people lived, worked, and governed. Inventions were sprouting up everywhere that allowed people to do more work in less time. It was an age of tremendous human empowerment when people acclaimed the accomplishments of the human race. Societies everywhere were wondering, "Do

---

88   White, 89.

I need the Bible anymore? Is it still accurate? Is it even the same book it was in the days of the early Christian Church?" Tischendorf's discovery of those ancient copies answered all these questions with a resounding, "Yes!" He found those ancient lines to be almost identical to the ones in your Bible sitting on your shelf right now. It's comforting to know that God has watched over the Bible all these years. The Word of God is reliable today.

However, with the explosion in earth's population during the last five centuries, and the need to take the gospel to every nation, kindred, tongue, and people, the former process of making hand copies of the scriptures changed. Johann Gutenberg in the mid-1400s began making copies of the Bible using a new invention called block printing. This new invention along with the Protestant Reformation helped bring the Bible to Europe and the World.

When the missionary movement began in the United States, the Bible became available like it had never been before. In 1816, delegates from 35 Bible societies met in New York City to form the American Bible Society. Protestant Americans felt the United States was being called by God to preach the gospel to the world and to make the Scriptures available in as many languages as possible. In that first year, 6,140 Bibles were either given to people on the streets of New York City or sent to overseas missions. By 1900 the organization had given away over 60 million Bibles. That's enough Bibles to make a stack 900 miles into the sky.

Today, the Bible is available to at least 98 percent of the world's people in the languages they speak. The Bible is by far the most published book in the history of the world, making it the undisputed best-seller of all time. More than four billion copies of the Bible have been printed in thousands of languages and editions. Bible societies the world over are working together to get the Bible printed in as many languages as possible. The Bible has been translated into 680 languages in Africa, 590 in Asia, 420 in the Pacific Islands, 420 in Latin America, 210 in Europe, and 75 in North America. The United Bible Societies are now assisting in over 600 Bible translation projects. In 1999, Wycliffe Bible Translators estimated that 2,251 languages on earth still need a Bible translation, with only 193 million people that don't have a Bible in their language. Their goal is that by the year 2025, a translation of the Bible will be started in every language. Truly the gospel has gone to almost every corner of the globe.[89]

Thank God for His precious Word! Today we can choose to read just about any kind of Bible we want—from copies in everyday English to versions that involve serious research. The wonder and blessing of the Bible is how the Holy Spirit speaks through it to give *us* exactly what we need, when we need it.

Thousands through the ages have valued God's Word more than jewels and gold. We may not be called to risk our lives for the Bible, but we can show our regard for it by safeguarding it at any cost. To be sure, its value is infinitely greater than rubies or silver or gold.

*The law of the Lord is perfect,*
*    Converting the soul;*
*The testimony of the Lord is sure,*
*    Making wise the simple.*

*More to be desired are they than gold,*
*    Yea than much fine gold,*
*Sweeter also than honey and the honeycomb.*

*The statutes of the Lord are right,*
*    Rejoicing the heart;*
*The commandment of the Lord is pure,*
*    Enlightening the eyes.*

*The fear of the Lord is clean,*
*    Enduring forever;*
*The judgments of the Lord are true*
*    And righteous altogether.*

*More to be desired are they than gold,*
*    Yea than much fine gold,*
*Sweeter also than honey and the honeycomb.*

—Psalm 19:7-10 as a song

---

89  Matthew Black and Robert Davidson, *Constantin von Tischendorf and the Greek New Testament* (Scotland: University of Glasgow Press, 1981).

**Spirit of the Living God—Reading #5**

"We cannot obtain wisdom without earnest attention and prayerful study. Some portions of Scripture are indeed too plain to be misunderstood, but there are others whose meaning does not lie on the surface to be seen at a glance. Scripture must be compared with scripture. There must be careful research and prayerful reflection. And such study will be richly repaid. As the miner discovers veins of precious metal concealed beneath the surface of the earth, so will he who perseveringly searches the word of God as for hid treasure find truths of the greatest value, which are concealed from the view of the careless seeker. The words of inspiration, pondered in the heart, will be as streams flowing from the fountain of life.

"Never should the Bible be studied without prayer. Before opening its pages we should ask for the enlightenment of the Holy Spirit, and it will be given. When Nathanael came to Jesus, the Savior exclaimed, *"Behold an Israelite indeed, in whom is no deceit!"* Nathanael said, *"How do you know me?"* Jesus answered, *"Before Philip called you, when you were under the fig tree, I saw you.'" John 1:47, 48.* And Jesus will see us also in the secret places of prayer if we will seek Him for light that we may know what is truth. Angels from the world of light will be with those who in humility of heart seek for divine guidance.

"The Holy Spirit exalts and glorifies the Savior. It is His office to present Christ, the purity of His righteousness, and the great salvation that we have through Him. Jesus says, *"He will take of what is Mine and declare it to you.'" John 16:14.* The Spirit of truth is the only effectual teacher of divine truth. How must God esteem the human race, since He gave His Son to die for them and appoints His Spirit to be man's teacher and continual guide!" [90]

**Illustrative Sketch:**

Vasili was stunned at the words of the Ukrainian evangelist! How could it be that there was a loving God in heaven, and he, an intelligent police officer, had not known it all these years? He could see that

---

90   White, 90.

the evangelist was sincere, and that the Bible from which he preached made sense. The gems of truth shown forth from this sacred Book like sparkling diamonds on the windswept sands of a desert.

With the words of the evangelist ringing in his ear, Vasili now felt more convicted than ever about Bible truth and this Advent message of a soon coming King. Jesus could come any day in the clouds of the sky, and Vasili wanted to a part of it. He wanted to go home to heaven to escape the hardship and superstition and spiritual darkness that had plagued him all his life in the former Soviet country of Moldova.

After studying the Bible for several months, Vasili decided he wanted to be baptized as a Sabbath-keeping Christian. Unfortunately, when he broke the news to his family about his decision, they were strongly against it. "You will no longer be considered family!" his brother and parents told him vehemently. "No one in our family is a Christian!" His wife Galina warned him that she would divorce him. "I'll not be married to a man crazy with religion!" she said coldly.

When Vasili told his police commander of his decision to honor the seventh-day Sabbath, the officer told Vasili he should look for another job. "Your responsibilities as a policeman require six days of work!" he frowned. "Monday through Saturday—I cannot give you another day off!"

Vasili agonized in prayer over his dilemma, and one night he asked God to give him a direct answer to help him decide what he should do. When he picked up his Bible, by God's grace it fell open to a famous passage in the book of Matthew. " 'He who loves father or mother more than me is not worthy of Me,'" it read. "'And he who loves his son or daughter more than Me is not worthy of me. And he who does not take his cross and follow after Me is not worthy of Me.'" Matthew 10:37, 38, NIV. Vasili was so surprised that God would answer his prayer by giving him such an appropriate text, that he felt impressed to step out in faith and make a decision for God. At all cost he must take up his cross and follow Jesus.

The next Sabbath Vasili went to the Seventh-day Adventist Church in town and was baptized. When he told Galina that he had been baptized, she wasn't angry, and that surprised him a little. However, when she said she already had divorce papers, he understood. Vasili didn't get upset. He just told Galina he loved her. Then the two of them went to Vasili's parents to give them the news. To her surprise, Vasili's family accepted his decision without objection. In fact, his parents and brother said they were proud of him for his decision to bravely follow God in the face of family rejection.

On Monday morning Vasili went to his commanding police officer to give him a letter of resignation. "I've been baptized and can no longer work on Saturday. It is now my Sabbath," he said gravely.

The officer told him to take a week off and think about the ramifications of such a decision. When Vasili returned a week later with his resignation, to his shock the commanding officer promoted him. "You can have your Sabbaths off," he smiled. "Do you think I would let a man of such integrity leave me to go work for someone else? I would be the loser in that arrangement!"

But Galina seemed unimpressed. In the face of such blessings from God she still stubbornly refused to accept Vasili's new-found faith. However during the next week, she got into trouble one day at the store where she worked as a cashier. The total cash receipts for the day didn't add up, and her boss said she would have to personally cover the amount that was missing.

She was frantic because it was a substantial amount. That night she asked Vasili to pray for her and the missing money. The next morning at work Galina found a mistake in the previous day's accounting. There was no error after all. Vasili invited her to give her heart to God for answering her prayer, but again she stubbornly refused, claiming it was a coincidence.

But, more trouble was on the way. Galina's mother became sick with cancer, and the doctors could do nothing. Galina begged her husband to pray for her mother, and to everyone's shock the cancer was miraculously healed. Galina could fight her secret convictions no longer. Her heart was softened, and she, too, decided to be baptized.[91]

With Galina we can all say, "Thanks be to God for His *indescribable gift!*" 2 Corinthians 9:15. *"The Lord is not slow in keeping his promise, as some understand slowness. Instead, He is patient with you, not wanting anyone to perish, but that everyone should come to repentance." 2 Peter 3:9 NIV.*

---

91  Ted Wilson, sermon for "General Conference Session," Atlanta, Georgia, 3 July 2010.

Spirit of the living God,
    fall fresh on me.
Spirit of the living God,
    fall fresh on me.
Melt me, mold me,
    fill me, use me.
Spirit of the living God,
    fall fresh on me.

—Daniel Iverson, "Spirit of the Living God"

# CHAPTER 11

# The Privilege of Prayer

**Sweet Hour of Prayer—Reading #1**

"Through nature and revelation, through His providence, and by the influence of His Spirit, God speaks to us. But these are not enough; we need also to pour out our hearts to Him. In order to have spiritual life and energy, we must have actual intercourse with our heavenly Father. Our minds may be drawn out toward Him; we may meditate upon His works, His mercies, His blessings; but this is not, in the fullest sense, communing with Him. In order to commune with God, we must have something to say to Him concerning our actual life.

"Prayer is the opening of the heart to God as to a friend. Not that it is necessary in order to make known to God what we are, but in order to enable us to receive Him. Prayer does not bring God down to us, but brings us up to Him.

"When Jesus was upon the earth, He taught His disciples how to pray. He directed them to present their daily needs before God, and to cast all their care upon Him. And the assurance He gave them that their petitions should be heard, is assurance also to us.

"Jesus Himself, while He dwelt among men, was often in prayer. Our Savior identified Himself with our needs and weakness, in that He became a suppliant, a petitioner, seeking from His Father fresh supplies of strength, that He might come forth braced for duty and trial. He is our example in all things. He is a brother in our infirmities, "in all points tempted like as we are;" but as the sinless one His nature recoiled from evil; He endured struggles and torture of soul in a world of sin. His humanity made prayer a necessity and a privilege. He found comfort and joy in communion with His Father. And if the Savior of men, the Son of God, felt the need of prayer, how much more should feeble, sinful mortals feel the necessity of fervent, constant prayer." [92]

**Illustrative Sketch:**

Letitia winced at the sharpness of the cold evening air as she stepped out the back door to get a bucket of coal from the woodshed. Tall chimneys spouted steady streams of gray smoke above the drab tints of the little village street where she lived. The December evening was bleak indeed, not a night for one to be out.

Times were hard, and food was scarce. At the moment there wasn't a morsel of food in the house, and there wouldn't be until payday at the end of the week. She hated to ask her neighbors for anything to help her get over the hump. She came from proud German stock and strength was a virtue to be prized. Everyone was suffering just now, and it wouldn't help much to go begging for even a crust of bread. Likely they had little or nothing to give.

She must simply do her part for the war effort in the small clothing factory where she worked. Letitia was an excellent seamstress, but was also a supervisor on the production line. The gray-green uniforms they made were in high demand to fill thousands of orders submitted each day by military operations in Berlin.

She sighed as she stoked the kitchen cook stove with a few lumps of coal. World War II was stretching on and on. Her only son was away in the war, serving somewhere in Africa, she thought, and that was depressing. He was only nineteen. To have such youth subjected to the horrors and indignities of war seemed so very wrong, especially to a mother. Her husband was in Homburg, working in a munitions factory, and could come home only when they would allow him a weekend pass, which wasn't very often anymore. Rumor had it that the Fuehrer's offensive on the Western Front was weakening, and Letitia wasn't sure whether that was good or bad.

She did not feel good about the war. She was proud to be a German indeed, but as a Christian she had to admit that war was evil, and the attempts of the Third Reich during the last five years had been revolting. First, Hitler had dominated Austria and Czechoslovakia, and then invaded Poland, prompting a war with France and Britain.

92   White, 93.

Letitia tried to quiet her growling stomach. She was hungry beyond words! The last potato had disappeared two days ago from the little bin beneath the kitchen cupboard, and for weeks there had been no onions, which she dearly loved. "Good for the heart," the town doctor always said.

"Please, Lord," Letitia prayed silently. "I know I must not complain, but with nothing to eat in the house, it is hard to be hopeful. I know I should be grateful for the little bit of heat I have. Thank you for the coal. Some have no heat at all." She glanced down at the few pieces of coal in the metal bucket and wished that it were food.

She went to her armchair and took up her Bible lying on the side board. "Help me to find comfort in Your Word!" she pleaded. "Help me to know that You are with me here tonight, and that You will sustain me. You are my only hope," she whispered.

The Bible fell open to a passage which she had often read, but now with more interest. It seemed perfectly crafted by God for this moment. "'Therefore I say to you, do not worry about your life, what you will eat or what you will drink; nor about your body, what you will put on. Is not life more than food and the body more than clothing? Look at the birds of the air, for they neither sow nor reap nor gather into barns; yet your heavenly Father feeds them. Are you not of more value than they?'" Matthew 6:25, 26.

Peace filled her heart as she closed her eyes in response to the wonderful promise. The crackling of the little fire in the stove bravely attempted to heat the kitchen, but it wasn't enough. Wartime rations of coal must be used sparingly in case the town supply should run out. There was nothing else for Letitia to do but retire early to bed for the night. At least I can stay warm there, she mused as she thought of the snug feather covering on the high backed bed in her bedroom.

It didn't take long to prepare for the night, and soon she was snuggled beneath the thick quilt, but it was hard to go to sleep. Her mind kept wandering to her son and her husband, and the growling of her empty stomach. "Give me rest," she prayed, "and help the hunger to go away. I know I am of more value than the birds to You, Lord."

Within a matter of minutes she dozed, hungry but warm under the softness of her comforter. And behold, she was standing in her kitchen, and on the table in plain sight was a large bowl of red-ripe strawberries. The scent of the strawberries permeated the room, their sweetness filling her nostrils with aromatic delight. The bowl of berries was so close she could reach out and touch them, and she did. They felt real, and soft, and she put one to her mouth to taste it. The sensation burst in her mouth like fireworks, and she took another. Its sweetness was as delicious as the first, and she found herself instinctively thanking God, though she knew it to be a dream. She took from the bowl again and again until it was empty.

And suddenly, amazingly she awoke, conscious that something wonderful had happened. "Thank you, Lord," she whispered again, but the strangest feeling came over her as she remembered the dream. The strawberries had seemed so real! Even now she could smell them and taste them in her mouth, if that were possible. And that was the odd part, for suddenly she sensed that the taste of strawberries was indeed on her tongue, their sweetness still on her breath, and—wonder of wonders—it felt like a piece of strawberry was still in her mouth.

She jumped out of bed, turned on the light, and ran to the little mirror in her room. She opened her mouth at the reflection in the mirror, and there on her tongue was a piece of ripe-red strawberry. She stared in dumbfounded astonishment and awe as a surreal sensation came over her. This was a miracle! An unexplainable, profound, true-to-life miracle God had given to encourage her and sustain her in time of need.

"Thank you, Lord!" Letitia fell to her knees beside her bed. "Thank you for Your watch care, for this incredible treat during these hard times! And thank you for your sense of humor Lord. I didn't even have to pick the berries! Truly I am a child of the King!"[93]

> Sweet hour of prayer! sweet hour of prayer!
>     That calls me from a world of care,
> And bids me at my Father's throne
>     Make all my wants and wishes known.
> In seasons of distress and grief,
>     My soul has often found relief,
> And oft escaped the tempter's snare,
>     By thy return, sweet hour of prayer!

93   This story was told to me in 1976 while I served as a student literature evangelist in Iowa.

Sweet hour of prayer! sweet hour of prayer!
    The joys I feel, the bliss I share,
Of those whose anxious spirits burn
    With strong desires for thy return!
With such I hasten to the place
    Where God my Savior shows His face,
And gladly take my station there,
    And wait for thee, sweet hour of prayer!

Sweet hour of prayer! sweet hour of prayer!
    May I thy consolation share,
Till, from Mount Pisgah's lofty height,
    I view my home and take my flight.
This robe of flesh I'll drop, and rise
    To seize the everlasting prize,
And shout, while passing through the air,
    "Farewell, farewell, sweet hour of prayer!"

—William W. Walford, "Sweet Hour of Prayer"

## Prayer Is the Key to Heaven—Reading #2

"Our heavenly Father waits to bestow upon us the fullness of His blessing. It is our privilege to drink largely at the fountain of boundless love. What a wonder it is that we pray so little! God is ready and willing to hear the sincere prayer of the humblest of His children, and yet there is much manifest reluctance on our part to make known our wants to God. What can the angels of heaven think of poor helpless human beings, who are subject to temptation, when God's heart of infinite love yearns toward them, ready to give them more than they can ask or think, and yet they pray so little and have so little faith? The angels love to bow before God; they love to be near Him. They regard communion with God as their highest joy; and yet the children of earth, who need so much the help that God only can give, seem satisfied to walk without the light of His Spirit, the companionship of His presence.

"The darkness of the evil one encloses those who neglect to pray. The whispered temptations of the enemy entice them to sin; and it is all because they do not make use of the privileges that God has given them in the divine appointment of prayer. Why should the sons and daughters of God be reluctant to pray, when prayer is the key in the hand of faith to unlock heaven's storehouse, where are treasured the boundless resources of Omnipotence? Without unceasing prayer and diligent watching we are in danger of growing careless and of deviating from the right path. The adversary seeks continually to obstruct the way to the mercy seat, that we may not by earnest supplication and faith obtain grace and power to resist temptation.

"There are certain conditions upon which we may expect that God will hear and answer our prayers. One of the first of these is that we feel our need of help from Him. He has promised, *"I will pour water upon him that is thirsty, and floods on the dry ground."* Isaiah 44:3. Those who hunger and thirst after righteousness, who long after God, may be sure that they will be filled. The heart must be open to the Spirit's influence, or God's blessing cannot be received.

"Our great need is itself an argument and pleads most eloquently in our behalf. But the Lord is to be sought unto to do these things for us. He says, *"Ask, and it will be given you."* And *"He who did not spare His own Son, but delivered Him up for us all, how shall He not with Him also freely give us all things?"* Matthew 7:7; Romans 8:32.

"If we regard iniquity in our hearts, if we cling to any known sin, the Lord will not hear us; but the prayer of the penitent, contrite soul is always accepted. When all known wrongs are righted, we may believe that God will answer our petitions. Our own merit will never commend us to the favor of God; it is the worthiness of Jesus that will save us, His blood that will cleanse us; yet we have a work to do in complying with the conditions of acceptance." [94]

### Illustrative Sketch:

Old Grumpy had been working as a hired hand on the homestead for as long as anyone could remember. Even longer than his boss John Taylor, who had been born on the farm. Old Grumpy seemed to be as much a part of the place as the big red barn. His real name was Silas, but no one called him that. The nickname given to him way back had stuck because he was—well—quite a grumpy old man.

---

94   White, 94.

Old Grumpy didn't have much in this world's goods. No land. No money in the bank. No buggy. Not even a horse. He wore the same old bib overalls day in and day out, and the same old sun bleached straw hat. "Just passin' through" was how he always put it, when anyone wanted to know.

But there was one thing Old Grumpy did have that meant something to him. In fact, it meant the world to him. It was a gold pocket watch with a glass front on it, and a long gold chain. It was his most prized possession. He wound it faithfully every night, and it kept perfect time. The sun might come up late, and the crowing of the rooster might be off by a few minutes, but not Grumpy's gold watch. It was so reliable everyone set their schedules by it.

And then one unforgettable day, Old Grumpy lost his gold watch. "Rubbish!" he all but shouted as he came in to supper that night. "I lost my gold watch!" he muttered more quietly, when he remembered that he was inside the house now.

"Where did you have it last?" little Gwen Taylor asked as she stared wide-eyed across the kitchen table at Grumpy.

"Well now, if I knew that I'd know where it was, wouldn't I?" he snapped gruffly, but one look from his boss, and Grumpy quieted down again. "Who knows!" he mumbled. "I've been all over the north forty this afternoon, cutting hay and hoeing corn."

They all let it drop, giving Grumpy his space, and ate their supper in silence. But that evening before bed, Gwen came to Grumpy's bedroom door and announced, "I'm going to ask God to help me find your watch!"

"Oh, no, you're not!" he growled. "No prayers ever did any good for me!"

But Gwen would not let it rest. She sensed from the look on his old face that he seemed totally lost without it. Life would be hard for Grumpy if he didn't have that watch. "Well, I'm going to pray anyway," she piped. "Jesus knows where that watch is, and I believe He'll show me."

"I say, don't go worrying your pretty little head over my watch," Grumpy softened a bit, and he still had an angry look in his eye.

Gwen danced off to bed, but she did kneel down by her bed as was her habit before going to sleep, and she did pray that God would show her exactly where the watch was. She didn't know exactly how God would do this, but her heart of faith needed little more than the assurance that Grumpy needed that watch, and more importantly that Grumpy needed Jesus.

He never had been one for religion. Truth was, he hadn't been to church since anyone could remember. After the War he seemed very stubborn about such things. The preacher had stopped him in town a few times to talk with him, but Old Grumpy refused to discuss spiritual matters.

The next morning Grumpy was out in the barn before breakfast sharpening a scythe, when Gwen came racing out to find him. "I know where your watch is!" she shouted excitedly. "I know where it is!"

"Oh go on!" Grumpy muttered, still very much out of sorts over the missing watch. "There ain't no watch, and there never will be! It's gone, I tell you! Gone for good!"

"No, really! I know where it is!" she kept shouting. "Jesus showed me right where it is in a dream last night!"

"Rubbish!" Grumpy began, but in his heart a faint glimmer of hope sprang up. Maybe, just maybe there was a chance she might really know where it was. "Oh alright, but I don't have much time!" he muttered. "Where is it!"

"It's down in the corn field near the end of one of the rows!" her eyes were fairly dancing.

"Well, I suppose it wouldn't hurt to look just a little bit!" he growled and allowed her to take him by the hand, but she had to fairly drag him to the cornfield out north of the barn. It was all she could do to get him to follow, because he kept holding back, growling about how he "didn't have time to go traipsing around creation looking for a dumb old watch." But Gwen knew he wanted to find it, too. She could tell by the strange light in his eyes.

Finally, he realized how silly this whole thing looked, and he stopped. "I'm not going any farther!" he snapped. "This is a wild goose chase!"

"No it's not!" Gwen pleaded. "It's just a little bit farther now. Down here on this row, near the end, I think," and with that she let go of his hand and raced ahead. Suddenly, she let out a scream. "I found your watch!" she shrieked. "I've found your watch!"

At this Old Grumpy jumped forward and literally ran to where Gwen was standing between the rows, her face radiant smiles. "There it is, just like I saw it in my dream!" she pointed at the gold watch where it rested in the dark soil. "In the sixth row, near the end, at the bottom of a cornstalk!"

And indeed it was. Old Grumpy reverently knelt in the damp earth to retrieve the gold watch. He cradled it to his heart and kept muttering to himself, "It's a miracle! It's a miracle! God does answer prayers!" But Gwen knew a greater miracle had happened that day, and it happened in Old Grumpy's heart. He became a changed man, his heart softened by the power of the Holy Spirit because of a little girl's prayer.[95]

"*Whatever things you ask in prayer, believing, you will receive.*" *Matthew 21:22.*

Change my heart oh God, make it ever true.
    Change my heart oh God, May I be like You.

You are the potter, I am the clay.
    Mold me and make me, this is what I pray

Change my heart oh God, make it ever true.
    Change my heart oh God, May I be like You.

—Eddie Espinosa, "Change My Heart, Oh, God"

**Abide With Me—Reading #3**

"Another element of prevailing prayer is faith. "*He who comes to God must believe that He is, and that He is a rewarder of those who diligently seek Him.*" *Hebrews 11:6.* Jesus said to His disciples, "*Whatever things you ask when you pray, believe that you receive them, and you will have them.*" *Mark 11:24.* Do we take Him at His word?

"The assurance is broad and unlimited, and He is faithful who has promised. When we do not receive the very things we asked for, at the

---

95   Arthur Maxwell, "Grumpy's Gold Watch," *The Children's Hour*, vol. 5 (Mountain View, CA: Pacific Press Publishing Association, 1949).

time we ask, we are still to believe that the Lord hears and that He will answer our prayers. We are so erring and short-sighted that we sometimes ask for things that would not be a blessing to us, and our heavenly Father in love answers our prayers by giving us that which will be for our highest good—that which we ourselves would desire if with vision divinely enlightened we could see all things as they really are.

"When our prayers seem not to be answered, we are to cling to the promise; for the time of answering will surely come, and we shall receive the blessing we need most. But to claim that prayer will always be answered in the very way and for the particular thing that we desire, is presumption. God is too wise to err, and too good to withhold any good thing from them that walk uprightly. Then do not fear to trust Him, even though you do not see the immediate answer to your prayers. Rely upon His sure promise, *'Ask, and it will be given to you.'* *Matthew 7:7.*

"If we take counsel with our doubts and fears, or try to solve everything that we cannot see clearly, before we have faith, perplexities will only increase and deepen. But if we come to God, feeling helpless and dependent, as we really are, and in humble, trusting faith make known our wants to Him whose knowledge is infinite, who sees everything in creation, and who governs everything by His will and word, He can and will attend to our cry, and will let light shine into our hearts. Through sincere prayer we are brought into connection with the mind of the Infinite. We may have no remarkable evidence at the time that the face of our Redeemer is bending over us in compassion and love, but this is even so. We may not feel His visible touch, but His hand is upon us in love and pitying tenderness.

"When we come to ask mercy and blessing from God we should have a spirit of love and forgiveness in our own hearts. How can we pray, *"Forgive us our debts, as we forgive our debtors,"'* and yet indulge an unforgiving spirit? *Matthew 6:12.* If we expect our own prayers to be heard we must forgive others in the same manner and to the same extent as we hope to be forgiven.

"Perseverance in prayer has been made a condition of receiving. We must pray always if we would grow in faith and experience. We are to be *"continuing steadfastly in prayer,"* to *"continue earnestly in prayer, being vigilant in it with thanksgiving."* *Romans 12:12; Colossians 4:2.*

Peter exhorts believers to be *"serious and watchful in your prayers."* 1 *Peter 4:7.* Paul directs, *"... In everything by prayer and supplication, with thanksgiving, let your requests be made known to God."* *Philippians 4:6.* *"But you, beloved,"* says Jude, *"... praying in the Holy Spirit, keep yourselves in the love of God ..."* *Jude 20, 21."* [96]

**Illustrative Sketch:**

George Mueller was a great man of faith in the Nineteenth Century. His ministry promoted faith-based evangelism projects that spanned seven decades of service for God. He traveled to over 40 countries in his work, served 17 years on a missionary assignment, beginning at 70 years of age, and is said to have read his Bible 200 times. His work included Bible distribution, missionary support, religious tract and book distributions, and the development of schools for children and adults to teach the Bible. However, he is best remembered for his efforts to house and clothe homeless orphans.

When he began this work in 1834, there was room for only 3,600 orphans in all of England's orphanages, and over 7000 children under eight years of age were in prison. By the end of his life, George built five large orphan houses, cared for over 10,000 orphans, and led over 3000 of them to accept Jesus as their personal Savior. Mr. Mueller's actions of reform consequently inspired England to build orphanages for 100,000 more children.

It was George's praying ministry that gave him real spiritual strength. He did not believe institutions should go into debt, and his faith experiences proved it down through the decades. He never took out a loan or went into debt. Money was usually in short supply for his various projects, but the heavenly Father always provided for the needs of George's ministry, and the orphans never went without food. He never took a salary during the last 68 years of his ministry, and trusted God to impress people to send him what he needed. While hundreds of thousands of dollars were donated to his causes, he never directly asked anyone for money.

One amazing example of his prayer life is illustrated in the following experience. Early one morning during a trip to America the ship on which he was sailing encountered heavy fog. When the mists

---

96   White, 96.

did not clear, the captain informed his passengers that because of the treacherous iceberg-filled waters ahead, he must stop the ship for lack of visibility. But, George Mueller told the captain that he needed to reach America on schedule for a speaking appointment. He went to his quarters below to pray for clear weather. The captain joined him, and when George had finished his simple prayer, the captain offered to pray, too.

"That won't be necessary," George informed the captain. "In the first place, you don't really believe God can do it for us, so our time is wasted. In the second place, the skies have already cleared. And when the two of them went on deck, the captain found it was true. Blue skies were everywhere, without a trace of the fog that had so recently crippled their voyage.[97]

Truly faith was the key that unlocked heaven's storehouses for George Mueller. He spent much time in prayer, a habit that gave him wisdom to deal with the challenges of his ministry, strength to endure hardship, and courage to stand faithfully for God during good times and bad.

*"'If you ask anything in My name, I will do it.'" John 14:14. "But these [things] are written that you may believe that Jesus is the Christ, the Son of God, and that believing you may have life in His name." John 20:31.*

Abide with me; fast falls the eventide;
    The darkness deepens; Lord, with me abide.
When other helpers fail and comforts flee,
    Help of the helpless, O abide with me.

I need thy presence every passing hour.
    What but thy grace can foil the tempter's power?
Who, like thyself, my guide and stay can be?
    Through cloud and sunshine, Lord, abide with me.

---

97  Basil Miller, *George Mueller: Man of Faith and Miracles* (Grand Rapids, MI: Bethany House, 1972).

I fear no foe, with thee at hand to bless;
    Ills have no weight, and tears not bitterness.
Where is death's sting? Where, grave, thy victory?
    I triumph still, if thou abide with me.

Swift to its close ebbs out life's little day;
    Earth's joys grow dim; its glories pass away;
Change and decay in all around I see;
    O thou who changest not, abide with me.

       —Henry F. Lyte, "Abide With Me"

**Walk and Talk With God—Reading #4**

"Unceasing prayer is the unbroken union of the soul with God, so that life from God flows into our life; and from our life, purity and holiness flow back to God.

"There is necessity for diligence in prayer; let nothing hinder you. Make every effort to keep open the communion between Jesus and your own soul. Seek every opportunity to go where prayer is wont to be made. Those who are really seeking for communion with God will be seen in the prayer meeting, faithful to do their duty and earnest and anxious to reap all the benefits they can gain. They will improve every opportunity of placing themselves where they can receive the rays of light from heaven.

"We should pray in the family circle, and above all we must not neglect secret prayer, for this is the life of the soul. It is impossible for the soul to flourish while prayer is neglected. Family or public prayer alone is not sufficient. In solitude let the soul be laid open to the inspecting eye of God. Secret prayer is to be heard only by the prayer-hearing God. No curious ear is to receive the burden of such petitions. In secret prayer the soul is free from surrounding influences, free from excitement. Calmly, yet fervently, will it reach out after God. Sweet and abiding will be the influence emanating from Him who seeth in secret, whose ear is open to hear the prayer arising from the heart. By calm, simple faith the soul holds communion with God and gathers to itself rays of divine light to strengthen and sustain it in the conflict with Satan. God is our tower of strength.

"Pray in your closet, and as you go about your daily labor let your heart be often uplifted to God. It was thus that Enoch walked with God. These silent prayers rise like precious incense before the throne of grace. Satan cannot overcome him whose heart is thus stayed upon God.

There is no time or place in which it is inappropriate to offer up a petition to God. There is nothing that can prevent us from lifting up our hearts in the spirit of earnest prayer. In the crowds of the street, in the midst of a business engagement, we may send up a petition to God and plead for divine guidance, as did Nehemiah when he made his request before King Artaxerxes. A closet of communion may be found wherever we are. We should have the door of the heart open continually and our invitation going up that Jesus may come and abide as a heavenly guest in the soul.

"Although there may be a tainted, corrupted atmosphere around us, we need not breathe its miasma, but may live in the pure air of heaven. We may close every door to impure imaginings and unholy thoughts by lifting the soul into the presence of God through sincere prayer. Those whose hearts are open to receive the support and blessing of God will walk in a holier atmosphere than that of earth and will have constant communion with heaven." [98]

**Illustrative Sketch:**
O Master, let me walk with Thee,
    As Enoch walked in days of old.
Place thou my trembling hand in Thine,
    And sweet communion with Thee hold.
Still thou the raging of the sea,
    Oh Master let me walk with Thee.

—Washington Gladden, "O Master, Let Me Walk With Thee"

Enoch is one of the most famous characters in biblical history, but who was he, really? Was he just a holy patriarch, the seventh in line from Adam, a man of great faith, and a prophet predicting the end of the world? He warned angry crowds in his day that a flood of waters

98   White, 98.

would one day destroy the planet, and he even prophesied the second coming of Jesus "with ten thousand of His saints." Jude v. 14.

To be sure Enoch was a man out of time and place, a misfit in a world gone crazy with wickedness. He was a man after God's own heart and must have had sterling qualities of character, for he was in constant communion with heaven. Daily he walked and talked with the Giver of life, drawing ever nearer heaven's gates, until God finally took him permanently into His presence.

Imagine what it must have been like to see such an event! Enoch's story wasn't a case of mysterious disappearance leaving everyone to wonder where he had gone. In fact, many were present to see the amazing phenomenon. Maybe it was in a public place, a city market on the outskirts of a coastal town. Quite a crowd might have gathered in the narrow street among the scattered vendors' stalls and piles of produce. Members of the Seth clan were present, no doubt Methuselah among them, but most of the listeners were probably nonbelievers.

As usual Enoch had been preaching against the world's increasing wickedness, and pleading with folks to turn back to God. Once again, he prophesied that if the world didn't repent of its evil ways, God would bring terrible judgments on the world.

Many in the crowd had been drinking, and at mention of God and his Divine judgments, they grew angry. A mob quickly formed and began to shout at Enoch. Some picked up bricks to throw at him, and others threatened to run him through with blades of steel.

"This is the last warning I'll be bringing!" Enoch stood his ground. "Hear me, my brothers! You are a perverted generation of stiff-necked people! You cannot hear the voice of God because your sins are an abomination to the Lord and have come between you and Him!"

The infuriated crowd could stand no more! Their eyes blazed red as they ground their teeth in a blinding rage. Instinctively, they clambered over one another to get to Enoch.

Then the unexpected happened, and the crowd fell back in surprise and fear! Suddenly Enoch's face was shining with a light like the noonday sun, and his clothes flashed and sparkled with a thousand bits of iridescent light. He raised a hand to point directly at the guilty crowd. "Like your fathers in ages past, you have always resisted the Holy Spirit! How many of God's messengers have you refused to obey! Which of

EVERY DAY WITH JESUS

the holy patriarchs have you not persecuted? The clans of Seth have instructed you, but you have not listened or cared! The holy angels of God have given you ample warning, but still you rush on blindly!"

By now the crowd was cowering on the ground, too frightened to move, but too riveted to turn away. Enoch stared into the blue of the sky, and it seemed he was looking straight into heaven. His eyes took on a strange light now, and he appeared to be lost in vision. "Hear now! I have given you fair warning! The day of the Lord is coming when neither forest nor mountain will be left to you for refuge. Like a thief in the night the day of reckoning will descend upon you as a flood of waters. In that day you will search for the Lord, but you will not find Him because you have rejected Him from ruling over you!"

A stiff wind suddenly began to build in the marketplace, kicking up dust on the street! It whipped its way through the crowd and vendor's stalls, sending baskets and clothing in every direction! The rushing current of air spun like a whirlwind as though it would seize the soul of every man present.

Enoch stood on the vegetable crate where he had been preaching. His arms were raised to the sky, his tunic snapping and whipping in the wind around his body. The look on his face was that of an angel's, and he was calling, "I see heaven opened and the Lord standing at the right hand of God Almighty!" Then a flash of light streaked down to that little marketplace and caught the prophet up in its glorious grasp. It never slowed its pace as it continued on its way in an arc of light that curved heavenward and out of sight somewhere among the clouds.[99]

*"Enoch walked faithfully with God; then he was no more, because God took him away." Genesis 5:24 NIV.*

**When You Call I Will Answer—Reading #5**
"We need to have more distinct views of Jesus and a fuller comprehension of the value of eternal realities. The beauty of holiness is to fill the hearts of God's children; and that this may be accomplished, we should seek for divine disclosures of heavenly things.

---

99  Based on Ellen G. White, "Enoch" in *Patriarchs and Prophets* (Mountain View, CA: Pacific Press Publishing Association, 1943).

"Let the soul be drawn out and upward, that God may grant us a breath of the heavenly atmosphere. We may keep so near to God that in every unexpected trial our thoughts will turn to Him as naturally as the flower turns to the sun.

"Keep your wants, your joys, your sorrows, your cares, and your fears before God. You cannot burden Him; you cannot weary Him. He who numbers the hairs of your head is not indifferent to the wants of His children. *"... The Lord is very compassionate and merciful."* *James 5:11.* His heart of love is touched by our sorrows and even by our utterances of them. Take to Him everything that perplexes the mind. Nothing is too great for Him to bear, for He holds up worlds, He rules over all the affairs of the universe. Nothing that in any way concerns our peace is too small for Him to notice.

"There is no chapter in our experience too dark for Him to read; there is no perplexity too difficult for Him to unravel. No calamity can befall the least of His children, no anxiety harass the soul, no joy cheer, no sincere prayer escape the lips, of which our heavenly Father is unobservant, or in which He takes no immediate interest. *"He heals the brokenhearted, and binds up their wounds."* *Psalm 147:3.* The relations between God and each soul are as distinct and full as though there were not another soul upon the earth to share His watch care, not another soul for whom He gave His beloved Son.

"Jesus said, *"'You will ask in My name, and I do not say to you that I shall pray the Father for you; for the Father Himself loves you.'"* *"'I chose you... that whatever you ask the Father in My name He may give you.'"* John 16:26, 27; 15:16.* But to pray in the name of Jesus is something more than a mere mention of that name at the beginning and the ending of a prayer. It is to pray in the mind and spirit of Jesus, while we believe His promises, rely upon His grace, and work His works." [100]

## Illustrative Sketch:

Koffi sat on his bed in the dormitory room staring out the window, the letter still in his hand. What should he do? The letter plainly said he was to come home. His mother was very ill, and the chances of her recovering were decreasing every day. If she should die, and he didn't see her one last time, that would be a shameful, unforgiveable thing. African

---

100 White, *Steps to Christ*, 99.

culture required that he go home to his village and his family immediately, to pay his proper respects while his mother was still living. That was the problem. He had no money, and no hope of getting any soon.

He put his head in his hands. What was he to do? His job as a colporteur selling religious books didn't pay much. In fact, sometimes he had to go weeks without pay of any kind. Right now he was in the coastal capital of Abidjan, Cote d'Ivoire, West Africa, studying at the literature evangelism seminary. Mornings he listened to lectures from his instructors about how to give Bible studies and how to preach sermons. That was the intention of the seminary—to teach young men to be evangelists by selling truth-filled books, giving Bible studies, and running evangelistic campaigns.

Afternoons Koffi and the other young men at the seminary usually went out to sell books and Bibles to folks on the street. He hadn't had much financial success lately. People were interested in the books, and sometimes they even purchased one or two, but no one had paid him for the sales he made during the previous week. He needed to revisit these homes, deliver the books, and try to collect the money.

He was in desperate straits. He needed cash to go see his mother and to get home on a bus cost 3000 Ivorian CFA, an equivalent of about ten dollars. But it might as well have been 30,000 CFA for all the chance there was that he was going to be able to raise that amount. Right now he had nothing!

He realized that he had not yet prayed about his problem. God could help him. Koffi had just read about this very kind of problem in his Bible that morning. "With God all things are possible." Matthew 19:26. God could give him the money to go home, or He could help him sell books to earn the travel money, or He could help his mother get well so Koffi wouldn't have to go home at all. God had a thousand ways to solve all of Koffi's problems, and this one was no different.

Dropping to his knees by his bed, he poured out his heart to God in simple faith. "I'm sorry I didn't bring this to you in prayer earlier," he said, bowing his head. "You own the cattle on a thousand hills, Lord, and this problem is just a tiny one for You. I know that prayer is the key to unlock heaven's storehouse. Please forgive me for my lack of faith. Help me to find a solution for this problem, to get some money so I can go see my mother. And bless her that she will be well soon." And with that Koffi snatched up his satchel to go out for an afternoon with his books. He would do his part, so that God could do His.

All that afternoon he visited with interested folks who loved his books. No one had money for the books, but one family did ask him to explain some important truths from the Bible. His session with the family ran long and before he realized it, the sun was going down. It was time to go home.

"Thank you Lord, for helping me to find a family that is seeking Your face," he prayed excitedly, as he walked back to the seminary. And then he remembered that he still had no money for bus fare back to his village. "But God will provide," he tried to console himself. "He always has, and He won't fail me now."

When he arrived back at the seminary, he found the small cafeteria empty. The evening meal was over and there was no food left except a little rice in the pot. He sat down to eat it and feel a little bit sorry for himself. He hadn't made any sales that day, he had no money to travel to see his mother, and now he had all but missed the evening meal.

Suddenly however, Alima, the seminary director's wife came in. "Koffi, I didn't hear you arrive," she smiled. "It's good to see you got home safely. Oh, and by the way, a letter arrived for you this afternoon. She brought the letter to Koffi and watched as he opened the envelope. He was shocked when 3000 CFA fell out, but he could only stare at it in surprise because he had no words for the feeling that came over him at that moment. "Thank you, Lord," was all he could say as he bowed his head reverently for several long minutes. "Who brought the money?" he finally asked Alima.

"A missionary lady from the Cocody Adventist Church," she replied. "Mrs. Chantel. She said she felt impressed that you needed some money so she brought it by."

"Praise God!" Koffi's eyes were shining in gratefulness. "How could she know that I needed exactly 3000 CFA?" His mind was in a whirl, but Alima had no answers, and Koffi had to make preparations to go home now anyway.

The next morning Koffi left, and thankfully was in his village by late afternoon. He spent a wonderful week with his mother during which time she recovered nicely, and then he returned to Abidjan in time for church the coming Sabbath.

During the service that day he stood up to give his testimony, and the church resounded with fervent amen's. Then Mrs. Chantel shared that she had had a dream in which she saw Koffi specifically, and that he needed money for some problem. Her dream didn't show her the details, but she decided to help him.

Overcome with emotion Koffi and the entire church bowed their heads as the pastor thanked God for this manifestation of His Spirit among them. Prayer had indeed been the key to unlock heaven's storehouse.[101]

*"'... When you pray, go into your room, and when you have shut your door, pray to your Father who is in the secret place; and your Father who sees in secret will reward you openly.'"* *Matthew 6:6.*

Whisper a prayer in the morning,
    Whisper a prayer at noon.
Whisper a prayer in the evening,
    To keep your heart in tune.

God answers prayer in the morning,
    God answers prayer at noon.
God answers prayer in the evening.
    To keep your heart in tune.

—Author unknown, "Whisper A Prayer in the Morning"

## Speak Lord—Reading #6

"God does not mean that any of us should become hermits or monks and retire from the world in order to devote ourselves to acts of worship. The life must be like Christ's life—between the mountain and the multitude. He who does nothing but pray will soon cease to pray, or his prayers will become a formal routine. When men take themselves out of social life, away from the sphere of Christian duty and cross bearing; when they cease to work earnestly for the Master, who worked earnestly for them, they lose the subject matter of prayer and have no incentive to devotion. Their prayers become personal and selfish. They

---

101 My family was involved in this incident in the Ivory Coast, West Africa in 1992.

cannot pray in regard to the wants of humanity or the upbuilding of Christ's kingdom, pleading for strength wherewith to work.

"We sustain a loss when we neglect the privilege of associating together to strengthen and encourage one another in the service of God. The truths of His word lose their vividness and importance in our minds. Our hearts cease to be enlightened and aroused by their sanctifying influence, and we decline in spirituality. In our association as Christians we lose much by lack of sympathy with one another. He who shuts himself up to himself is not filling the position that God designed he should. The proper cultivation of the social elements in our nature brings us into sympathy with others and is a means of development and strength to us in the service of God.

"If Christians would associate together, speaking to each other of the love of God and of the precious truths of redemption, their own hearts would be refreshed and they would refresh one another. We may be daily learning more of our heavenly Father, gaining a fresh experience of His grace; then we shall desire to speak of His love; and as we do this, our own hearts will be warmed and encouraged. If we thought and talked more of Jesus, and less of self, we should have far more of His presence.

"If we would but think of God as often as we have evidence of His care for us we should keep Him ever in our thoughts and should delight to talk of Him and to praise Him. We talk of temporal things because we have an interest in them. We talk of our friends because we love them; our joys and our sorrows are bound up with them. Yet we have infinitely greater reason to love God than to love our earthly friends; it should be the most natural thing in the world to make Him first in all our thoughts, to talk of His goodness and tell of His power.

"The rich gifts He has bestowed upon us were not intended to absorb our thoughts and love so much that we should have nothing to give to God; they are constantly to remind us of Him and to bind us in bonds of love and gratitude to our heavenly Benefactor. We dwell too near the lowlands of earth. Let us raise our eyes to the open door of the sanctuary above, where the light of the glory of God shines in the face of Christ, who *"... is able also to save to the uttermost those who come to God through Him ..." Hebrews 7:25.*"[102]

---

102 White, 101.

**Illustrative Sketch:**

Simon bowed his head dejectedly and laid his hand on the Holy Book. He loved God with all his heart. He loved his time in prayer each day with the Lord, and he loved his Bible, but he felt cursed! How could he really teach the Bible to his children properly when he couldn't read? He was a grown man, an intelligent chap, and an elder in the local church. But he couldn't read. Never had been able to, and it had brought him no end of troubles. When he was giving Bible studies to interested folks in town, they would sometimes ask where verses of Scripture could be found. He could quote the verses for them, and he could point them out, but he couldn't read them. In church he was often asked to read the verses for the divine service, but he had to have the verses ahead of time in order to make sure they were memorized properly. He knew his Bible well, so most folks didn't know of his problem, but it bothered him just the same.

Many a time he had prayed that God would somehow remove this thorn from his flesh, but he had no idea how God might do this. He was too old to go to school, and even his son's attempts to teach him the basics had failed.

One morning he prayed as he had a thousand times before on the veranda of his little bungalow. It was an early hour, and the sun was not yet peeking over the amber horizon of Jamaica's shimmering ocean to the east. "Lord, make me an instrument of Thy peace," he held his Bible in his hands. "If I can serve You without the skill of reading, let it be so. But if it is Your will, change this stubborn old mind and help me learn how to read. Thy will be done."

He contemplated that thought in silence, and then it was he heard the voice. Clear, resonant, and full of authority. "Take your Bible and go to the river," it said distinctly. Simon opened his eyes and glanced around him in the shadows of dawn. There was no one with him on the veranda, and yet he had undoubtedly heard a voice. He bowed his head again, closing his eyes momentarily. Was God trying to speak to him? Could it possibly be?

And then the voice came again, this time quite conspicuous in the quietness of the morning hour. "Take your Bible and go to the river." That was it. Nothing more, nothing less, and he knew he had to obey. Putting on his sandals he picked up his Bible and went through the house and out the back door. The way to the river bottom was still quite shadowy, but he knew it well. He'd been running this path since he was a barefoot boy.

When he reached the river, he sat down on a log and closed his eyes to pray. "Lord, what will you have me to do?" he held his Bible tight in his hands.

"Open your Bible to Genesis, chapter one," came the voice again loud and clear.

Simon turned the pages breathlessly, wondering at the voice so kind and full of purpose.

"Repeat the words after me, 'In—the—beginning.'"

Simon hesitated only a moment, and then traced the familiar line with his fingers, "In—the—beginning."

"God—created," the voice continued.

"God—created," Simon traced the words again with his fingers, repeating the letters and sounds as they passed before his eyes.

"the—heavens,"

"the—heavens," Simon kept going,

"and—the—earth."

"and—the—earth." Simon could not believe what was happening. The words and letters were fairly streaming along on the page, feeding into his brain, and he was remembering them by sound and sight. He was ecstatic hardly daring to breathe lest he awake and find it was all a dream!

But it was not a dream, and it was becoming more and more clear to him this was instead a miracle of the most wonderful sort!

The mysterious voice continued on reading the rest of the verses in chapter one, and as each verse passed, Simon was remembering words from previous verses. He was beginning to recognize the sounds and letters in sequence enough to repeat them on his own. It was a wonderfully, glorious experience, and by the time he finished with chapter one, he could read. He read chapter two, and then three, and he knew what the strange marks on the page were saying. He was tempted to believe that it couldn't be quite this easy, that it would be a temporary skill he would soon lose, but to his delight he found he did not forget.

Several times he went back to his Bible that day and found he could still read the words and sentences, and verses from new chapters, too.

It was astounding! It was magnificent! It was an amazing experience sent straight from heaven to cheer him in his humble life.[103] "*Call to Me, and I will answer you, and show you great and mighty things, which you do not know." Jeremiah 33:3.*

Open our eyes, Lord
    We want to see Jesus,
To reach out and touch Him,
    And say that we love Him.

Open our ears, Lord
    And help us to listen.
Open our eyes, Lord
    We want to see Jesus.

—Author unknown, "Open Our Eyes, Lord"

## The Science of Salvation—Reading #7

"We need to praise God more *"for His goodness, and for His wonderful works to the children of men." Psalm 107:8.* Our devotional exercises should not consist wholly in asking and receiving. Let us not be always thinking of our wants and never of the benefits we receive. We do not pray any too much, but we are too sparing of giving thanks. We are the constant recipients of God's mercies, and yet how little gratitude we express, how little we praise Him for what He has done for us.

"Anciently the Lord bade Israel, when they met together for His service, *"'You shall eat before the Lord your God, and you shall rejoice in all to which you have put your hand, you and your households, in which the Lord your God has blessed you.'" Deuteronomy 12:7.* That which is done for the glory of God should be done with cheerfulness, with songs of praise and thanksgiving, not with sadness and gloom.

"Our God is a tender, merciful Father. His service should not be looked upon as a heart-saddening, distressing exercise. It should be a

---

103 Isaac Lewis, as told to author in 2000. The man in the story is Isaac's father.

pleasure to worship the Lord and to take part in His work. God would not have His children, for whom so great salvation has been provided, act as if He were a hard, exacting taskmaster. He is their best friend; and when they worship Him, He expects to be with them, to bless and comfort them, filling their hearts with joy and love. The Lord desires His children to take comfort in His service and to find more pleasure than hardship in His work. He desires that those who come to worship Him shall carry away with them precious thoughts of His care and love, that they may be cheered in all the employments of daily life, that they may have grace to deal honestly and faithfully in all things.

"We must gather about the cross. Christ and Him crucified should be the theme of contemplation, of conversation, and of our most joyful emotion. We should keep in our thoughts every blessing we receive from God, and when we realize His great love we should be willing to trust everything to the hand that was nailed to the cross for us.

"The soul may ascend nearer heaven on the wings of praise. God is worshiped with song and music in the courts above, and as we express our gratitude we are approximating to the worship of the heavenly hosts. *"Whoever offers praise glorifies"* God. *Psalm 50:23.* Let us with reverent joy come before our Creator, with *"thanksgiving, and the voice of melody." Isaiah 51:3."* [104]

**Illustrative Sketch:**

The praise of heavenly music has always been a comfort to God's people. Through the ages of sacred history they have used it to cheer themselves and express heartfelt gratitude for the incredible blessings God lavishes on them. Miriam led the women in songs of praise on the shores of the Red Sea after the destruction of the Egyptian army. David played his harp and sang sweet songs in the royal palace to soothe King Saul's troubled spirit. Jesus' voice was heard singing in the streets of Nazareth when he was just a boy, and many a soul drew inspiration from it.

When Paul and Silas were on a missionary trip to Philippi, they were thrown into prison for healing a demon possessed woman. But, they didn't let that discourage them. Instead, they turned their jail time into a revival meeting.

---

104 White, 102.

---

"About midnight Paul and Silas were praying and singing hymns to God, and the other prisoners were listening to them. Suddenly there was such a violent earthquake that the foundations of the prison were shaken. At once all the prison doors flew open, and everybody's chains came loose. The jailer woke up, and when he saw the prison doors open, he drew his sword and was about to kill himself because he thought the prisoners had escaped. But Paul shouted, 'Don't harm yourself! We are all here!'

"The jailer called for lights, rushed in and fell trembling before Paul and Silas. He then brought them out and asked, 'Sirs, what must I do to be saved?' They replied, 'Believe in the Lord Jesus, and you will be saved—you and your household.' ... At that hour of the night the jailer took them and washed their wounds; then immediately he and all his family were baptized. The jailer brought them into his house and set a meal before them; he was filled with joy because he had come to believe in God—he and his whole family." Acts 16:25-34, NIV.

Praises to God certainly proved to be a positive force in lifting the spirits of Paul and Silas that night, and indeed a blessing to those who listened. Instead of complaining, the two missionaries found reasons to be happy as they witnessed for Jesus.

During times of spiritual darkness in Medieval Europe the Waldenses suffered much for the sake of the gospel, but they also learned to use music to cheer them on their spiritual journey. It was a time of castles and moats and Knights of the Round Table, a time of poverty and disease when men were so poor that they could be bought and sold with the land they farmed. It was an era of great ignorance and superstition.

When persecution arose against the Waldenses because of their faith, they fled to the mountain valleys of the Alps. Behind the lofty bulwarks of these ancient summits the Waldenses found a hiding place where they could practice their religion and raise their families according to conscience. Here the light of truth was passed from generation to generation, and when times were darkest, the keepers of God's flame were encouraged by reciting passages of Scripture put to music that had been with them for a thousand years. Often, one could hear the people going to and from their work with a song on their lips. Mothers taught their children great Bible truths by putting the words to music, and hymns of faith were a part of the simple worship services held in the fortresses of the mountains.

When religious persecution arose again, this time reaching into the mountain valleys, the Waldenses fled into the forests and caves of the highest peaks. They were hunted nearly to extinction, and though they suffered the worst that Satan could plot against them, still their voices were heard in praise to God.

Sometimes we may be tempted to doubt God's goodness, but we must remember that a song of praise can do wonders to lift the cloud of doom that surrounds us. Music inspired by the Spirit of God can give us energy to stand for Jesus and make us fit to sing with the angel choirs. When Jesus comes again, and we finally reach the celestial shore, we will sing a new song on a very old topic, and the science of salvation will be its central theme.

> Blessed assurance, Jesus is mine!
>> Oh, what a foretaste of glory divine!
> Heir of salvation, purchase of God,
>> Born of His Spirit, washed in His blood.
>
> Perfect submission, perfect delight,
>> Visions of rapture now burst on my sight;
> Angels, descending, bring from above
>> Echoes of mercy, whispers of love.
>
> Perfect submission, all is at rest,
>> I in my Savior am happy and blest,
> Watching and waiting, looking above,
>> Filled with His goodness, lost in His love.
>
> This is my story, this is my song,
>> Praising my Savior all the day long;
> This is my story, this is my song,
>> Praising my Savior all the day long.
>
> —Frances J. Crosby, "Blessed Assurance, Jesus Is Mine"

# CHAPTER 12

# What to Do With Doubt

**All Thing Work Together for Good—Reading #1**

"Many, especially those who are young in the Christian life, are at times troubled with the suggestions of skepticism. There are in the Bible many things which they cannot explain, or even understand, and Satan employs these to shake their faith in the Scriptures as a revelation from God. They ask, "How shall I know the right way? If the Bible is indeed the word of God, how can I be freed from these doubts and perplexities?"

"God never asks us to believe, without giving sufficient evidence upon which to base our faith. His existence, His character, the truthfulness of His word, are all established by testimony that appeals to our reason; and this testimony is abundant. Yet God has never removed the possibility of doubt. Our faith must rest upon evidence, not demonstration. Those who wish to doubt will have opportunity; while those who really desire to know the truth will find plenty of evidence on which to rest their faith.

"It is impossible for finite minds fully to comprehend the character or the works of the Infinite One. To the keenest intellect, the most highly educated mind, that holy Being must ever remain clothed in mystery. *"Can you search out the deep things of God? Can you find out the limits of the Almighty? They are higher than heaven—what can you do? … What can you know?" Job 11:7, 8.*

"The apostle Paul exclaims, *"Oh the depth of the riches both of the wisdom and knowledge of God! How unsearchable are His judgments, and His ways past finding out!" Romans 11:33.* But though *"clouds and darkness surround Him, righteousness and judgment are the foundation of His throne." Psalm 97:2.* We can so far comprehend His dealings with us, and the motives by which He is actuated, that we may discern boundless love and mercy united to infinite power. We can understand as much of His purposes as it is for our good to know; and beyond this we must still trust the hand that is omnipotent, the heart that is full of love." [105]

**Illustrative Sketch:**

"Cornelius, have you given your two sons the Hezekiah Woodbridge test yet?" the railroad president lowered his reading glasses, to stare at his son at a desk nearby. "Cyrus has real strength of character, but I'm afraid I can't say the same for Conrad. He seems to be quite stuck on himself, and lacking in self-discipline. Undesirable, I say! Quite undesirable!"

Cornelius glanced up at his father. "Quite right! I suppose I should be getting to it."

"Well it is a family tradition worth keeping, you know."

"I'll make the plans right away," Cornelius smiled at the railroad tycoon!

"Good. You know your boys, so make it a tough one like I did for you! Cyrus will do well, but Cornelius?" the railroad boss frowned again and put his reading glasses back on. "Say, why don't you do it this coming Thursday?" he suddenly added. "That way the boys can go with us on our inspection tour around the country. That should be reward enough, don't you think?"

"What a splendid idea!" Cornelius smiled again at his father's enthusiasm.

And so on Thursday morning after breakfast Cyrus Woodbridge was called to his father's library. He was a bright-eyed lad of fifteen, and intelligent in every way, it seemed. "I've got a job for you," his father said, "but I don't have time to explain the directions. Please take this packet and follow its instructions to the letter. Do I have your word of honor that you'll do this?"

Cyrus had plans for the day, since it was the first week of summer vacation, but then he saw the look in his father's eye. "Alright sir, I'll do it." The boy went to his room and opened the large packet. Inside it were many smaller envelopes numbered in order. He pulled out a letter

105 White, 105.

that read, "Go to the Westchester Library and open envelope number one. Be sure to keep the contents of all envelopes secure." Cyrus whistled, "Well, I guess that ends my plans for today," he hesitated only a moment, and then was off at a run. He hopped on a Westchester Avenue streetcar, and in fifteen minutes was at the library where he opened envelope number one.

"Head for the office of W.K. Crandon, room 503, ninth floor of the Norfolk Building on Elm Street. Check in by 9:30 am and ask for a letter addressed to Cornelius Woodbridge. You may read envelope number two when you get back on the elevator." Cyrus began to laugh. "What's this all about, he wondered? I'm all the way over here, and now I have to go back across town again? Oh well, I'd best do it! Father's got a reason for everything!"

Meanwhile, back at home Mr. Woodbridge had called for his older son, Cornelius. He was a tall lad of seventeen with a strong family resemblance, and a lazy manner about him. He leaned against the open doorway of his father's library, but didn't enter.

"I've got a task for you, Cornelius," the father was direct. "I need you to go on an errand for me, and it promises to be of possible inconvenience to you. I don't have time to give you instructions, but they are here in this envelope. Keep the business of its contents in the strictest confidence. Do I have your word of honor that you will do as I have asked to the last detail?"

The boy put on his glasses and reached for the envelope, but Mr. Woodbridge waited for his response. "You cannot look at the instructions until you have given me your word of honor."

"Well, I don't know, sir, that's asking much. How long will it take?"

"That's none of your concern," Mr. Woodbridge frowned. "Certainly no more time than I would expect of any messenger I hire."

Something in his father's voice made Cornelius stand up straighter. "I'll go," he replied almost wearily. "On my word of honor," he slowly added.

"Here's the instructions then," Mr. Woodbridge handed his older son the envelope. "Read them before you leave." The instructions told him to go to a remote suburb within forty minutes.

By now Cyrus was on another assignment. His instructions had told him to "Take a streetcar to K Street, transfer to Kentucky Avenue, and then go on out to Balder Flats. Find the corner of North and Kensington Streets before opening envelope number three."

"What is going on!" Cyrus was clearly annoyed as he tore open the next envelope. "Take the underground train to Clarke Street Station," it said. "Then proceed to the Daily Tribune office, and pick up a copy of yesterday's newspaper. While there open envelope number four."

"This is getting ridiculous!" he almost shouted. "What is father thinking? Is this some kind of a joke?" He looked at the large packet of unopened envelopes. "It would be easy enough to just open the whole bunch of 'em and see what this is all about," he mumbled, but he realized that would be breaking his word to his father.

Next he was sent up a fourteen-story building where the elevator was out of order. Then he was ordered twice across town again, with one of the stops at a Café on Webster Square. He took a seat hungrily, but before he could order lunch, a waitress brought him a card from his father which sent him downtown to hear a lecture by a famous scientist. Disappointed, he left the café and headed for the lecture hall, but half way through the lecture the next envelope sent him to a football field four miles away. However, before the game got started, the next message called him away again. All afternoon he raced back and forth across the city, once to his house, and then away again, all the while growing more tired with every trip. There seemed no purpose behind any of this, except maybe to test his patience and endurance. Several times he wanted to cheat on the directions and take shortcuts, but he remembered his promise to his father.

The last envelope, number twenty, ordered him to "go to Humboldt Street Station, B&O Railroad, arriving no later than 8:10. To his surprise when he arrived he was asked by a porter to give him all the things he had collected that day—the card from the café, the lecture coupon, the newspaper. Then he was escorted to his grandfather's private railroad car.

"Cyrus, my boy," his father and grandfather greeted him with a smile, "You have passed the famous Hezekiah Woodbridge Test, and you can be proud of it! Now you are to go with us on a trip through eighteen States and Mexico. Is that reward enough for the day's troubles?"

Cyrus could only grin because he was so very tired, but he noticed his grandfather searching the station platform as if waiting for someone else. Suddenly, the porter entered the train car again with an armful of envelopes. And as the train began to move and slowly pull away from the station, Conrad entered the car, too.

"You made it, young man!" grandfather congratulated his older grandson. "Welcome aboard," and they all headed off for a well-deserved meal in the dinner car. Only then did the two boys get a chance to talk, and Cyrus found out that his brother's regiment for the day was quite different from his own. Conrad spent the whole day in a little room at the top of a vacant building, with twelve trips down the stairs at specific times during the day to get envelopes from messengers sent his way. There was nothing to do, nothing to eat, and "I was so afraid I was going to fall asleep and miss one of my appointments," Conrad said in exasperation.

So, the first real test of their young lifetimes ended. The boys had not known what their father had in mind, but they did know they could trust him to do only what was good for them.[106] *"And we know that all things work together for good to those who love God, to those who are the called according to His purpose." Romans 8:28.*

**Born Again—Reading #2**

"The word of God, like the character of its divine Author, presents mysteries that can never be fully comprehended by finite beings. The entrance of sin into the world, the incarnation of Christ, regeneration, the resurrection, and many other subjects presented in the Bible, are mysteries too deep for the human mind to explain, or even fully to comprehend.

"But we have no reason to doubt God's word because we cannot understand the mysteries of His providence. In the natural world we are constantly surrounded with mysteries that we cannot fathom. The very humblest forms of life present a problem that the wisest of philosophers is powerless to explain. Everywhere are wonders beyond our ken. Should we then be surprised to find that in the spiritual world also

---

106 Grace S. Richmond, "Their Word of Honor," *Their Word of Honor and Other Stories* (Washington D. C.: Review and Herald Publishing Association, 1940), reprinted from *Youth's Companion*.

there are mysteries that we cannot fathom? The difficulty lies solely in the weakness and narrowness of the human mind. God has given us in the Scriptures sufficient evidence of their divine character, and we are not to doubt His word because we cannot understand all the mysteries of His providence.

"The apostle Peter says that there are in Scripture "... *things hard to understand, which untaught and unstable people twist to their own destruction." 2 Peter 3:16*. The difficulties of Scripture have been urged by skeptics as an argument against the Bible; but so far from this, they constitute a strong evidence of its divine inspiration. If it contained no account of God but that which we could easily comprehend; if His greatness and majesty could be grasped by finite minds, then the Bible would not bear the unmistakable credentials of divine authority. The very grandeur and mystery of the themes presented should inspire faith in it as the word of God.

"The Bible unfolds truth with a simplicity and a perfect adaptation to the needs and longings of the human heart, that has astonished and charmed the most highly cultivated minds, while it enables the humblest and uncultured to discern the way of salvation. And yet these simply stated truths lay hold upon subjects so elevated, so far-reaching, so infinitely beyond the power of human comprehension, that we can accept them only because God has declared them.

"Thus the plan of redemption is laid open to us, so that every soul may see the steps he is to take in repentance toward God and faith toward our Lord Jesus Christ, in order to be saved in God's appointed way; yet beneath these truths, so easily understood, lie mysteries that are the hiding of His glory—mysteries that overpower the mind in its research, yet inspire the sincere seeker for truth with reverence and faith. The more he searches the Bible, the deeper is his conviction that it is the word of the living God, and human reason bows before the majesty of divine revelation." [107]

**Illustrative Sketch:**

Harry Orchard was one of the most notorious assassins in American history, but his conversion story is a phenomenal testimony to what the Spirit of God can do to change the heart of a man.

[107 White, 106.]

During his crime spree from 1896 to 1905 he killed at least 20 people and wreaked untold damage to millions of dollars' worth of property. Harry became a specialist in crimes associated with labor union leaders, especially those who sought to gain more political power in the mining industry in the western part of the United States. He lived the life of a paid assassin and conducted his business without remorse or regret. By his standards any enemy of the labor unions was considered fair game—State Supreme Court justices, governors, and greedy mining officials.

Orchard was unorthodox in his methods. Instead shooting the victim, he used a trip wire on a bomb, or sometimes slow burning acid on blasting caps to trigger explosions. This gave him time to be somewhere else at the time the bomb exploded, so he could establish an alibi for himself if necessary.

However, when Mr. Orchard assassinated Frank Steunenberg in 1905, a former Governor of Idaho, the authorities suspected him. They tracked Harry down, captured him, convicted him, and sent him to prison for the rest of his life. When the trial was over, Governor Steunenberg's son visited Harry Orchard in prison and gave him some religious reading material. He said his mother wanted Harry to have the books and pamphlets because she thought he needed God. When Harry asked for a Bible, she sent him one, and eventually came several times to see him. She said she forgave Harry because Jesus had asked that we forgive our enemies.

Because of Mrs. Steunenberg's touching testimony and her spirit of kindness, Harry Orchard accepted Jesus as his personal Savior. The warden and guards could see that Harry was "born again", and when he asked to be baptized, they agreed to take him to the Boise, Idaho, Seventh-day Adventist church where he became a member in absentia.[108]

Does this amazing conversion story somehow do away with Harry's long list of crimes? Of course not, but it does spell out one very important message. We must never give up on anyone's salvation, no matter what they've done, or how bad we think they are. "'Man looks on the outward appearance, but the Lord looks on the heart.'" 1 Samuel 16:7.

---

108 Leroy Froom, *Harry Orchard, The Man God Made Again* (Mountain View, CA: Pacific Press Publishing Association, 1954).

That's exactly what God was thinking when He stopped Paul on the road to Damascus. Like Harry Orchard, Paul was zealous in his chosen cause. He was passionate in his persecution of the early Christian Church, but it was a misguided passion. He was not motivated by the Spirit of God, and that put him in enemy territory. As Paul neared Damascus on his journey, suddenly a light from heaven flashed around him. He fell to the ground and heard a voice say to him, "Saul, Saul, why do you persecute me? ... I am Jesus, whom you are persecuting. Now get up and go into the city, and you will be told what you must do."[109]

Paul became a new man! Completely changed under the commission issued by God Himself. "'This man is My chosen instrument to carry my name before the Gentiles and their kings and before the people of Israel. I will show him how much he must suffer for my name.'" *Acts 9:15, 16 NIV.* And truly he was a new man, born again by the power of the Holy Spirit.

> I hear the children playing
> And think of younger days,
> When I was just a child back then
> Still had my childish ways.
>
> The childhood years they come and go
> Like ashes in the wind,
> But simple faith of childhood days
> It can live on within.
>
> Born again—Born as a mother's child.
> Born again—A child of the King.
> Born again—Born for a brand new life.
> Born again—For what it may bring.
>
> I want to be a child again,
> But not as I was before,
> To have the faith of little ones,
> To trust Thee more and more.

109 Based on Acts 9:3-7.

To be a child of God again,
   A brother to the Son,
Will give me grace to live for Him,
   Oh Lord Thy will be done.

Born again—Born as a mother's child.
   Born again—A child of the King.
   Born again—Born for a brand new life.
   Born again—For what it may bring.

—Take Three

**Open My Eyes, Lord—Reading #3**

"To acknowledge that we cannot fully comprehend the great truths of the Bible is only to admit that the finite mind is inadequate to grasp the infinite; that man, with his limited, human knowledge, cannot understand the purposes of Omniscience.

"Because they cannot fathom all its mysteries, the skeptic and the infidel reject God's word; and not all who profess to believe the Bible are free from danger on this point. The apostle says, *"Beware, brethren, lest there be in any of you an evil heart of unbelief, in departing from the living God."* Hebrews 3:12. It is right to study closely the teachings of the Bible and to search into *"the deep things of God"* so far as they are revealed in Scripture. 1 Corinthians 2:10. While *"the secret things belong to the Lord our God, but those things which are revealed belong to us ..."* Deuteronomy 29:29.

"But it is Satan's work to pervert the investigative powers of the mind. A certain pride is mingled with the consideration of Bible truth, so that men feel impatient and defeated if they cannot explain every portion of Scripture to their satisfaction. It is too humiliating to them to acknowledge that they do not understand the inspired words. They are unwilling to wait patiently until God shall see fit to reveal the truth to them. They feel that their unaided human wisdom is sufficient to enable them to comprehend the Scripture, and failing to do this, they virtually deny its authority. It is true that many theories and doctrines popularly supposed to be derived from the Bible have no foundation in its teaching, and indeed are contrary to the whole tenor of inspiration. These things have been a cause of doubt and perplexity to many minds. They are not, however, chargeable to God's word, but to man's perversion of it.

"If it were possible for created beings to attain to a full understanding of God and His works, then, having reached this point, there would be for them no further discovery of truth, no growth in knowledge, no further development of mind or heart. God would no longer be supreme; and man, having reached the limit of knowledge and attainment, would cease to advance. Let us thank God that it is not so. God is infinite; in Him are *all the treasures of wisdom and knowledge.* *Colossians 2:3.* And to all eternity men may be ever searching, ever learning, and yet never exhaust the treasures of His wisdom, His goodness, and His power.

"God intends that even in this life the truths of His word shall be ever unfolding to His people. There is only one way in which this knowledge can be obtained. We can attain to an understanding of God's word only through the illumination of that Spirit by which the word was given. *No one knows the things of God except the Spirit of God.* *For the Spirit searches all things, yes, the deep things of God.* *1 Corinthians 2:11, 10.* And the Savior's promise to His followers was, *"When He, the Spirit of truth, has come, He will guide you into all truth... for He will take of what is Mine and declare it to you."* *John 16:13, 14.*"[110]

### Illustrative Sketch:

Lloyd Mitchell and his wife Jean owned a small farm near Spokane, Washington. The farm was a successful enterprise with a good crop each year, and a few head of livestock. They had avoided debt and felt financially secure. Life couldn't be better, but then tragedy struck.

One afternoon their son Leon came home with a pounding headache and felt quite sick. The next morning he felt even worse, so Lloyd and Jean took him to the doctor who admitted him to a hospital immediately. To their horror Leon was diagnosed with meningitis, a bacterial infection in the brain. Leon's condition worsened. The doctors said

110 White, 108.

the family should expect the worst. Treatment for meningitis in the 1950s was minimal, and soon Leon's life was teetering in the balance. Jean tried to be brave, but she finally broke down and cried in Leon's hospital room.

"Don't worry, Mom," he assured her. "I'll be alright. I'm not afraid to die," but she refused to be consoled. "Really, Mom, if I die, it will just be like I'm sleeping, and then when Jesus comes He'll resurrect me, and I'll live forever with Him in heaven."

Jean blinked back the tears, "Where are you getting all this stuff?" she asked wiping her eyes with a handkerchief.

"I've met this guy in the hospital who told me all about heaven and Jesus and what it's like to die. He's a nurse. We've been talking quite a bit, and we're the best of friends now. So really, Mom, don't worry about me. I'll be Okay."

Jean and Lloyd met Oscar, the nurse who had given their son such hope, and it gave them some comfort to hear the way he described the hereafter. But, it didn't soften the blow much when Leon died two days later. They were heartbroken, and life began to fall apart for them. Nothing was the same without their Leon.

Jean decided to go to church. Maybe it would help ease the pain. She chose a church near their house, but nothing brought them comfort or made sense at the church. The pastor explained that Leon was in heaven looking down on them. "I'm going to look these things up in the Bible myself," she told Lloyd. What she found greatly surprised her. She learned the truth about where people go when they die—exactly what Oscar had said. She learned other things too, like the truth about the seventh-day Sabbath, Jesus' second coming, and the eternal destruction of the wicked, not an eternally burning hell.

Excited about all this new information from the Bible, she shared it with Lloyd. Their search for a church that taught all these things led them to a Seventh-day Adventist Church where they were baptized a few weeks later.

Feeling the joy of a new found faith, and the desire to share it, Jean and Lloyd decided to go into missionary work full time. They sold their farm and moved to a small town along the coast of Oregon where they bought a little cottage. Since there was no Adventist church in the area, they devised a plan to share Jesus' love in their new community.

Jean was the brave one of the two who visited her neighbors. She studied the Bible with several of her new friends who were baptized by an Adventist pastor in another town. Within a few months a small company of believers sprang up, and then it grew big enough for them to rent space for a church.

But Satan wasn't happy about their newfound joy in witnessing. Tragedy struck again. One night when Lloyd was on the way home, a car hit him head on and nearly killed him. When Jean reached the hospital, she found her husband near death. He had several fractures on his skull, his jaw was broken, his ear disfigured, and his ribs and legs were broken. In fact, he had so many broken bones that the doctors could not understand how he had survived the accident. All they could do was shake their heads and try to prepare Jean for the worst.

But Jean wasn't ready to give up, and she called for their pastor to come and pray for Lloyd. She also wanted the pastor to anoint Lloyd, as the Bible suggests. "Is anyone among you sick? Let him call for the elders of the church, and let them pray over him, anointing him with oil in the name of the Lord." James 5:14. Several key people gathered for the special service, and they knelt in a circle around Lloyd as Pastor Jones prayed for him and anointed him. The group dispersed, and Jean went out for a walk to clear her head in the cool evening air. When she came back about an hour later, the nurse excitedly met her at the door.

"Your husband is asking for you," she looked like she had seen a ghost. "He says he's hungry and wants to eat."

Jean rushed into Lloyd's room where he was trying to sit up. He kept trying to pull tubes and bandages off his head and arms, worrying the nurse. "We need to wait for the doctor," she said. When the doctor came in, he was as shocked as the nurse. Everybody in the hospital came to see the miracle, and Jean was just beaming. "Praise God!" she kept saying. "Praise God for His goodness!"

Truly it was a miracle straight from heaven. God healed Lloyd. Lloyd and Jean had accepted the light of truth, stepped out in faith to witness for Jesus, and God had restored Lloyd to perfect health.[111]

---

111 Rose Slaybaugh, *Escape from Death* (Nashville: Southern Publishing Association, 1953).

Open mine eyes that I may see glimpses of Truth Thou hast for me.
Place in my hand the precious key that shall unclasp
and set me free.
Silently now I wait for Thee, ready my God Thy will to see.
Open mine eyes; illumine me, Spirit divine.

Open my ears that I may hear voices of Truth Thou sendest clear.
And while the glad notes fall on my ear, everything false
will disappear.

Open my mouth and let me bear gladly the Christ,
Truth everywhere.
Open my heart; let me prepare Love with Thy children
thus to share.

Silently now I wait for Thee, ready my God Thy will to see.
Open mine eyes; illumine me, Spirit divine.

—Charles H. Scott, "Open My Eyes That I May See"

**Stand Up for Jesus—Reading #4**

"God desires man to exercise his reasoning powers; and the study of the Bible will strengthen and elevate the mind as no other study can. Yet we are to beware of deifying reason, which is subject to the weakness and infirmity of humanity. If we would not have the Scriptures clouded to our understanding, so that the plainest truths shall not be comprehended, we must have the simplicity and faith of a little child, ready to learn, and beseeching the aid of the Holy Spirit. A sense of the power and wisdom of God, and of our inability to comprehend His greatness, should inspire us with humility, and we should open His word, as we would enter His presence, with holy awe. When we come to the Bible, reason must acknowledge an authority superior to itself, and heart and intellect must bow to the great I AM.

"There are many things apparently difficult or obscure, which God will make plain and simple to those who thus seek an understanding of them. But without the guidance of the Holy Spirit we shall be continually liable to wrest the Scriptures or to misinterpret them. There is much reading of the Bible that is without profit and in many cases a positive injury. When the word of God is opened without reverence and without prayer; when the thoughts and affections are not fixed upon God, or in harmony with His will, the mind is clouded with doubts; and in the very study of the Bible, skepticism strengthens. The enemy takes control of the thoughts, and he suggests interpretations that are not correct.

"Whenever men are not in word and deed seeking to be in harmony with God, then, however learned they may be, they are liable to err in their understanding of Scripture, and it is not safe to trust to their explanations. Those who look to the Scriptures to find discrepancies, have not spiritual insight. With distorted vision they will see many causes for doubt and unbelief in things that are really plain and simple.

"Disguise it as they may, the real cause of doubt and skepticism, in most cases, is the love of sin. The teachings and restrictions of God's word are not welcome to the proud, sin-loving heart, and those who are unwilling to obey its requirements are ready to doubt its authority. In order to arrive at truth, we must have a sincere desire to know the truth and a willingness of heart to obey it. And all who come in this spirit to the study of the Bible will find abundant evidence that it is God's word, and they may gain an understanding of its truths that will make them wise unto salvation.

"Christ has said, '*If anyone wills to do His will, he shall know concerning the doctrine.*' John 7:17. Instead of questioning and caviling concerning that which you do not understand, give heed to the light that already shines upon you, and you will receive greater light. By the grace of Christ, perform every duty that has been made plain to your understanding, and you will be enabled to understand and perform those of which you are now in doubt." [112]

**Illustrative Sketch:**
Adamu was a cotton farmer in Togo, West Africa, where a majority of people worship animals and spirits, and diseases like hepatitis,

---

112 White, 109.

malaria, and yellow fever are still considered dangerous enemies. Life was hard for him and his family, and he knew there had to be more to life than just farming and going through the motions of life.

When a traveling colporteur came through town selling religious books, Adamu became interested in his message and began studying the Bible. After he was baptized, he became a dynamic young Christian, and together with the colporteur and a local pastor, built a sizeable church group in the town of Natigou where he lived. Adamu's wife and his best friend Hassan were also brought to Jesus as a result of Bible studies and evangelistic crusades Adamu helped conduct in the community.

One of the greatest blessings for Adamu and his friends when they became Seventh-day Adventists was the good news of the Sabbath. As Adventists they could rest from all their labors, and appreciate a day to commune with their Heavenly Father.

The villagers raised two crops of cotton a year, but until the crop was sold, there was no money for extras. Money was usually tight. They survived on the vegetables and other basics they raised in their gardens.

Harvest time was always a good time with lots of hard work and a little money to put in their pockets for the coming year. Everyone turned out to help—grownups, kids, and the old folks, too. They walked the long rows dragging their large sacks behind them, snatching the cotton from the bolls, one ball at a time. When a sack was full, they took it to the sheds to be tied up in big bales of clean, white cotton. It usually took the village folks several days to pick the fields clean.

But, one year at harvest time a real test of faith came for Adamu and the other Adventist Christians in the village of Natigou. When the cotton had all been picked and tied up into bales, a government agricultural representative came to town to announce arrangements for the purchase and transport of their cotton. A big truck was scheduled to arrive in two weeks on November 21.

However, when Adamu and his good friend Hassan saw the date on the form the purchasing agent gave them, they realized the 21st of November fell on Saturday. For them this was big trouble! None of the Adventists would be able to do business with the government agent on that day. "The seventh day is the Sabbath, God's holy day," Adamu told Hassan, "and we must honor it." If they didn't sell their cotton to the agent when he came, they would have to wait until the next harvest when the trucks returned.

Adamu called a special meeting that night. There were 16 families in the church who were cotton farmers. Worried, they debated the issue for several hours that night, with some arguing one thing and some another. Finally, Adamu advised everyone to pray about it and wait to make their decision until the church service on the coming Sabbath.

He and Hassan knew this was going to be a real struggle for many of the farmers who couldn't afford to wait, and they prayed for their fellow church members. When Sabbath came, there was much debate again, but most of the people felt this case was an exception. They would sell their cotton to the government agent on the appointed day. It would only take a few minutes to complete the transaction. Adamu and Hassan begged everyone to give their decision some more thought, to consider the importance of the Sabbath and their vows at baptism to honor the Sabbath.

The week flew by and the dreaded day finally arrived. Adamu, Hassan, and three other families decided to go to church as usual and let God take care of them and their cotton. The rest of the members hauled their cotton out to the road to await the arrival of the big truck. The morning passed and the members along the road could hear their fellow Adventists down the road, singing the familiar hymns of worship.

Noon came and went. The worshipping Adventists finished their church service and went home, and still the truck hadn't come. By now the Adventist farmers waiting beside the road were wishing they had been true to their convictions, but still they waited.

Late in the afternoon a sudden rainstorm blew in without warning! Before the farmers could get their bales of cotton under cover, a downpour descended from the heavens, totally dousing their precious cotton! The cotton was damaged, and though the farmers opened the bales of cotton and tried to dry the cotton out after the rains had passed, it was obvious most of the cotton was ruined. Still the truck hadn't come. Discouraged the Adventist farmers finally went home, taking their damaged cotton and their guilty consciences with them.

The next morning before it was hardly light someone came running through the village announcing that the cotton truck was coming.

The five faithful Adventist families loaded their bales of cotton on carts and hauled them to the pick-up point, where the agent apologized for his late arrival. Several repairs to the truck the day before kept him from arriving on Saturday as previously scheduled. Adamu and the faithful few received a good price for their cotton, but when the rest of the villagers brought out their damaged, rain-soaked cotton, it sold for a pittance.

In the weeks and months that followed, times were hard for the villagers who sold the damaged cotton. It was a reminder to all that faithfulness to God is of great importance, and honoring the Sabbath indeed brings the promise of spiritual and material blessings.[113]

"'*If you turn away your foot from the Sabbath, from doing your pleasure on My holy day, and call the Sabbath a delight, The holy day of the Lord honorable, And shall honor Him, not doing your own ways, Nor finding your own pleasure, Nor speaking your own words, Then you shall delight yourself in the Lord; And I will cause you to ride on the high hills of the earth, and feed you with the heritage of Jacob your father. The mouth of the Lord has spoken.'*"Isaiah 58:13, 14.

**My Redeemer Is Faithful and True—Reading #5**

"There is an evidence that is open to all—the most highly educated, and the most illiterate—the evidence of experience. God invites us to prove for ourselves the reality of His word, the truth of His promises. He bids us '*taste and see that the Lord is good.*'" *Psalm 34:8.* Instead of depending upon the word of another, we are to taste for ourselves. He declares, "'*Ask, and you will receive.*'" *John 16:24.* His promises will be fulfilled. They have never failed; they never can fail. And as we draw near to Jesus, and rejoice in the fullness of His love, our doubt and darkness will disappear in the light of His presence.

"The apostle Paul says that God "*has delivered us from the power of darkness and conveyed us into the kingdom of the Son of His love.*" *Colossians 1:13.* And everyone who has passed from death unto life is able to "*certified that God is true.*" *John 3:33.* He can testify, "I needed help, and I found it in Jesus. Every want was supplied, the hunger of

---

113 Marenas DePaula, as told to author, 1991.

my soul was satisfied; and now the Bible is to me the revelation of Jesus Christ. Do you ask why I believe in Jesus? Because He is to me a divine Savior. Why do I believe the Bible? Because I have found it to be the voice of God to my soul." We may have the witness in ourselves that the Bible is true, that Christ is the Son of God. We know that we are not following cunningly devised fables.

"Peter exhorts his brethren to *"grow in the grace and knowledge of our Lord and Savior Jesus Christ." 2 Peter 3:18*. When the people of God are growing in grace, they will be constantly obtaining a clearer understanding of His word. They will discern new light and beauty in its sacred truths. This has been true in the history of the church in all ages, and thus it will continue to the end. *"The path of the just is like the shining sun, that shines ever brighter unto the perfect day." Proverbs 4:18*

"By faith we may look to the hereafter and grasp the pledge of God for a growth of intellect, the human faculties uniting with the divine, and every power of the soul being brought into direct contact with the Source of light. We may rejoice that all which has perplexed us in the providences of God will then be made plain, things hard to be understood will then find an explanation; and where our finite minds discovered only confusion and broken purposes, we shall see the most perfect and beautiful harmony. *"Now we see in a mirror, dimly, but then face to face. Now I know in part, but then I shall know just as I also am known." 1 Corinthians 13:12."*[114]

**Illustrative Sketch:**

There was a man in the Land of Uz whose name was Job. He was a pious man of influence, blameless and upright, one who feared God and spurned evil. He had seven sons and three daughters and in all the land were found no men so noble, no women so beautiful as the children of Job. And Job was exceedingly wealthy. His possessions included 7,000 sheep, 3,000 camels, 500 teams of oxen, and 500 donkeys. He also had many servants, a very large household, and was in fact the richest man in all the East. But troubling times were coming for Job, and his faith in God would be severely tested. He could not see the future, and it was just as well for him that he could not.

114 White, 111.

Now it happened one day while Job was sitting in judgment at the city gate that a messenger arrived all out of breath, with his clothes torn and dirt on his head. "I have bad news!" he bowed his head with grief. "The Sabeans have invaded the land and stolen all your teams of oxen that were plowing in the fields! They also ran off with the donkeys pasturing nearby, and killed all the farmhands, and I alone have escaped to tell you."

Job jumped to his feet in alarm. "How can this be!" he exclaimed. "We've always had good relations with the Sabeans!" but even as he spoke, another messenger came running in, his eyes wide with fear. He too was dressed in mourning.

"Lightening has struck and burned up your sheep and all the shepherds," he gasped, "but I'm the only one alive to bring the news!"

"Can it be true?" Job stammered. "I was with the shepherds just this morning, and all was well!" But there was more to come.

Within a few minutes a third messenger arrived in a state of panic with the latest news: "Three bands of Chaldean marauders have stolen your camels and killed your caravan drivers. I am the only one left to bring you the report!" the messenger was clearly in a state of shock.

Job had to steady himself, and others helped him sit down again on his judgment seat by the city gate. This was preposterous! How could all these bad things be happening in one day? He had suffered misfortune before, but never anything like this! But even as he was reeling from the latest of the three catastrophes, the worst news of all came! "Your sons and daughters were feasting in your oldest son's home," a fourth messenger began, and Job jumped to his feet in protest.

"No, please! Not my children! Tell me it isn't so!"

The messenger remained on his face in the dust and waited. "Master Job," he finally said with bitter tears, "It is as you say! The worst of news, and I am the sad bearer of the calamity! A wind storm has hit the house where your children were feasting! The house collapsed, and all is lost! Your children are dead!"

"All of them!" Job groaned in bewilderment, his eyes rolling back in his head.

"All of them!" tears ran freely down the messenger's dirt-streaked face. "I was at the feast, and I am the only one who remains to bring you the details!"

Job felt his head begin to spin. This was the end of all things! The world as he knew it was gone! The loss of his oxen, sheep and camels was bad enough, but the death of his children was a tragedy beyond compare! He was too stunned to speak, and his breath came in short rasping gasps, until he finally fell to the pavement in a dead faint. He awoke a few minutes later in his own bed at his estate, and his first thought was that the news had been a horrible dream. But as he saw the smitten looks of his servants, he knew it must be true. All was lost.

Job fell to the floor on his knees again, and tore his robe in grief. Then he took a razor and shaved his head. "Naked came I from my mother's womb," he prayed, "and naked I'll be when I leave this world. The Lord has given, and the Lord has taken away!" There was no stopping his tears now. "And yet, in spite of all this I cannot doubt the Lord is good!" he said with great sadness.

He continued on his knees in mourning for several days, but by the end of the week, more misfortune came his away. Ugly sores began forming all over his body until they became great oozing ulcers from the crown of his head to the soles of his feet. He was in great pain. To make matters worse, his wife finally came in to tell him what she thought of the whole thing. "Why don't you just curse God and be done with this life!" she wailed in anger and grief. "There's nothing more to live for anyway!"

Job understood that his wife's anguish had shattered her confidence in God, but he refused to relinquish his own faith experience. His friends came to share in his grief, but they did more damage than good. "God is not happy with you," one of them said, "He is punishing you for your sins." Another friend insisted, "You are too proud Job, and God is waiting for you to humble yourself before Him."

Job didn't know what to think, but he was sure that God was in control. "The wicked sometimes prosper and the righteous often suffer, but God is the great equalizer in the battle between good and evil," Job replied. "In the end evil will be punished and good will prevail. Good and bad folks will receive their just rewards. I don't know why God is allowing these events in my life, but I know my Redeemer lives, and even if I die, He will raise me up in the last resurrection. In that glad morning I will be justified and God's good name will be vindicated."

Job didn't understand everything about God, but in the end it was his faith that kept him trusting in God's goodness. God was pleased with Job. and the blessings of his latter days were more than his beginning. As our story ends, we read that he had 14,000 sheep, 6,000 camels, 1,000 teams of oxen, and 1,000 donkeys. He also was blessed with more children—seven sons and three daughters, and in all the land were none so noble, and none *so* beautiful as the children of Job. And Job served God all the days of his life, and he lived one hundred and forty years after his days of tribulation and saw his children and grandchildren *for* four generations.[115]

> I do not know oh Lord, why it should be Thy will
>> For me to bear so much heartache and pain.
> I do not know oh Lord, why it should be Thy will
>> For me to suffer loss when I had prayed for gain.
> But I do know Thou wilt not let me go
>> Thy way is always best, no matter what the test.
> And I do know if I but trust in Thee
>> All the darkness soon will pass, and I shall see
>
> I do not know oh Lord, why it should be Thy will
>> For me to walk this valley dark so lonesome drear
> I do not know oh Lord, why it should be Thy will
>> For me to turn from all the dreams I held so dear
> I do not know oh Lord, why it should be Thy will
>> Thy way is always best, no matter what the test.
> And I do know if I but trust in Thee
>> All the darkness soon will pass, and I shall see.

—Ruth Harms Calkin

---

115 Based on Job 1, 2, 42.

# CHAPTER 12

# Rejoicing in the Lord

**Have Faith Dear Friend in God—Reading #1**

"The children of God are called to be representatives of Christ, showing forth the goodness and mercy of the Lord. As Jesus has revealed to us the true character of the Father, so we are to reveal Christ to a world that does not know His tender, pitying love. "*As You sent Me into the world,*" said Jesus, "*I also have sent them into the world.*" "*I in them, and You in Me ... that the world may know that You have sent Me, and have loved them as You have loved Me.*" *John 17:18, 23.* The apostle Paul says to the disciples of Jesus, "*clearly you are an epistle of Christ,*" "*known and read by all men.*" *2 Corinthians 3:3, 2.*

"In every one of His children, Jesus sends a letter to the world. If you are Christ's follower, He sends in you a letter to the family, the village, the street, where you live. Jesus, dwelling in you, desires to speak to the hearts of those who are not acquainted with Him. Perhaps they do not read the Bible, or do not hear the voice that speaks to them in its pages; they do not see the love of God through His works. But if you are a true representative of Jesus, it may be that through you they will be led to understand something of His goodness and be won to love and serve Him.

"Christians are set as light bearers on the way to heaven. They are to reflect to the world the light shining upon them from Christ. Their life and character should be such that through them others will get a right conception of Christ and of His service.

"If we do represent Christ, we shall make His service appear attractive, as it really is. Christians who gather up gloom and sadness to their souls, and murmur and complain, are giving to others a false representation of God and the Christian life. They give the impression that God is not pleased to have His children happy, and in this they bear false witness against our heavenly Father.

"Satan is exultant when he can lead the children of God into unbelief and despondency. He delights to see us mistrusting God, doubting His willingness and power to save us. He loves to have us feel that the Lord will do us harm by His providences. It is the work of Satan to represent the Lord as lacking in compassion and pity. He misstates the truth in regard to Him. He fills the imagination with false ideas concerning God; and instead of dwelling upon the truth in regard to our heavenly Father, we too often fix our minds upon the misrepresentations of Satan and dishonor God by distrusting Him and murmuring against Him. Satan ever seeks to make the religious life one of gloom. He desires it to appear toilsome and difficult; and when the Christian presents in his own life this view of religion, he is, through his unbelief, seconding the falsehood of Satan."[116]

**Illustrative Sketch:**

Years ago when the West was being settled, a young Christian book salesman moved to the San Francisco area to try his hand at selling Bibles and religious books. We don't know his real name, so we'll call him Alex Clemson.

Reading material was scarce in those days and people were always on the lookout for good books, but times were hard. Because he hadn't had much success, Alex was disheartened. As Satan to discourage him more and more, he considered quitting the business.

One day he was getting on a streetcar when a stranger stepped up to him and asked what he did for a living. When he told the stranger he was a religious book salesman, the stranger asked him if he had been out to the Sacramento Valley.

"I can't say that I have," Alex replied.

"You should visit that valley someday," the stranger said. "You would do well there."

Alex tipped his hat. "Thank you," he said, "I'll keep that in mind." But the days and weeks passed, and Alex quite forgot the stranger on the streetcar. Then one day he was walking along the street when the same man stopped to chat.

116 White, 115.

"Have you been to the Sacramento Valley with your Bibles yet?" the stranger asked again.

"I'm sorry to say that I've not gone yet," Alex grinned sheepishly. "I've been so busy here in San Francisco, but I'm sure the valley must be a wonderful place to sell books. I'll try to make it out there as soon as I can," Alex shook the man's hand, and turned to go.

"By the way," Alex asked, once again turning to the stranger. "Do you have anyone specific that I should be looking for?" but the man was nowhere in sight. Alex looked both ways on the sidewalk and across the street too, but the man had vanished. There was only a high stone wall bordering the sidewalk, so it he couldn't have jumped over the wall, and it was too far in either direction for him to slip away that quickly. Alex shook his head in bewilderment as he continued on his way.

However, he couldn't get the stranger out of his mind, so that night he made plans to leave for the Sacramento Valley. The next morning he took a trolley to the edge of town, and then borrowed a horse to make the half-day trip to the river. However, there was no bridge to cross the river, and no ferryboat service. It was late in the day and he wondered how he would get across the river, or where he would stay for the night when he saw a rowboat coming down the river.

"How much will you charge to take me across the river?" he called to the gentleman in the boat.

"A dollar," the man replied, as he pulled the boat to the river bank.

Alex got into the boat, grateful for a way to get across the river after all. While he waited for the crossing, he pulled out a silver dollar from his pocket and turned the coin over in his hand. The coin was dated 1896, and had a big scratch on it over the eagle's eye.

When they reached the other side of the river Alex gave the man the silver dollar and thanked him again. As he turned to leave, the man in the boat said, "Be sure to stop at the first house up the valley."

Alex thanked the man again and headed up the valley until he saw a country lane leading to a small cottage. As he neared the house, a little girl came running out to meet him, shouting all the while, "Mommy! Mommy! The man with the Bible is here!"

Moments later a young woman came hurrying out, wiping her hands on her apron. "Thank God, you've come!" she said, her face flushed with excitement. "Do you have a Bible for us?"

"Yes, but how did you know that?" Alex asked in surprise.

"Well, we've been praying for a Bible for quite some time, but really had no idea how we'd get one. And then I had a dream the other night and saw you, of all people, coming up our lane with a Bible for us."

Alex was so surprised he didn't know what to say.

"How much do the Bibles cost?" she added.

"One dollar."

"Wonderful," the young woman added, her face glowing, "because that's exactly what we have, and that's the best part of all. We didn't even have the money, and then this morning my daughter found a silver dollar lying out here in the yard. We have no idea how it got here!"

She pulled it from her apron pocket. "Thank you so much for bringing our Bible," she handed him the coin.

"Praise God," Alex smiled, and as he took the dollar to put it in his pocket, he happened to notice that the coin had been minted in the same year as the coin he had given the man at the boat—1896. He turned it over, and to his utter amazement there was a scratch on the coin right over the eagle's eye.[117]

"The eyes of the Lord *are on the righteous, and His ears are open to their cry." Psalm 34:15. "This was the Lord's doing; It is marvelous in our eyes." Psalm 118:23.*

I trust in God wherever I may be,
    Upon the land or on the rolling sea,
For, come what may, from day to day,
    My heavenly Father watches over me.

He makes the rose an object of His care,
    He guides the eagle thru the pathless air,
And surely He remembers me,
    My heavenly Father watches over me.

I trust in God, for in the lion's den,
    On battlefield, or in the prison pen,

---

117 Arthur Maxwell, "The Mystery of the Silver Dollar," *Uncle Arthur's Bedtime Stories,* vol. 4 (Washington D. C.: Review and Herald Publishing Association, 1976).

Thru praise or blame, thru flood or flame,
    My heavenly Father watches over me.

The valley may be dark, the shadows deep
    But O, The Shepherd guards His lonely sheep;
And thru the gloom, He'll lead me home
    My heavenly Father watches over me.

I trust in God, I know He cares for me,
    On mountain bleak or on the stormy sea;
Though billows roll, He keeps my soul,
    My heavenly Father watches over me.

—W.C. Martin, "My Heavenly Father Watches Over Me"

**Under His Wings—Reading #2**

"Many, walking along the path of life, dwell upon their mistakes and failures and disappointments, and their hearts are filled with grief and discouragement. While I was in Europe, a sister who had been doing this, and who was in deep distress, wrote to me, asking for some word of encouragement. The night after I had read her letter I dreamed that I was in a garden, and one who seemed to be the owner of the garden was conducting me through its paths. I was gathering the flowers and enjoying their fragrance, when this sister, who had been walking by my side, called my attention to some unsightly briers that were impeding her way. There she was mourning and grieving. She was not walking in the pathway, following the guide, but was walking among the briers and thorns. "Oh," she mourned, "is it not a pity that this beautiful garden is spoiled with thorns?" Then the guide said, "Let the thorns alone, for they will only wound you. Gather the roses, the lilies, and the pinks.""

"Have there not been some bright spots in your experience? Have you not had some precious seasons when your heart throbbed with joy in response to the Spirit of God? When you look back into the chapters of your life experience do you not find some pleasant pages? Are not

God's promises, like the fragrant flowers, growing beside your path on every hand? Will you not let their beauty and sweetness fill your heart with joy?

"The briers and thorns will only wound and grieve you; and if you gather only these things, and present them to others, are you not, besides slighting the goodness of God yourself, preventing those around you from walking in the path of life?

"It is not wise to gather together all the unpleasant recollections of a past life—its iniquities and disappointments—to talk over them and mourn over them until we are overwhelmed with discouragement. A discouraged soul is filled with darkness, shutting out the light of God from his own soul and casting a shadow upon the pathway of others.

"Thank God for the bright pictures which He has presented to us. Let us group together the blessed assurances of His love, that we may look upon them continually: The Son of God leaving His Father's throne, clothing His divinity with humanity, that He might rescue man from the power of Satan; His triumph in our behalf, opening heaven to men, revealing to human vision the presence chamber where the Deity unveils His glory; the fallen race uplifted from the pit of ruin into which sin had plunged it, and brought again into connection with the infinite God, and having endured the divine test through faith in our Redeemer, clothed in the righteousness of Christ, and exalted to His throne—these are the pictures which God would have us contemplate."[118]

**Illustrative Sketch:**

Steven Kovalski was one of the most self-sacrificing Catholic priests in the modern era. After much prayer, he decided to renounce his citizenship and immigrate to India. He arrived in Calcutta penniless and chose to live among the lepers in the backstreet slums of Anand Naghar. The little shack he lived in was tiny—only four feet by six—but he cared nothing for his own comforts, citing Jesus as his example, who came to live a life of poverty for His people.

Daily Steven served the lepers, dressing like them and eating their food. He prayed for them, helping them find treatment for the living death that had come to inhabit their bodies. When mothers came to

118 White, 116.

him with dying children, he prayed over them. When parents wanted his blessing on the marriages of their young people, he honored them with a simple ceremony. When the floods of monsoon descended upon the streets of Calcutta, he gladly assisted the helpless to higher ground and shelter from the storm. When an American doctor came to Calcutta for several months to help the wretched lepers, Steven Kovalski became his right-hand man.

In all his years of service to the church, Steven considered the lepers to be the most unusual people he had ever met. They were saddled for life with a double curse—the loathsome disease of leprosy, and the social caste system of India that would never allow them to rise above their station in life—and yet they still managed to remain buoyant in their love of life.

Leprosy would eat away at their skin and fingers and toes, eroding their flesh and their self-respect. Eventually nerve damage would set in, circulation would grow sluggish, and living limbs would literally rot as though part of a dead corpse. If this were not enough, they remained burdened by the curse of their religious philosophy, that reincarnation for them is a must if they would escape this miserable existence here. If they are good enough and lucky enough, somewhere in the hundreds of thousands of lives stretching out before them, they might attain a better existence, whether it be in the life of a worm or a cow or a god.

To Steven Kovalski the leper slum of Calcutta came to be known as the "City of Joy." Because of the indomitable spirit of hope and love he found in the lives of the Indian people he came to serve, his perspective on life was changed forever. He experienced their joy for life, though he could not comprehend it. In spite of such seemingly insurmountable odds in the cycle of their pitiful lives, the lepers still found much to be grateful for.[119]

And through Steven's ministry, they learned of God's love for them in sending Jesus. The incarnation of God's only Son was truly marvelous! That Jesus had touched lepers and healed them and accepted them when he walked the earth, was truly a comfort to their souls. But, that he came to save them and die for their sins personally was almost incomprehensible!

---

119 Dominique Lapierre, *Story of Steven Kovalski and Lepers* (New York: Doubleday, 1985).

The crowning concept of all was the hope that the life, death and resurrection of Jesus could lift them from their lives of suffering and depravity to become children of the heavenly Father. What a notion! What an awesome, incredible, eternal plan that gave them peace of mind and hope for a brand new body when Jesus comes again! *"For this corruptible must put on incorruption, and this mortal must put on immortality." 1 Corinthians 15:53.*

The lyrics to the following hymn were penned by Ira Sankey, a well-known musician of the late 1800s who worked with Dwight Moody the famous evangelist. The simplicity of the hymn's message and the beauty of its lines can be an inspiration to all who have ever looked for comfort in Jesus. His wings of righteousness can do for us what nothing else ever could—enfold us in His arms of love now and in the life to come.

Under His wings I am safely abiding,
    Though the night deepens and tempests are wild,
Still I can trust Him; I know He will keep me,
    He has redeemed me, and I am His child.

Under His wings, under His wings,
    Who from His love can sever?
Under His wings my soul shall abide,
    Safely abide forever.

Under His wings, what a refuge in sorrow!
    How the heart yearningly turns to His rest!
Often when earth has no balm for my healing,
    There I find comfort, and there I am blessed.

Under His wings, oh, what precious enjoyment!
    There will I hide till life's trials are o'er;
Sheltered, protected, no evil can harm me,
    Resting in Jesus, I'm safe evermore.

Under His wings, under His wings,
    Who from His love can sever?
Under His wings my soul shall abide,
    Safely abide forever.

—Ira David Sankey, "Under His Wings"

**What A Friend We Have in Jesus—Reading #3**

"When we seem to doubt God's love and distrust His promises we dishonor Him and grieve His Holy Spirit. How would a mother feel if her children were constantly complaining of her, just as though she did not mean them well, when her whole life's effort had been to forward their interests and to give them comfort? Suppose they should doubt her love; it would break her heart. How would any parent feel to be thus treated by his children? And how can our heavenly Father regard us when we distrust His love, which has led Him to give His only-begotten Son that we might have life? The apostle writes, *"He who did not spare His own Son, but delivered Him up for us all, how shall He not with Him also freely give us all things?"* Romans 8:32. And yet how many, by their actions, if not in word, are saying, "The Lord does not mean this for me. Perhaps He loves others, but He does not love me."

"All this is harming your own soul; for every word of doubt you utter is inviting Satan's temptations; it is strengthening in you the tendency to doubt, and it is grieving from you the ministering angels. When Satan tempts you, breathe not a word of doubt or darkness. If you choose to open the door to his suggestions, your mind will be filled with distrust and rebellious questioning. If you talk out your feelings, every doubt you express not only reacts upon yourself, but it is a seed that will germinate and bear fruit in the life of others, and it may be impossible to counteract the influence of your words. You yourself may be able to recover from the season of temptation and from the snare of Satan, but others who have been swayed by your influence may not be able to escape from the unbelief you have suggested. How important that we speak only those things that will give spiritual strength and life!

"Angels are listening to hear what kind of report you are bearing to the world about your heavenly Master. Let your conversation be of Him who liveth to make intercession for you before the Father. When you take the hand of a friend, let praise to God be on your lips and in your heart. This will attract his thoughts to Jesus.

"All have trials, griefs hard to bear, temptations hard to resist. Do not tell your troubles to your fellow mortals, but carry everything to God in prayer. Make it a rule never to utter one word of doubt or discouragement. You can do much to brighten the life of others and strengthen their efforts, by words of hope and holy cheer." [120]

**Illustrative Sketch:**

The morning had not yet dawned, but the last of the cool shadows were quickly melting away in the promise of another hot day. From where he sat on his floor mat, Joseph could see the sky now turning cerulean blue above him through an opening in the prison roof. Snowy egrets winged their way across this patch of blue on their way to the Nile River, and sparrows chattered noisily somewhere in the vines crawling up the prison walls.

It was depressing sitting in prison day after day, week after week, month after month. Would justice never come, or would he spend the rest of his days in this hole in the ground? He closed his eyes as he remembered his father Jacob and the hills of his homeland in Canaan. In those days he loved running through the grassy pasturelands with his little brother Benjamin. He loved helping shear the sheep and gathering the spring harvest of golden grain during the month of Zif.

But that was before his ten older brothers maliciously sold him into slavery. He knew he had been partly to blame for the animosity festering toward him. He knew he had been the favored one of his father. Still, it hadn't been fair with the odds stacked against him ten to one. He had begged his brothers to be compassionate, pleaded with them just to send him home. There was too much hatred, and they had gone too far to turn back! He was lucky they sold him outright, instead of killing him as some of them had suggested.

Arriving in Egypt, he was sold as a slave to Potiphar, captain of Pharaoh's royal guard. But God guarded his every step, and his

120 White, 118.

industrious attitude finally earned him the supervisor's position of Potiphar's entire estate. "The touch of his fingers turns my properties to gold," Potiphar would often tell his friends. "I don't even know the extent of my wealth!" "The Lord was with Joseph, ... and the blessing of the Lord was on all that he had in the house and in the field." Genesis 39:2, 5.

For a while it had looked as if he might even become a free man and rise among the ranks of Egyptian society. But, Joseph should have known it wouldn't last. A slave was a slave and would always be a slave. He could no more change his status than a leopard could change his spots. Of course, there was Potiphar's wife. She had had her eye on Joseph from the start. For months, maybe years, she had been watching him. A woman could be very patient when she wanted something badly enough. To comply with her wishes would have been unthinkable in the eyes of the Lord His God. It would have been unethical, immoral, and treacherous since his master Potiphar trusted Joseph with all that he had.

To refuse Potiphar's wife her desires was to sacrifice his career. He was true to his God and his convictions, and the seductive, spiteful woman robbed him of his position in the estate, his liberty, and who knew, maybe someday soon even his life.

Joseph's thoughts strayed to another morning in prison. Two prisoners shared their dreams with him. The dreams troubled them greatly since Egyptians put confidence in dreams. Joseph himself knew the importance a dream could have, especially if it were given by God.

The first prisoner shared a dream about grapes and wine, and the Pharaoh's royal chalice. The second prisoner spoke of baskets and pastries and birds. Joseph at once realized these dreams had crucial messages sent by God to these prisoners who had once been officers in Pharaoh's royal court. The news was good for one and bad for the other. Because God had revealed the meaning of the dreams to Joseph, his interpretation proved accurate. The first officer was restored to his position in the court. The other was executed.

But, the correct interpretations hadn't changed Joseph's fate. Some two years later he still languished in prison, and wondered now more than ever, if God had forsaken him. He knew better than that, but the temptation was strong and real.

The sun had risen fully now, and Joseph was suddenly jarred from his reverie by the squeak of the outer prison gate as it opened on rusty hinges. "Get yourself cleaned up!" an excited guard rushed in to tell Joseph. "The pharaoh himself has ordered you to appear before him within the hour."

"The Pharaoh? What does he want with me?" Joseph stammered, blinking his surprise.

"I know few details. Only that he had a dream and it troubles him greatly!" the guard clapped his hands together. "Hurry now, take a bath and get shaved. When the Great Pharaoh of upper and lower Egypt has dreams in the night, all our futures hang in the balance. He has been told that you hold the keys to divine interpretation, and I trust for all our sakes it is so."

But Joseph could only wonder at God's providence and the mysterious ways in which He works. Through divine insight the son of Jacob interpreted the Pharaoh's dreams, and by royal decree was launched to a position of almost limitless power and prestige in Egypt. The headlines of the day would have read: "A Lowly Slave Comes to the Rescue of Egypt's Mighty Pharaoh."

Joseph was definitely the man for the job. Torn from his family and country for most of his adult life, he nevertheless maintained an unswerving faith in the God of his fathers. Daily Joseph was dependent on the will of his Father in heaven. Through divine intervention he became the savior of the Egyptians and his own people, an apt symbol of Jesus who would come to deliver His people from their sins. Joseph testified about the God of heaven at a crucial time in Middle Eastern history. Because he learned to call on the Lord in times of need, he became a friend of God as had His great-grandfather Abraham before him.

What a friend we have in Jesus,
    All our sins and griefs to bear!
What a privilege to carry
    everything to God in prayer!
O what peace we often forfeit,
    O what needless pain we bear,
all because we do not carry
    everything to God in prayer.

Have we trials and temptations?
    Is there trouble anywhere?
We should never be discouraged;
    take it to the Lord in prayer.
Can we find a friend so faithful
    who will all our sorrows share?
Jesus knows our every weakness;
    take it to the Lord in prayer.

Are we weak and heavy laden,
    cumbered with a load of care?
Precious Savior, still our refuge;
    take it to the Lord in prayer.
Do thy friends despise, forsake thee?
    Take it to the Lord in prayer!
In his arms he'll take and shield thee;
    thou wilt find a solace there.

—Joseph M. Scriven, *"What A Friend We Have in Jesus"*

**I Cast All My Cares Upon You—Reading #4**

"There is many a brave soul sorely pressed by temptation, almost ready to faint in the conflict with self and with the powers of evil. Do not discourage such a one in his hard struggle. Cheer him with brave, hopeful words that shall urge him on his way. Thus the light of Christ may shine from you. *"None of us lives to himself." Romans 14:7.* By our unconscious influence others may be encouraged and strengthened, or they may be discouraged, and repelled from Christ and the truth.

"There are many who have an erroneous idea of the life and character of Christ. They think that He was devoid of warmth and sunniness, that He was stern, severe, and joyless. In many cases the whole religious experience is colored by these gloomy views.

"It is often said that Jesus wept, but that He was never known to smile. Our Savior was indeed a Man of Sorrows, and acquainted with grief, for He opened His heart to all the woes of men. But though His life was self-denying and shadowed with pain and care, His spirit was not crushed. His countenance did not wear an expression of grief and repining, but ever one of peaceful serenity. His heart was a wellspring of life, and wherever He went He carried rest and peace, joy and gladness.

"Our Savior was deeply serious and intensely in earnest, but never gloomy or morose. The life of those who imitate Him will be full of earnest purpose; they will have a deep sense of personal responsibility. Levity will be repressed; there will be no boisterous merriment, no rude jesting; but the religion of Jesus gives peace like a river. It does not quench the light of joy; it does not restrain cheerfulness nor cloud the sunny, smiling face. Christ came not to be ministered unto but to minister; and when His love reigns in the heart, we shall follow His example.

"If we keep uppermost in our minds the unkind and unjust acts of others we shall find it impossible to love them as Christ has loved us; but if our thoughts dwell upon the wondrous love and pity of Christ for us, the same spirit will flow out to others. We should love and respect one another, notwithstanding the faults and imperfections that we cannot help seeing. Humility and self-distrust should be cultivated, and a patient tenderness with the faults of others. This will kill out all narrowing selfishness and make us large-hearted and generous." [121]

## Illustrative Sketch:

Sarah Camden trudged along the three-mile stretch of road to school. Things were falling apart at school because of Clarice Borden. She was the meanest girl in town, and everyone knew it. Her razor sharp tongue could cut like a knife, and if looks could have killed, her dark sinister eyes would have already committed murder many times over. She was new in town, but that didn't seem to make any difference. Her father had bought the feed store in the small town of Dorchester, and Clarice had discovered that money could buy friends anywhere.

It hadn't always been like this, Sarah admitted. A stray tear stole its way down her cheek, and the lump in her throat just wouldn't go away. The hours spent in the little red school house had always been the bright spot in Sarah's day, but since Clarice came, all that had changed. School days had become almost unbearable.

---

121 White, 120.

Clarice wasn't the most beautiful girl in the school, but her family was rich, and she reminded the others of it continually. "My father owns the feed store, so you'd better be nice," she would retort. "If you're lucky, I may invite you to the store after school to get some candy." Sarah was sure she would scream if she had to hear that line one more time!

Clarice considered herself an excellent speller and whenever spelling bees were held, she liked to brag, "I won the county spelling contest two years in a row in the last school I was at."

Sarah was a good speller too, but she was interested in other things as well. She could hit a baseball as well as any boy, and could outrun every kid in the school. "Oh, she just thinks she's Miss Olympics!" Clarice had snapped one day after Sarah had won yet another race. Sarah had ignored her, but she couldn't help noticing Clarice's legs and arms were as skinny as toothpicks.

One day Clarice begun dictating who could be friends with whom at school. As one of the oldest girls in the school, Sarah had dared to challenge Clarice on this issue. Offering the girls candy was one thing and bragging about spelling rights was another, but interfering in friendships was the limit. Too late Sarah realized what a mistake that had been, and now she was paying a heavy price for it! Clarice used her power effectively. For the last two weeks none of the other girls would even talk to her.

Spring break started tomorrow, and though she should have been excited about the coming vacation, Sarah found herself dragging her footsteps along the roadway. What new stab of cruelty would Clarice have ready for her today? The morning was a bright one with the first hint of spring in the air. Wild crocuses pushed their way up along the hedgerows, and chickadees called to one another in the hazelnut bushes near Colton's pond, but Sarah hardly noticed.

Then she remembered that any day now thousands of sheep would be coming through Dorchester. All the farmers banded together to transport their sheep to the shearing sheds in Greenfield. It was a fun time of year, but it could also be trouble because the herders didn't like slowing down for anyone who got in the way. For a moment Sarah forgot her problems as she thought of the excitement the sheep always brought to town.

All too soon she arrived at school, and who should happen to meet her at the door, but Clarice. "My, what a pretty red coat!" the new girl paused in derision. "Looks big enough for Santa Claus and all his elves!"

The words stung, in part, perhaps because Clarice was right. The coat was too big, a hand-me-down from Sarah's sixteen-year-old sister. Money was tight, and Sarah's parents could not afford a new one for her. Sarah's face turned red with embarrassment as she hung up the coat. She knew she should have been used to Clarice by now, but the words cut deeply.

Through arithmetic, grammar and history Sarah thought about Clarice and her cruel words. The more she thought about them, the angrier she became. What right did Clarice have to make fun of other people! What right did she have to be so cruel! Just because her parents could afford to give her nice things didn't mean she should make life miserable for other people who were doing their best to get along! By the time school let out, Sarah was so angry she wanted to find Clarice and beat her with sticks. She knew this wasn't right, but she didn't care! She wanted to take her face and rub it in the mud, and she knew she could, too. Clarice was just a little scrawny thing. "Where's Clarice?" she asked the other girls, her eyes blazing as she left the school building.

"She left already, a little bit before school was out," they said. "She wasn't feeling well." Without another word Sarah turned and ran. She would catch Clarice before she got home and make her pay for all the mean things she had done. Sarah knew Clarice lived on the other side of town, across the river, and there was only one way to get there. The bridge. She had to cross the big bridge that spanned the river. Sarah ran and ran. She got tired, but she kept running. The day had turned cold, and her lungs hurt from the icy afternoon air, but she kept running.

As she came down Main Street, she could hear people shouting at her. "Get off the streets! The sheep are coming!" A shock wave went through Sarah's body as she realized what they were saying. The big day had finally arrived! The huge flocks of sheep must be coming through town for shearing! That could be a dangerous thing! People had been known to get trampled to death beneath the thousands of pounding feet when they didn't get out of the way! Gone was her anger and the planned vengeance against Clarice. She must get out of the way! She could see the long bridge ahead, stretching a hundred fifty yards across the river, and on the other side she could see the sheep just now coming onto the bridge. As their feet hit the wooden planking she could hear the distant rumble of their little hooves.

But then she noticed something else—a dark shape huddled out on the bridge. She strained her eyes to see what it was, and suddenly realized it was a person. Who could it be? Who would be foolish enough to be out on the bridge when the sheep were coming? "Get off the bridge!" she heard herself screaming, but she was too far away to be heard. Instinctively, she ran onto the bridge, ignoring the frantic shouting of the people in the streets behind her. As she drew near the forlorn figure, she couldn't believe her eyes. It was Clarice, huddled silent and unmoving against the railing. "Please Lord," Sarah prayed, her heart now moved with compassion for Clarice, "forgive me for letting myself get so angry!"

The sheep were coming along fast now, but Sarah was faster. She knew it would be a race to the middle, and she made it. She reached Clarice with a few seconds to spare and managed to pull her up onto the bridge railing. "Hang on tight!" she shouted above the noise of the thundering sheep, as she put her arms around Clarice's frail body. Only then did she feel the girl relax and begin to sob. "I've been so awfully mean to you!" Clarice stammered in Sarah's ear. "All those horrible things I said! I guess I was jealous of you because you were so good at everything! Can you ever forgive me?"

Sarah forgave her, and they became best friends.[122] The lesson they learned that day echoes the words of Jesus. "*And be kind to one another, tenderhearted, forgiving one another, even as God in Christ forgave you.*" *Ephesians 4:32.*)

**Be Thou Faithful—Reading #5**

"The psalmist says, *"Trust in the Lord, and do good; dwell in the land, and feed on His faithfulness."* Psalm 37:3. *"Trust in the Lord."* Each day has

---

122 Lilith Sanford Rushing, "the Day the Sheep Came Through," in *The Sorry Potato* (Washington D. C.: Review and Herald Publishing Association, 1965).

its burdens, its cares and perplexities; and when we meet how ready we are to talk of our difficulties and trials. So many borrowed troubles intrude, so many fears are indulged, such a weight of anxiety is expressed, that one might suppose we had no pitying, loving Savior ready to hear all our requests and to be to us a present help in every time of need.

"Some are always fearing, and borrowing trouble. Every day they are surrounded with the tokens of God's love; every day they are enjoying the bounties of His providence; but they overlook these present blessings. Their minds are continually dwelling upon something disagreeable which they fear may come; or some difficulty may really exist which, though small, blinds their eyes to the many things that demand gratitude. The difficulties they encounter, instead of driving them to God, the only source of their help, separate them from Him because they awaken unrest and repining.

"Do we well to be thus unbelieving? Why should we be ungrateful and distrustful? Jesus is our friend; all heaven is interested in our welfare. We should not allow the perplexities and worries of everyday life to fret the mind and cloud the brow. If we do we shall always have something to vex and annoy. We should not indulge a solicitude that only frets and wears us, but does not help us to bear trials.

"You may be perplexed in business; your prospects may grow darker and darker, and you may be threatened with loss; but do not become discouraged; cast your care upon God, and remain calm and cheerful. Pray for wisdom to manage your affairs with discretion, and thus prevent loss and disaster. Do all you can on your part to bring about favorable results. Jesus has promised His aid, but not apart from our effort. When, relying upon our Helper, you have done all you can, accept the result cheerfully.

"It is not the will of God that His people should be weighed down with care. But our Lord does not deceive us. He does not say to us, "Do not fear; there are no dangers in your path." He knows there are trials and dangers, and He deals with us plainly. He does not propose to take His people out of a world of sin and evil, but He points them to a never-failing refuge. His prayer for His disciples was, "*I do not pray that You should take them out of the world, but that You should keep them from the evil one.*" "*In the world,*" He says, "*you will have tribulation; but be of good cheer, I have overcome the world.*" John 17:15, 16:33."[123]

---

123 White, 121.

---

**Illustrative Sketch:**

How far would you be willing to go today to express your love for God? What trials would you be willing to suffer in order to honor the biblical truths you love so dearly?

From the old regime of the Soviet Union comes a tale about a Pastor who sacrificed everything to remain faithful to Jesus and the gospel commission to which he had been called. Nickolai, a Seventh-day Adventist Russian pastor, was arrested by the KGB because he refused to divulge the names of the members who were secretly meeting with him each week in his underground church. For this he was exiled from home and sent to the very edges of Soviet civilization.

On the wide-open wastelands of Siberia Nickolai was put to work in a prison camp. As was his custom, he did not work on the seventh day because it was God's holy Sabbath. The prison warden was furious and ordered him to report for work at once, but when Nickolai refused, the guard beat him and left him lying unconscious on the ground. The next Sabbath when he refused to work, Nickolai was beaten again and then locked up in a small wooden crate. There was just enough room to sit, but not to stand or move around much. For ten days the warden left him there with water only—no food and no trips out of the crate to use a bathroom.

Nickolai suffered in such tight quarters, and his faith in God was the only thing that carried him through the ordeal. When the guards finally came to take him out, he could hardly move from the stiffness in his joints and lack of circulation in his legs. He resumed his duties as a carpenter, but the following Sabbath he again refused to work. Again, he was put back into the crate. Week after week Nickolai refused to work on the Sabbath, and always he was returned to the crate. For two years this episode was reenacted over and over again.

During these hard times an ox named Maksim was stabled in the shed each night where Nickolai's crate was kept, and throughout these trying times the two of them became friends. At night when Maksim was in the shed, Nickolai would talk to him through the cracks in the box, preaching him sermons and reciting long passages of Scripture.

When a military official on an inspection tour from Moscow discovered Nickolai in the crate, he asked the warden about him. The warden told the official of Nickolai's strange religious belief about resting on the seventh day of the week. When questioned by the officer, Nickolai assured him he was willing work at any job in the prison for as many hours as the warden asked, if he could just have his Sabbaths off.

To Nickolai's surprise he was given the opportunity to haul water from a nearby lake in large barrels carried on Maksim's ox cart—two barrels on the cart per trip. If he and Maksim could haul seven days' worth of water in six, then Nickolai would be given his Sabbaths off. However, the challenge wasn't as simple as Nickolai had hoped. He worked hard all that first week, most days long after dark, only to reach Thursday night with the number of barrels far short. With one day left he was still 16 barrels short of his quota. On Friday morning, to Nickolai's surprise, Maksim began to run. In a strange feat of endurance the old ox trotted his legs off, and amazingly, by sunset the barrels were all in as the warden had ordered.

Nickolai wondered if it might be a fluke of nature that Maksim ran all day, but the next week the same scenario was repeated. He realized that God was indeed helping him reach his goals so he could keep the Sabbath. On Fridays the other prisoners gathered to watch the old ox run. As the weeks passed, God continued to bless Nickolai and Maksim with energy to do seven days' work in six, always finishing by sunset Friday evening. For eight years man and beast worked together, never failing to make their quota of water barrels, always getting their Sabbath day's blessing and serving as God's witnesses to the sacredness of the Holy Sabbath.

One day the same military official from Moscow returned for another inspection of the prison. He witnessed Pastor Nickolai doing the job as originally planned and was amazed at Nickolai's faithfulness. The credit for such a phenomenon was all God's, of course, and Nickolai made sure the officer understood it. So impressed was the officer with Nickolai's integrity that he authorized the pastor's release so he could return home to his family and church.

The members of his Church rejoiced that God had brought him home from his long ordeal, and thanked Jesus for Nickolai's faithfulness under fire. Nickolai returned to the life of a Pastor, and continued to witness for God. Thus ends the saga of a man who would rather suffer persecution and hardship than break his covenant with God and desecrate the holy hours of the Sabbath. Like God's faithful ones down through the ages, Nickolai withstood the furnace of affliction and come out shining like gold.

But, the story doesn't end there. Another prisoner arrived at the prison where Nickolai had been incarcerated all those years, and was given Nickolai's job to haul water from the lake. All week he worked, and when Friday came, the man could hardly keep up with old Maksim. And when Sabbath arrived, Maksim refused to get up and go to work. When asked about the ox's strange behavior, the warden replied, "That's the preacher's fault who worked here for ten years. He made a Sabbath keeper out of Maksim and now nothing can get that old ox to work on the Sabbath. We call him the seventh-day Ox."

The influence of Nickolai's life lived on through the testimony of an ox. Old Maksim continued to be true to his duties and to his witness for the Sabbath. Nickolai was gone, but there was still Maksim, the seventh-day ox.[124]

> *"'Do not fear any of those things which you are about to suffer. Indeed, the devil is about to throw some of you into prison, that you may be tested … Be faithful until death, and I will give you the crown of life.'" Revelation 2:10.*

Faith of our fathers, living still,
    In spite of dungeon, fire, and sword;
Oh, how our hearts beat high with joy
    Whene'er we hear that glorious Word!
Faith of our fathers, holy faith!
    We will be true to thee till death.

Our fathers, chained in prisons dark,
    Were still in heart and conscience free
How sweet would be their children's fate
    If they, like them, could die for thee

---

124 John McGhee as told to the author, 1994. John McGhee worked in Russia and knew these individuals.

Faith of our fathers, we will love
   Both friend and foe in all our strife;
And preach Thee, too, as love knows how
   By kindly words and virtuous life.
Faith of our fathers, holy faith!
   We will be true to thee till death.

—Frederick W. Faber, "Faith of Our Fathers"

**All Things Bright and Beautiful—Reading #6**

"In His Sermon on the Mount, Christ taught His disciples precious lessons in regard to the necessity of trusting in God. These lessons were designed to encourage the children of God through all ages, and they have come down to our time full of instruction and comfort. The Savior pointed His followers to the birds of the air as they warbled their carols of praise, unencumbered with thoughts of care, for "'*they neither sow nor reap.*'" *Matthew 6:26.* And yet the great Father provides for their needs.

"The Savior asks, "'*Are you not of more value than they?*'" *Matthew 6:26.* The great Provider for man and beast opens His hand and supplies all His creatures. The birds of the air are not beneath His notice. He does not drop the food into their bills, but He makes provision for their needs. They must gather the grains He has scattered for them. They must prepare the material for their little nests. They must feed their young. They go forth singing to their labor, for "'*your heavenly Father feeds them.*'" And "*… are you not of more value than they?*'" *Matthew 6:26.* Are not you, as intelligent, spiritual worshipers, of more value than the birds of the air? Will not the Author of our being, the Preserver of our life, the One who formed us in His own divine image, provide for our necessities if we but trust in Him?

"Christ pointed His disciples to the flowers of the field, growing in rich profusion and glowing in the simple beauty which the heavenly Father had given them, as an expression of His love to man. He said, "Consider the lilies of the field, how they grow." The beauty and simplicity of these natural flowers far outrival the splendor of Solomon. The most gorgeous attire produced by the skill of art cannot bear comparison with the natural grace and radiant beauty of the flowers of God's creation. Jesus asks, *"If God so clothes the grass of the field, which today is, and tomorrow is thrown into the oven, will He not much more clothe you, O you of little faith?" Matthew 6: 28, 30.* If God, the divine Artist, gives to the simple flowers that perish in a day their delicate and varied colors, how much greater care will He have for those who are created in His own image? This lesson of Christ's is a rebuke to the anxious thought, the perplexity and doubt, of the faithless heart.

"The Lord would have all His sons and daughters happy, peaceful, and obedient. Jesus says, *"… My peace I give to you; not as the world gives do I give to you. Let not your heart be troubled, neither let it be afraid." "These things have I spoken unto you, that My joy may remain in you, and that your joy may be full." John 14:27; 15:11."*[125]

**Illustrative Sketch:**

The Lord wants us to count our blessings. All have been adopted as sons and daughters of the King, the Giver of every good thing. Creatures of nature accept without question the loving care of their Creator. Although this old world is under the curse of sin, the Master Designer has given each bird and tree and flower the gifts it needs to survive. Their very existence is a testimony to the power of God.

Beautiful though it is, our world has environments and zones that provide a real challenge for survival. Frigid glaciers sit atop the world and cover out tallest mountains for much of the year—and yet animals flourish there. Bears and many rodents sleep away the cold winter months, their heart rates slowing drastically as their body temperatures drop. Many insects hibernate to survive the cold winter months, too. Wooly caterpillars stay warm in their fuzzy coats, while other insects replace the water in their bodies with glycerol, a type of antifreeze! Some grubs burrow deeper into the soil to escape the cold.

In hot or dry weather many animals learn to adapt, too. Some creatures go through a process of dormancy called estivation, otherwise known as summer sleep. Some species of fish and frogs do this when their ponds dry up. In harsh habitats many creatures survive long

---

125 White, 123.

periods without food or water. Reptiles, amphibians, and insects can exist for months without eating. Camels store water in their humps for treks across long stretches of desert. Some varieties of cicada live underground in the pupae stage for as much as seventeen years.

Animals have been created with the ability to progress through various stages in order to develop and survive. Most insects go through stages of metamorphosis in which their bodies change from one form to another. Grasshoppers go through three stages of development, while butterflies and moths go through four—from eggs to larvae to pupae to mature adults. Most amphibians lay eggs that develop into tadpole-like creatures, and then develop into full-sized adults. Some fish lay eggs, and some give birth to fish on a miniature scale. Mammals carry their young for a period of days or months or even years, and then give birth in varying stages of ability to cope. Newborn puppies and kittens are completely helpless with eyes undeveloped and completely shut. Pronghorn antelopes and giraffes, on the other hand, produce babies ready to run with the herd in a matter of hours.

Some animals have developed natural camouflage. They survive best when they adapt to their changing environment. Arctic foxes and hares change color to match their tundra surroundings. Stick bugs and leaf beetles blend in with their habitat of twigs and leaves. Chameleons change color to match the hues of their setting, turning shades of pink, blue, red, orange, green, yellow, and even purple.

Caribou, Canadian geese, monarch butterflies, and whales are examples of creatures that migrate to adapt to changing temperatures, water supplies, food sources, or breeding grounds. Many species of fish migrate to better feeding grounds, or up rivers and streams to spawn, like salmon. A few unique species of fish are even known to migrate across land for short distances from one body of water to another.

Because of the sinful word in which we live, some creatures have developed dangerous weapons so they can repel attackers. Blowfish swell to appear like a giant swimming pincushion, with some species having poison on the tips of their spines. Some types of toads and snakes shoot poisons from glands on their bodies. Bees and scorpions sting, snakes bite injecting venom, and skunks shoot a vile odor that can cause their victim to go temporarily blind.

Plants have also developed abilities to survive. In colder or drier climates trees and flowers often settle into a state of dormancy, while others develop seeds that can withstand amazing extremes in cold, heat, and moisture content. Some seeds found in tombs thousands of years old still possessed the ability to germinate. Pine cones can withstand forest fires and then germinate the next spring to reforest the landscape. Plants like poison ivy have developed toxins in their leaves to keep from being eaten or destroyed, and yet jewelweed which grows in the vicinity of poison ivy, has developed an antidote to neutralize the toxin. Orchids of the Amazon rainforest contain life-giving properties that can help heal many forms of cancer. Penicillin was discovered in a blue mold that was growing on a piece of fruit in a produce market.

But perhaps one of the rarest and most amazing illustrations of God's creative genius is the tale of a tiny fish that lives in the rain forest canopy of Hawaii. The uninterrupted rain in this unusual habitat allows a type of fish to live out their entire life cycle in the cups of unique leaves holding tiny pools of water. The males deposit their sperm in the little pools, and birds coming to drink the water carry the sperm on their feet to other leaves where the females live and lay their eggs. Because of the eternal rains, the water never dries up, thus providing for the reproduction of the species in a unique way. Truly our Creator is a marvelous God. *"Then God saw everything that He had made, and indeed it was very good." Genesis 1:31.*

Since the days of creation God has given animals and plants the ability to adapt in the environments where they live. Conditions aren't always ideal, but they learn to survive and live to praise their Creator in their rare beauty, amazing antics, and magnificent song.

All things bright and beautiful, All creatures great and small,
    All things wise and wonderful, The Lord God made them all.

Each little flower that opens, Each little bird that sings,
    He made their glowing colors, He made their tiny wings.

The purple-headed mountains, The river running by,
    The sunset and the morning That brightens up the sky.

The cold wind in the winter, The pleasant summer sun,
 The ripe fruits in the garden, He made them every one.
The tall trees in the greenwood, The meadows where we play,
 The rushes by the water, To gather every day.

He gave us eyes to see them, And lips that we might tell
 How great is God Almighty, Who has made all things well.

All things bright and beautiful, All creatures great and small,
 All things wise and wonderful: The Lord God made them all.

 —Cecil F. Alexander, "All Things Bright and Beautiful"

**Redeemed—Reading #7**
 "Happiness that is sought from selfish motives, outside of the path
of duty, is ill-balanced, fitful, and transitory; it passes away, and the soul
is filled with loneliness and sorrow; but there is joy and satisfaction in
the service of God; the Christian is not left to walk in uncertain paths;
he is not left to vain regrets and disappointments. If we do not have the
pleasures of this life we may still be joyful in looking to the life beyond.
 "But even here Christians may have the joy of communion with
Christ; they may have the light of His love, the perpetual comfort of
His presence. Every step in life may bring us closer to Jesus, may give
us a deeper experience of His love, and may bring us one step nearer
to the blessed home of peace. Then let us not cast away our confidence,
but have firm assurance, firmer than ever before. "*Thus far has the
Lord helped us,*'" and He will help us to the end. *1 Samuel 7:12.*
 "Let us look to the monumental pillars, reminders of what the Lord
has done to comfort us and to save us from the hand of the destroyer.
Let us keep fresh in our memory all the tender mercies that God has
shown us—the tears He has wiped away, the pains He has soothed, the
anxieties removed, the fears dispelled, the wants supplied, the blessings bestowed,—thus strengthening ourselves for all that is before us
through the remainder of our pilgrimage.

"We cannot but look forward to new perplexities in the coming conflict, but we may look on what is past as well as on what is to come, and say, "*Thus far has the Lord helped us.*" "*As your days, so shall your strength be.*" *1 Samuel 7:12, Deuteronomy 33:25.* The trial will not exceed the strength that shall be given us to bear it. Then let us take up our work just where we find it, believing that whatever may come, strength proportionate to the trial will be given.

"And by and by the gates of heaven will be thrown open to admit God's children, and from the lips of the King of glory the benediction will fall on their ears like richest music, "*Come, you blessed of My Father, inherit the kingdom prepared for you from the foundation of the world.*" *Matthew 25:34.*

"Then the redeemed will be welcomed to the home that Jesus is preparing for them. There their companions will not be the vile of earth, liars, idolaters, the impure, and unbelieving; but they will associate with those who have overcome Satan and through divine grace have formed perfect characters. Every sinful tendency, every imperfection, that afflicts them here has been removed by the blood of Christ, and the excellence and brightness of His glory, far exceeding the brightness of the sun, is imparted to them. And the moral beauty, the perfection of His character, shines through them, in worth far exceeding this outward splendor. They are without fault before the great white throne, sharing the dignity and the privileges of the angels.

"In view of the glorious inheritance that may be his, "*... what will a man give in exchange for his soul?*" *Matthew 16:26.* He may be poor, yet he possesses in himself a wealth and dignity that the world could never bestow. The soul redeemed and cleansed from sin, with all its noble powers dedicated to the service of God, is of surpassing worth; and there is joy in heaven in the presence of God and the holy angels over one soul redeemed, a joy that is expressed in songs of holy triumph." [126]

**Illustrative Sketch:**

Long ago, Jesus told a famous story about two brothers: the restless prodigal son and his committed, stay-at-home brother. The young men in that story come to us with a very different set of problems. They were worlds apart, opposites like night and day. Their dreams

---

126 White, 124.

and aspirations diverged in the woods of life like two pathways. And yet, though the young men made vastly different choices, in some ways these brothers were very much the same.

Which are we? If we are to be completely honest with ourselves, we will realize that we are either the wayfaring prodigal, or the predictable older brother.

Do we chafe under the restrictions of a home or church that we feel dictates the right and wrong in our lives? Then maybe Jesus' story speaks to us. It speaks to us when we feel the passions of the young and restless, those who find themselves wanting to leave all that is familiar. It speaks to us when we grit our teeth to faithfully perform some duty, but long to spread our wings and soar into the unknown. It speaks to us when we are the risk takers who receive fulfillment from doing the unconventional—who feel the urge to experience the pain and sorrow of disappointment for themselves—who cannot seem to learn from the mistakes others have made, and who are destined to reinvent their own wheel of misfortune. It touches us when we don't understand heaven's lavish love.

Jesus told this story for that prodigal son among us who knows that stubborn pride is not productive and rarely satisfying. It is for the daughters among us who have come to grips with the reality that independence is not everything we once thought it would be. It is about our embracing the elements of the cruel, cold world that never responds affectionately. It is for those among us who eventually admit that the smart thing to do is to just go home to the love of a compassionate, supportive, heavenly Father.

Then there is the older brother in our midst. He has always been considered the more faithful of the two. He is the reliable one among us, waking up with the dawn to make his contributions. He works for the benefit of us all, giving of himself. He sacrifices for his local church. He asks little in return for his efforts, and because he expects little, he receives even less. At times we feel with him his resignation to a life of mediocrity. We feel his rebellious spirit creep forward, and we feel his bitterness, resentment, cynicism, and anger.

But there is an unfamiliar side to our second brother. Lurking beneath the disguised exterior we see someone longing for recognition. We sense his need for acceptance, gratitude and affirmation. Do we see our sons and daughters for their true value to the church as a whole? Do we pigeon-hole them to the roster of the ninety and nine, who have no conspicuous need of a shepherd?

Can we feel the needs of these two brothers? The story Jesus shares invites us to take the road less traveled, the road to redemption. Today, He invites us to be rescued from our lives of reckless adventure and misfortune, to be saved from our pitiful lives of quiet desperation.

Amazingly, this salvation comes with no strings attached. Jesus accepts us just as we are, and for all that we can become through His righteousness. We accept this offer of great mercy and love. As Jesus opens wide His arms, we can almost hear the angels singing, "Rejoice for another child has come home." It is a prelude to a time when we shall pass through those pearly gates to meet our Savior, the One who died so we could be with Him in glory. What greater reward could we have than to see His broad smile and the tears of joy that have carved our names forever on His glorious face.

"My sons and daughters have come home!" Jesus' voice will ring out across the Sea of Glass. "Praise to the Father!" He raises His hands to the Great white throne. "'Come! … Blessed of my Father! Inherit the kingdom!'" Matthew 25:34. "Let us partake of a feast prepared for us from the foundation of the world! Let us eat and rejoice, for my sons were dead and are alive again!" His voice echoes and reechoes out over the walls of the New Jerusalem, "My daughters were lost and are found!" And the angels strike a note higher on the heavenly scale as all creatures across the expanse of God's wide universe rejoice in its glad song of harmony.[127]

*"'I have loved you with an everlasting love … with loving kindness I have drawn you.'" Jeremiah 31:3*

Redeemed, how I love to proclaim it!
   Redeemed by the blood of the Lamb;
   Redeemed through His infinite mercy,
      His child, and forever, I am.

127 Ellen G. White, *God's Amazing Grace* (Washington D. C.: Review and Herald Publishing Association, 1973) 356.

Redeemed and so happy in Jesus,
    No language my rapture can tell;
I know that the light of His presence
    With me doth continually dwell.
I think of my blessed Redeemer,
    I think of Him all the day long;
I sing, for I cannot be silent;
    His love is the theme of my song.

I know I shall see in His beauty
    The King in whose way I delight;
Who lovingly guardeth my footsteps,
    And giveth me songs in the night.

Redeemed, redeemed,
    Redeemed by the blood of the Lamb;
Redeemed, redeemed,
    His child, and forever, I am.

—Charlotte Martin, "Redeemed, How I Love to Proclaim It"

---— ⊛ —---

# EPILOGUE

## Master the Tempest Is Raging!

*E*very *Day With Jesus* has been written to help readers stay in touch with Jesus. If we will spend a thoughtful hour each day with Jesus, we will understand something of His great sacrifice for us. Step by step we will find ourselves being drawn closer and closer to His infinite arms of love, and the protection He would give us against the forces of evil. Jesus wants to forgive our sins, cleanse us from all unrighteousness, and give us courage to fight the good fight of faith. 1 John 1:9, 1 Timothy 6:12.

If we would have victory in our lives, we must understand that there is a battle raging for our souls behind the scenes. It is the battle between good and evil, called the great controversy between Christ and Satan. The object of Satan's very existence is to cast reproach upon the Father. He will do everything in his power to destroy God's good name and separate Christians from the love of the Father. However, when we surrender our lives to Jesus and put ourselves entirely within His care, the evil one cannot touch us. With Paul we can say, "For I am persuaded that neither death nor life, nor angels nor principalities nor powers, nor things present nor things to come, nor height nor depth, nor any other created thing, shall be able to separate us from the love of God which is in Christ Jesus our Lord." Romans 8:38, 39.

The following hymn contains a profound storyline for God's people today. Painted in lyrics that poetically describe the battle of elements at sea, we see Jesus and his disciples caught in the vortex of a storm. But the contrast between Jesus and the demons of destruction in this setting is stark, and immediately we recognize on whose side we must be.

Master, the tempest is raging!
    The billows are tossing high!
The sky is o'ershadowed with blackness.
    No shelter or help is nigh.
Carest Thou not that we perish?
    How canst Thou lie asleep?
When each moment so madly is threatening
    A grave in the angry deep?

Master, with anguish of spirit
    I bow in my grief today.
The depths of my sad heart are troubled.
    Oh, waken and save, I pray!
Torrents of sin and of anguish
    Sweep o'er my sinking soul!
And I perish! I perish! dear Master,
    Oh, hasten, and take control.

Master, the terror is over,
    The elements sweetly rest.
Earth's sun in the calm lake is mirrored,
    And heaven's within my breast.
Linger, O blessed Redeemer!
    Leave me alone no more!
And with joy I shall make the blest harbor,
    And rest on the blissful shore

The winds and the waves obey Thy will, Peace, be still!
    Whether the wrath of the storm tossed sea,
Or demons or men, or whatever it be.
    No waters can swallow the ship where lies
The Master of ocean, and earth, and skies!
    They all shall sweetly obey Thy will.
Peace, be still! Peace, be still!
    They all shall sweetly obey Thy will.
Peace, peace, be still!

    —Mary A. Baker, "Master the Tempest is Raging"

When the storms of life are raging all around us, it's good to know we have the Master of ocean and earth and skies in the boat with us. The elements of spiritual warfare may take their toll, but if we rely on the Man from Galilee, we can be sure we are protected by the Infinite One. The winds and waves of doubt may assail us, but we will be convinced of His goodness. The lightning strikes of misfortune may be thrown against us by the prince of darkness, but we will stand tall with Jesus. The waves of despair may threaten to overtake us, but our Savior has gone this way before us, and He will help us conquer evil with His righteousness. He will ride out the waves with us 'til we reach that heavenly shore.

Thanks be to God for this incredible gift! *"Therefore, having been justified by faith, we have peace with God through our Lord Jesus Christ."* Romans 5:1.